I
see a
new India

A book by Preeti Mahurkar

Text copyright © 2017 Preeti Mahurkar
All Rights Reserved

To,

India - our motherland and to all those sung and unsung heroes who sacrificed their lives to free India, so that people of India could live in freedom, peace, and prosperity, and to all those who are working tirelessly to make this dream come true….

All rights reserved. No part of this publication may be reproduced, stored in or introduced into a retrieval system, or transmitted, in any form, or by any means (electrical, mechanical, photocopying, recording or otherwise) without the prior written permission of the publisher.
Any person who does any unauthorized act in relation to
this publication may be liable to criminal prosecution
and civil claims for damages.

First Edition
July 2017
Angels Creations
Pune ,India

Thank you God, for guiding me and making this book happen.

Thank you my angels, Ashok, Aahan for your unconditional love and support.
Without you, this book would not be complete.
Thank you, my family and friends for your love, support and patience.

Where the mind is without fear and the head is held high;
Where knowledge is free;
Where the world has not been broken up into fragments by narrow domestic walls;
Where words come out from the depth of truth;
Where tireless striving stretches its arms towards perfection;
Where the clear stream of reason has not lost its way into the
dreary desert sand of dead habit;
Where the mind is led forward by thee into ever-widening thought and action,
Into that heaven of freedom father let us all be awake

Rabindranath Tagore

Igniting minds...Illuminating hearts.....Inspiring hands.....

Prologue

As is the atom, so is the universe
As is the human body, so is the cosmic body
As is the human mind, so is the cosmic mind
As is the microcosm, so is the macrocosm
-The Upanishads

This book is a quest towards finding the ultimate reality that is based on the oneness of spirit, love and wisdom. It is a quest to find the highest truth in its pure glory without any biases or prejudices tinted perspective that goes beyond all personal truths, preferences or loyalties. It is a quest to find the true Dharma that is based on Sarva-dharma (highest collective good) and goes beyond sva-dharma (personal good).

The purpose of this book is not to criticize or condemn any person, group or ideology but to present the current reality and things as they are and identify those unconscious patterns, paradigms and practices that do not serve our highest collective good. As, unless we accept and acknowledge what is not working or serving anymore, we would not be able to choose better ways and means that work for all….

"It shall be the duty of every citizen of India to develop the scientific temper, humanism and the spirit of inquiry and reform." – The Constitution of India

This is the purpose of this book - to invite the people of India with scientific temper, human values to inquire and reform and usher our country into a new era of social and conscious evolution.

Chapters

1. From Revolution to Conscious Evolution
2. Vision: A new India Arising
3. The choice
4. India - Taking stock of the Journey so far
5. The Dream of freedom
6. The Failure
7. India- A reality check
8. The promise
9. Who are we?
10. Where are we going wrong?
11. What can we do?
12. What are we missing?
13. How do we do it?
14. Means and tools
15. Team India – An idea whose time has come

    - Creating an India -Think Tank (Expert team)
    - Creating a National Integrity Infrastructure
    - Creating a National Public Information and social accountability Infrastructure
    - Creating a National resources pool
    - Creating a National Action Plan (sustainable development goals and prosperity for all)
    - Creating review, monitoring, public awareness teams and task forces

16. Convergence is the key!
17. Yes, we can India …. Let's do it NOW!
18. Building a new India
19. Take a pledge India

References

Table of Content

Chapter links:

From Revolution to Conscious evolution

"THE CHOICE"

Taking stock of the journey so far....

The dream of freedom

A country of contrasts

India- A reality Check

The failure

Where are we going wrong?

What Are We Doing?

Who Are We?

What are we missing?

Means and Tools

Reforming and transforming India

Team India- An Idea whose time has come!

Yes we can Team India!

Convergence is the key!

Creating a new Paradigm

Building A New India

Take a Pledge India

Epilogue - Yes, we can India....Let's do it NOW!

Index

From Revolution to Conscious Evolution

Conscious evolution - evolution by choice, not by chance.

-Barbara Max Hubbard

"Occasionally in the course of human events, a new worldview emerges that transforms society. It occurred in the Renaissance when the idea of progress through knowledge was born. It took place in the world through various revolutions and uprising. Now, once again a new worldview is arising. This idea is the culmination of all human history. It holds the promise of fulfilling the high aspirations of the past and heralds the advent of the next phase of our evolution. It is the idea of conscious evolution.

"Conscious Evolution is at the core a spiritually motivated endeavor. Its precepts reside at the heart of every great faith, affirming that humans have the potential of being co-creators with Spirit, with the deeper patterns of nature and universal design."

We are now changing our understanding of how nature evolves; we are moving from unconscious evolution through natural selection to conscious evolution by choice. With this increased knowledge and the power that it gives us, we can destroy the world or we can participate in a future of immeasurable dimensions. Into our hands has been given the power of co-destruction or co-creation.

I believe that the crises and opportunities we face today are triggering the next stage of planetary evolution and that we, as individual members of the planetary body, are now being awakened to our new personal and social capacities to participate in our evolution. This is not a plan imposed by any group or individual, but rather a design of evolution, a tendency toward a higher, more complex order and consciousness, with which we can cooperate and align ourselves to repattern our social systems and evolve ourselves.

Social Evolution is a vast field designed to guide ourselves through this "crisis of the birth of a new humanity" such that we can co-create a future equal to our spiritual, social and scientific potential. In order to get through our current crisis of entangled problems, we need to cultivate SOCIAL SYNERGY, the coming together of separate groups, initiatives, and ideas to form a new whole system different from and greater than the sum of its parts or competing factions. We have the knowledge, the skill and the resources to create the world that works for everyone. Do we have the will to do so?

-- Excerpts on social and conscious evolution by Barbara Marx Hubbard.[1]

This Conscious evolution urges us to accept our higher and ultimate truth that is based on the oneness of spirit and takes us beyond all those old beliefs and practices that were rooted in ignorance or misinterpretations. It calls us to wake up, and create our future consciously by choosing what serves us collectively and reject all those inhumane systems, structures and processes that created a dysfunctional society with all sorts of discriminations and divisions. It asks us to move over those lower emotions and beliefs and embrace our highest truth to acknowledge that omnipresent, omniscient and omnipotent spirit pervading all things and all beings.

It pushes us to cultivate our social energy to initiate a social revolution and evolution for co-creating our collective future by developing individual and collective consciousness and potential, design new systems, processes and paradigms that work for all, not just for some selective sections of society. It asks us to accept out greatest truth and dharma (duty) that is to serve the highest collective good and move above all personal motives, preferences or loyalties. It urges us to develop a scientific temper to question, reform and reject every such choice or action that is not good for the collective well-being of society.

As we evolve, we are becoming more aware and intolerant of social, economical, and environmental injustices, imbalances, degradations and longing for a radical transformation in our obsolete and old social systems that are beginning to disintegrate and becoming dysfunctional day by day. As Barbara suggests, there is an awakening happening that is propelled by various civil and human rights movements, spiritual transformational literature, new age philosophy, music, yoga, meditation nudging us to wake up and become the harbinger of a new world.

This awakening is urging us to explore more, know more, do more, come out and declare that this is not the way……things don't have to be like this! This new consciousness that is evolving is giving birth to new social movements that are revolutionary yet, this revolution is not destructive rather it is constructive and evolutionary. This movement is here not to destroy but to fulfill the past inspirations and dreams of our previous generations, and to use the accumulative wisdom and resources for greater common good. It is here to assist our collective evolution and fulfill our highest collective potential.

We are at a pivotal point in history where the future of India would not happen by chance; rather it would depend upon the choices and decisions we make collectively today. The further course of evolution of India will be determined by our conscious decisions to utilize our powers and resources intelligently for a happy, positive and prosperous future for all and that calls for massive reforms and transformation of the existing systems and processes. We must let go what no longer serves us, break the systems that no longer work and change our democratic and political structure to take part in this movement of conscious evolution that is so radically changing our consciousness and our world.

70 years back our previous generation started a revolution by choosing a new vision and made a conscious effort to secure a better future for all of us. They rose and revolted against oppressive forces, fought to break free from the chains of repression and bondage to make the dream of a free India come true. After years of slavery and humiliation, they envisioned an India where all Indians are free, equal, happy, healthy and prosperous and are living in peace and harmony ever after. As the inheritors of their hard-earned legacy of freedom and the last generation to witness their struggles and sacrifices, now it is our turn! Now it is our responsibility as a nation to make their dream turn into reality and pass the

legacy to our children. We need to rise again and unite for another revolution and start a new freedom movement to create a new India. Only this time the enemies are within!

This is the time to break old destructive patterns, paradigms that created separatism, inequalities, conflicts, and a dysfunctional society and build a new evolved, empowered and enlightened society where we all work together purposefully, harmoniously and cooperatively to create a model country that our children and future generations will be proud of!

This is the time to create a whole new India. We need to dismantle the existing inhumane systems, structures and processes that gave rise to hunger, diseases, poverty , inequality, communal disharmony and violence , degraded so many human lives and environment; and come together to create new social processes, structures, and systems that provide better education, healthcare, social - economic justice, equal opportunities, peace, progress and prosperity for all. We must redesign our social and economic system to create a new society that is based on compassion, cooperation, creativity and encourages all to explore their unique potentials and purposes. A society where everyone has equal opportunity to live a life of dignity, to work, to thrive and equal access to national resources.

A new India is emerging as millions of us are awakening to our spiritual and human potentials individually and collectively. Our collective wisdom body that has been built over the years by our collective human efforts and intelligence calls us to share our gifts, pool our resources and expertise to bring out the glory of our individual and magnificent collective future. A glorious future that calls us to collaborate effectively and intelligently to create a social revolution that is not destructive but constructive, and would fulfill the promises of the past and our collective potential. A revolution that would transform the crises and adversities into opportunities to create a better and higher order. And as we cooperate and align ourselves to re-pattern our existing systems and processes, we too consciously evolve to a higher level.

India has finally come of age as centuries of discoveries, inventions, experiments, explorations, technological and intellectual advancements have opened doors to unlimited possibilities and potentials and have presented a new insight and choice to us – to choose from our collective experiences and create a better tomorrow for all. This is a glorious opportunity to take a pause.... take stock of the discoveries and developments till now.... ponder over the infinite potentials and possibilities.... select the best course and come together to choose- create - claim our highest potential as a nation to make India the supreme power of Asia and the crown of the world again.

The time is just right and we have all that is needed i.e. resources, manpower, means and tools to create a new India that works for all! It would just require our collective will, wisdom and actions to create an intellectual revolution to transform our country into a heaven on earth!

A new consciousness is arising and a new India is being born.....

Let us all come together and create a new India ...

A new India that is free of poverty, hunger, violence, communalism, terrorism, unemployment, illiteracy, unhygienic conditions etc.

A new India, where every citizen enjoys freedom, equity, justice, peace, harmony, progress and prosperity regardless of what class, caste or creed he belongs to. Where the fruits of nation's growth benefit all sections of the society, not a few chosen ones.

A new India, where there is no social, economic, communal division or discrimination and all people have enough opportunities, privileges to thrive and achieve their highest potential.

A new India, where the whole nation has awakened and overcome all differences and divisions and is united as one body, one mind and one soul. Where all collectively strive to create a developed India with a booming economy, sound infrastructure, progress, prosperity, social and national security for all.

A new India, where there is dignity of labor and the gaps between rich and poor, rural and urban do not exist. Where all have access to enough food, water, housing, quality education, health care and justice.

A new India, where all the resources are properly conserved, managed, fairly distributed and all people are living in perfect health, wealth, peace, harmony and are experiencing creative and holistic fulfillment.

A new India, where all children are provided quality education, skills and moral values... youth are provided best opportunities and employment.....women are provided equal opportunities, security and respect.....elders are provided care and dignified living....poor and vulnerable are provided basic necessities and better livelihood opportunities and all sections of the society co-exist in peace and harmony.

A new India, where the government is people's true representative, accountable, reliable, transparent and incorrupt. Where there is a perfect symphony between governments, public, private and various sectors and all work towards the common goal of co- creating a new India.

A new India, where every part of our great country is united and synchronized to optimize its full potential and India has achieved its final destiny as the super power and the crown of the world.

Now let's ask ourselves some questions:

Are we asking for too much?

Does a new India with such a vision still look like a pie in the sky or a far-fetched dream?

For how long are we going to wait for a better establishment or better leaders to come and change the face of India?

Do we really think that such an India will happen only in future...that proverbial always-on-the-horizon-yet-unachievable utopian dream?

Are we still waiting for some supernatural higher power or superheroes to come, save the world- save our country, and transform it?

Do we still think that we don't have enough resources, means or tools to create a new India that works for all?

I mean, do we really....really... think we don't have enough..........

Enough means or tools?
Enough opportunities?
Enough intelligence?
Enough manpower?
Enough youth power?
Enough resources?
Enough ideas?
Enough technology?
Enough Capacity?

Come on India!

are we fooling??

The truth is ....

That we all know in our heart of hearts, that never before have we been so resourceful, powerful and capable as today and science and technology so advanced that recreating our country was so practical and achievable!

The truth is……

That we all know, the only thing we lack is - the will! The collective will to take responsibility of creating a new India that works for all!

Let us face it ……

A new India is not a future idea…it is a reality waiting to be realized by all of us, for all of us, through all of us! It will take a revolution to create a new India that would lead us to our conscious evolution and by consciously choosing what works and rejecting what does not, we can transform our country into a heaven.

Now the only questions we must ask ourselves should be:

If not HERE then WHERE??

If not NOW then WHEN???

If not WE then WHO??

"THE CHOICE"

'Heaven on Earth' is a choice you must make, not a place you must find.-Dr. Wayne Dyer

"Ask yourself whether the dream of heaven and greatness should be waiting for us in our graves - or whether it should be ours here and now and on this earth."- Ayn Rand

The journey of India's evolution through eons of struggle, internal and external assaults- from the golden bird of east to the captured bird in the cage and its freedom- has been long and tedious. Civilization after civilization, generation after generation, so many seen and unseen heroes worked tirelessly and sacrificed their lives for India's freedom and victory. They all had a vision – to see our mother India sitting on its throne again free, victorious, proud and joyous. As their successors and the last link between our past and future generation, it is time to take the journey further and make their dreams come true. It is time to re-calibrate, re-create and re-surrect our country by conscious evolution and take it to greater heights.

We are living in radically paradoxical times. On one hand, India is being hailed as the fastest growing economy and next superpower, poised to take a mammoth leap; on the other hand, our internal economic and social inequalities and conflicts are weakening and threatening the very foundation of our country. We have never been so free, technologically and intellectually advanced, capable and resourceful as today yet mismanagement and misuse of national wealth and resources has created a great deal of oppression, keeping millions of our poor and deprived living below poverty line... starving... malnourished ....waiting for better social and economic opportunities. Our bright brains from esteemed institutions i.e. IITs and IIMs are wowing the world with their intelligence and acumen yet; millions of our young talents are being wasted due to lack of quality education, skills and employment opportunities. Our healthcare and Medical services have become world class and highly advanced, yet millions of our children are still dying due to ill health, unhygienic conditions and malnourishment. We have made remarkable strides in Science, research and information technology yet, communal discrimination and violence is deteriorating and disintegrating our communities. Our robust private sector is flourishing and scaling great heights yet, corruption, mismanagement of power and politics have hollowed the very roots of our public infrastructure, pulling India's potential down. All these issues have made India a country of extreme contrast. This dichotomy pervades every nook and corner of our country!

Years of neglect of our lower economic strata have created severe inequalities and imbalance in our society, and the result is that poverty and deprivation exist side by side in modern cities with developed industrial and commercial infrastructure. Our wealth distribution is insanely disproportionate and distorted and is considered as one of the most unequal economic structures in the world, with extreme contrast and contradictory conditions existing simultaneously. Ultra luxurious high-rises with the state-of- art amenities and guttery, dingy slums…… swanky imported cars and begging bowls….. lavish international schools and laboring children…… outrageously rich billionaires and debt-ridden dying farmers…… copious wealth and wretched poverty, show an ironical picture of a suffering Bharat hidden beneath the glitter and glamour of a much-hyped shining India. A Bharat that our mainstream India, politicians, policy-makers and elite are ashamed to acknowledge. This paradox has created a highly dysfunctional and divided society that puts a question mark on our intellectual capabilities and on the promise of India as an emerging superpower!

At this critical point, we must come together to make a conscious decision to co-create our future by choice- by using our collective power to effect sustainable and inclusive positive growth and changes in our country to achieve our highest potential. For so long we have been learning, it is time for action! We must choose now as inaction and lack of retrospection has already cost us dearly. Any more delay would create further distortion and imbalance. Any uneven growth will disrupt the momentum so like a gardener we must make snips & cuts to ensure that the growth is well rooted and all the branches are given proper attention and are growing healthy. We must take stock of our nation and co-create a new India where we all, through our individual and collective actions and creative capabilities; build a new vibrant society that is cohesive and cooperative.....a new human economy that works for all ....a new conscious, participatory democracy that brings social and political transformation ....a new sensitive, alert media and a responsible private sector that works with integrity and purpose for betterment of all.

"We must, therefore, act together as a united people, for national reconciliation, for nation building, for the birth of a new world. Let there be justice for all. Let there be peace for all. Let there be work, bread, water and salt for all." Nelson Mandela

For ages, our great Indian psyche and resilience have been misused and abused by numerous external invaders and internal power mongers. Our great tolerance, unconditional acceptance of all, flexibility, adaptability, lack of rebellion against oppression, obedience to higher authorities and lack of adventure have turned us into a submissive society that turns a blind eye to so many atrocities and social ills and is somehow unable to take a firm stand against repression and injustice. As a nation, we have lost the fire that prompted our previous generations to rise and rebel. Moreover, our great Indian spirit is lying dormant with a lack of national integrity and a national vision. This is time to rekindle that fire....this is time for impatience and determination not resilience as a nation and take concrete actions to make India a piece of heaven on earth.

The time has come for all of us to reunite for a new national vision and a national action plan. What we need today is an all-inclusive, comprehensive growth plan which uplifts not just a section of society but ensures prosperity and happiness for all... right from the bottom of the pyramid to the top. A multilateral, multi-dimensional approach and framework that ensures food, water, housing, job, education, health and social security to all.

As we know, Evolution always works on some basic principles that are sustainable and inclusive. It operates through the trinity of create-sustain-destroy (recreate) process and creates variety….diversity…… selects and sustains the best and destroys-recreates from the rest. Let us follow the process…. select what is best for all…. let go what is not inclusive or sustainable, and above all let this unity of diversity be our biggest strength and tool to transform our country.

For eons, all spiritual scriptures, religions and Avatars have been asking us to know ourselves, to overcome duality and find the unity in "ALL THAT IS." The same truth has been handed over to us by all the prophets and masters in various languages, cultural hues and shades that we all are one! The same consciousness that pervades the entire creation is expressing itself through all things and all beings. It does not matter what we call it - Brahma, Shiva, Allah, Christ, Jehovah or what today's scientists and quantum physicists call - the unified field or the singularity. The truth is that the same creative intelligence that created the entire universe……the suns, the moons and the stars has endowed us with the position of its most creative and supreme creations with highly developed brains and complex bodies. It has bestowed upon us the same creative intelligence and mighty powers of wisdom, actions and discernment; empowering us to play our role as conscious co-creators in the collective evolution of our country and planet.

It is high time we realized and accepted the truth. We all are parts of one collective body of creation. Each one of us forming different cells of this amazing creation - each one has a definite purpose and role in the entire creative evolutionary process. We can no longer behave or carry on as single, isolated identities as no cell can operate individually in a body lest creating havoc and driving the whole body doomed to destruction! Every creation…. be it a bird, an animal, a plant or a human; is a part of the whole cosmic body and has its specific place, purpose and role to play in this highly synchronized dance of creation…..ever evolving. Any step missed would disrupt the dance, so let us be careful, aware, mindful of our steps as the most intelligent and responsible players; we only have the ability to guide, maneuver and consciously drive our collective evolution to its perfect destination.

Denial of this great truth would lead to further imbalance and deterioration. Behaving as single entities, ignoring or refusing to see the cancers of poverty, hunger, illiteracy, inequalities, communal discrimination, terrorism, eco - imbalance, global warming etc. spreading in the body unless they attack us directly, would result in destruction only. We all know nothing can prevent the destruction of the body when each cell exists and works for itself heedless to the wellbeing of the whole body. Too late an action would only result in irreversible destruction. We must wake up and make the choice life wants us to make. We cannot deny our greatest truth anymore as time is running out. Life gives us only two choices – get in sync or get out of the way! We must act and play our role through conscious evolution or face dire consequences.

Acceptance, on the other hand, would lead us to create a heaven on this earth. A heaven, where each one glorifying his true essence and playing his part with perfect synchrony in the dance of evolution, individually and collectively. Self-realization of our oneness and empowerment of self and of others are the keys to ultimate happiness. Accepting and living our highest truth and helping others to do the same. Every small step taken towards real empowerment of fellow humans and ourselves will pave the path to real and lasting happiness for ages to come.

No more hunger...no more poverty....no more conflicts.....no more killings....no more scarcity....no more lack of anything to exist and survive....just joy and abundance that is the natural birthright of each creation. Does it sound too good to be true? No matter how mammoth the task of creating a new India seems, it is actually very simple as the truth is always simple yet profound. Once we accept and hold our greatest truth as one body.... each individual a cell in the body of creation ....everything will fall in place. The whole Universe will deploy its forces and resources to help us achieve our perfect collective evolution.

It is as if the creative intelligence is patiently waiting for us – human beings to accept our highest truth and participate in the evolutionary process to unleash the full potential and possibilities to achieve our perfect future.

The road where we are today, therefore, leads us to two destinations... unconscious destruction or conscious evolution!

In short, make a heaven or a hell out of it!!

Well, frankly……..do we really have a choice?

It is high time we stopped criticizing the system or blaming the government for every ill that is happening in the country and playing the victim card. For, governments, bureaucrats are just a tiny part of the system, but as the primary stakeholders in the world's largest democracy we, the people of India, all 1.3 billion of us, are the system itself.

The government is just the representative of the people of India, to serve India not to rule or dictate. Unless we take a collective social responsibility for the growth and development for all and change the system, nothing would change. Only the faces will keep on changing. The point is not what this or that government did, or how they are doing better or worse than the others. The point here is what India can and must do with all her resources- huge skilled and raw manpower pool, great knowledge pool, vibrant technology and abundant land area and bio- mineral resources.

As Mandela said – "No political democracy can flourish if the mass of the people remains in poverty, without food, shelter and tangible prospects for a better life. Attacking poverty and unemployment must, therefore, be the priority of a democratic government and the entire nation. And to do it successfully a collective intention and a comprehensive program is required that is achievable, sustainable, and meets the objectives of a stable, thriving economy and an improved standard of living and quality of life for all people within a peaceful and stable society."[2]

Just what do we lack today...natural resources? Manpower? Brain power? Technology? Visionaries? Youth power? Means? Tools? No we have everything in abundance ...so many visionaries, illuminated and enlightened minds have already presented brilliant blueprints for India's overall growth and success....we have the brightest brains on earth with us, the largest pool of skilled and unskilled manpower at our disposal, best financial and technical institutions, science and technology at our fingertips, abundance of bio, mineral and chemical resources, service and strategic sectors, massive youth power, largest agriculture resources, brightest economists, scientists, entrepreneurs, intellectuals, analysts, academia, a robust and successful private sector, global support etc. We have it all! We just lack the collective will and vision to turn India into a developed country and the happiest place on earth to live in.

We need to unite as one mind, one soul, and one body as Mother India with a multi-dimensional and multi-lateral approach in form of effective strategies, action and implementation plans to eradicate the monsters of corruption, poverty, illiteracy, unhygienic conditions, poor infrastructure, communalism, unemployment etc. destroying our country; once and for all. Yes, It calls for a revolution ....indeed every revolution is good. Anything that asks for a change – a fundamental change- any adversity that comes to shake our base is an opportunity to rule out what is not working and start all over again with a sound foundation for a sound outcome. It is a call to let go the past and create a new future…..bigger, better, brighter with the experiences, inventions, discoveries, technology advancements our country has acquired. We have the best of means and tools to choose and create the best. All we need is a spiritual, intellectual, social revolution that would lead us to our collective conscious evolution. Today we are a step away from making the changes for the betterment of our entire country.

We must focus on the need to achieve a more balanced and equitable development by promoting inclusive, sustainable and equitable economic growth; raising basic standards of living, developing better social and physical infrastructure; creating greater opportunities and reducing inequalities by leveling playing fields. We must strive to create a healthy and harmonious environment by conserving, restoring and promoting sustainable and integrated management of natural resources and ecosystems that in turn would support overall economic, social and human development.

We must create an enlightened, evolved and empowered society and play our roles and responsibilities in nation building through cooperation, contribution and collaboration. We must participate and demand the highest levels of governance based on trust, integrity, transparency and accountability. Such efforts combined with good governance and unity in our dynamic cultural diversity would create a healthy social and economic environment in the country that will nurture abundance and contentment and promote peace and harmony with nature, others and ourselves, which is the very essence of true happiness.

That is what real growth, advancement and evolution mean. Social, economic empowerment, peace and happiness for all. Not only we live in abundance and joy but help others do the same. We need not do any charity as that would mean making others dependent on us and cripple them for life. Real charity means empowerment, making people self-dependent, showing them the strength, which is inherent in every human. Those who discovered their power must empower others by sharing the wealth of their ideas, expertise and work through collective will and efforts to make it work for all.

Ask not what your country can do for you; ask what you can do for your country- JFK

Again, the question is not that whether our governments will do it or not....the question is whether we, the people of India as a team , will do it or not? We saw what a feat team Gandhi had accomplished to free our country. Imagine what our team India can accomplish if united!

We must rise above all divisions, differences and work as one body, one mind, as one India. Our only "Dharma" should be our duty towards our country, our people and our environment and our only "Karma" should be creating happiness and prosperity for ourselves and for all. Let us all become India's head, heart and hands and make it whole, free and victorious again. Let not a single of its children go without food, shelter, education or clothing. Let not even one of its youth go without skills or job opportunities. Let not even a single one lose life over petty issues and insane differences.

Let this vision be our collective national vision. Let us all come together to make this vision a reality.... the government, public sector, judiciary, , academia, businesses, media, intellectuals, industry, professionals, workers, farmers, women and the youth of our country– all working towards the same goal of creating a heaven on earth and making India a shining inspiration and a force to reckon with in the entire world. The land of wise and the bird of gold... let us all put India on her throne again.

Let us all become the harbingers and light bringers for our future generations- history will always remember us for the courage.....for making the right choice at the right time.

To quote **Vivekananda:**

"Let us all work hard, my brethren; this is no time for sleep.
On our work depends the coming of the India of the future.
She is there ready waiting. She is only sleeping.
Arise and awake and see her seated here on her eternal throne,
rejuvenated, more glorious than she ever was — this motherland of ours."

Arise…..Awake…..Stop not till the goal is reached.

Taking stock of the journey so far....

Let us take stock of India's journey so far .....

How far have we come?

What have we learned?

Where are we going wrong?

What are we doing?

What are we missing?

What should we do?

How should we do it?

India's journey started with a dream of freedom and the promise of democracy. Let us have a recap.....

The dream of freedom

The Swaraj of my...our...dream recognizes no race or religious destinations. Nor is it to be the monopoly of the lettered persons nor yet of moneyed men. Swaraj is to be for all, including the farmer, but emphatically including the maimed, the blind the starving toiling millions. We should wipe away tears from every eye." We should be messengers of peace for our country and we should work and die for our country.

I shall strive for a constitution, which will release India from all thralldom and patronage, and give her, if need be, the right to sin, I shall work for an India, in which the poorest shall it is their country in whose making they have an effective voice; an India in which there shall be no high class and low class of people; an India in which all communities shall live in perfect harmony. This is the India of my dreams....I shall be satisfied with nothing less. - **Mahatma Gandhi**

In 1947, after a long period of inner and outer assaults, struggles and innumerable sacrifices, a free India was born. For the first time in the history, people of India finally made their dreams of Swaraj (self –rule) a reality. On the cornerstones of freedom, equality, justice and dignity, the foundation of world's largest democracy was laid. After years of slavery and humiliation, the excitement about the idea of a free and self-governed India was palpable. The leaders who ushered India into a new dawn of freedom had a vision of a new India with a self-elected government, which was of the people, by the people and for the people.

This vision became the beacon of light for drafting the Constitution of India and our founding fathers ensured that the Constitution of India secures the fundamental rights, social, economic and political justice, freedom of thought, belief, religion, equality of opportunity, status and right to life with dignity to all the citizens. To make sure that every citizen of India as the primary stakeholder of democracy is empowered to participate in the growth story of a new free India, they included the "Directive Principles" in the Constitution like right to life with dignity, right to quality education, right to quality health services, right to food and right to employment etc. They cherished the dream of democracy and envisaged India as a socialist country and a welfare state where these directives became the national conscience and guideposts of our constitution ensuring 'inclusive growth and development' for all the citizens.

The Constitution further evolved and directed that it must be the duty and social responsibility of the governments (central & states') to apply the Directive Principles in making laws and policies to ensure social and economic justice and inclusion to all like securing right to work, to education, to health and to public assistance in cases of unemployment, provide social security for old age, sickness and disabilities, promote small scale industries, securing all workers a living wage and work opportunities, ensuring a decent standard of life . It further directed that the primary aim of elected governments should be to establish a welfare state and strive to remove inequalities of income, employment, status, living standards and distribution of economic resources for an even and orderly growth and development and for the empowerment of every citizen ensuring that no one is left behind.

These welfare policies and inclusive development strategies were later integrated and laid the foundation of the National Planning Commission and guided various policies, programs and schemes for the first 5-year plan and all successive plans thereafter.

Today, as we celebrate the 68th anniversary of our republic, against this vibrant democratic framework of these fundamental rights, directive principles and successive plans and policies; let us take stock of the journey so far- how far have we come to fulfill this vision of our founder fathers and how sustainable and inclusive our growth has been ? What are the achievements or missed opportunities and where do we stand globally in our quest? Let us find out what distances need to be covered, select the best course that works for all and reject what is not working.

A country of contrasts

"Economic equality is the master key to non-violent independence .Working for economic equality means abolishing the eternal conflict between capital and labor. It means the leveling down of the few rich in whose hands is concentrated the bulk of the nation's wealth on the other hand , and a leveling up of the semi starved naked millions on the other hand naked millions on the other .

A non – violent system of governments is clearly an impossibility so long as the wide gulf between the rich and the hungry millions persists. The contrast between the palaces of New Delhi and the miserable hovels of the poor, laboring class cannot last one day in a free India in which the poor will enjoy the same power as the richest in the land." - **Mahatma Gandhi** [3]

In 1930 when India was under British rule, Jawaharlal Nehru wrote about the pathetic conditions and suffering as: "A servile state, with its splendid strength caged up, hardly daring to breathe freely, governed by strangers from afar; her people poor beyond compare; short-lived and incapable of resisting disease and epidemic; illiteracy rampant; vast areas devoid of all sanitary or medical provision; unemployment on a prodigious scale, both among the middle classes and the masses."[4]

In 1947, after getting independence, he said in his famous speech - Long years ago we made a tryst with destiny, and now the time comes when we shall redeem our pledge, not wholly or in full measure, but very substantially .The ambition of the greatest man of our generation has been to wipe every tear from every eye. That may be beyond us, but as long as there are tears and suffering, so long our work will not be over.[5]

In 1962, the Nobel-winning Mexican poet and Ambassador Octavio Paz traveled to India and wrote about India's incredible opulence surrounded by equally unbelievable poverty. Yet, even after many years of steady growth and development, that shocking observation of the travelers about India being a "land of extreme contrasts" and its unusual patterns of unequal development still persists.

In 2017, many successive governments later alas, our work is still not over yet. Unfortunately, the contrast " **between the palaces of New Delhi and the miserable hovels of the poor, laboring class"3** ;that our father of nation so hopefully predicted would not last even for a single day in a free India ; has lasted seven long decades!

No man is an island quoted John Donne famously but anyone visiting India, treated by the sights of island of ridiculous wealth and luxury surrounded by filth and abject poverty... worth thousand crores' mansions and penthouses of stinking rich surrounded by miserable, dingy slums would never agree with him...welcome to the country of contrasts! The ever-growing inequality between the rich and the poor is striking and disturbing. A tiny section of India is shining and celebrating its success, but the majority of Indians are still waiting and hoping against hope for their turn. These extreme poverty and miserable slum conditions existing in the midst of ultra-luxurious high-rises and five-star hotels show a contrasting picture of India's growth story, that famous Nobel prize winner economist Amartya Sen and Jean Dreze' described as **"making the country look more and more like islands of California in a sea of sub-Saharan Africa".**[6]

Today, Indian economy is hailed as the world's fastest growing economy poised to become a superpower in the world. However, these seven decades have been full of contradictory growth measures and outcomes, making India a country of extreme contrast. While India has taken great strides from where we stood in 1947, there are still many other areas where things have not improved much. The objectives of the liberalization and globalization that were sought with the hope that the fruits of high growth would trickle down and would bring prosperity to all in terms of inclusive and sustainable social and economic development of the nation, unfortunately, have not been realized.

Though it's a fact that after the economic reforms in 1991, the GDP of our country is on rise and India has emerged as a leading world economic power attracting a great deal of foreign investment, increased international trade output and climbing up global competitiveness charts but the global indexes and indicators show that while India is going up the ladder in macroeconomic rankings, its performance on social indicators is going down. In fact, in many areas, it is almost at the bottom of the indexes which reminds us that we still have a great distance to cover before we can claim to have arrived.

Today, India is one of the fastest growing countries in the world and its growth story is attracting great attention globally yet, this high growth remains a paradox as it has failed to translate into higher and sustainable development and a huge section of the country is still suffering badly due to critical socio –economic issues like poverty, unemployment, inequalities, low levels of human development and slow infrastructure.

Of course, India has performed well in many areas post-reform, mainly in higher economic growth, trade and exports, increased growth in service sector, telecommunications & information technology (IT), improved foreign exchange reserves, stock market etc. and what India has achieved cannot be undermined but at the same time, there have been some massive failures in some crucial areas like slow development in social, agriculture, infrastructure, manufacturing sectors topped with public sector's failure of service delivery, mismanagement of national resources and revenue, misplaced priorities and policies, faulty processes, huge gaps between targets and outcomes etc. that led to widespread destitution, hunger and malnourishment, lack of basic facilities like housing, electricity and other essential infrastructure, poor health and education infrastructure, slow growth and growing socio-economic inequalities; that can't be ignored either. It makes India a country of extreme contrast.

This paradox exists in all spheres of growth and development in India, from poverty to inequality, health, education, jobs, infrastructure, public and private sectors etc. It made **Amartya Sen comment- "The history of world development**

offers few other examples, if any, of an economy growing so fast for so long with such limited results in terms of reducing human deprivations or improving social progress." He further wonders- Something must have gone terribly wrong in the past decades of Indian democracy, for our record in the social sector - be it healthcare, education or gender justice - is dismal; we are even worse than Bangladesh in living standards. [7]

Moreover, the GDP of a country does not really give a clear picture of its growth story. Around the world Gross Domestic Product (GDP), and growth rate have been extensively used to measure economic progress over the years yet, amid this GDP hoopla and growth rate obsession, we tend to forget that these measures were never intended for this purpose! GDP merely gives a partial, short-term measure of the amount of the final goods and services produced in a country in a particular year or any given period but what matters is not just how much is produced but how the gains are distributed and utilized to improve the lives of all citizens rather than some selective sections of the society.

GDP growth must translate into inclusive, sustainable economic and social progress, equitable development, increased opportunities, and uplifting living standards for all. In this regards, GDP is not an effective metric to determine the well-being of people in a country.

Robert F. Kennedy famously quoted - "Yet the gross national product does not allow for the health of our children, the quality of their education or the joy of their play. It does not include the beauty of our poetry or the strength of our marriages, the intelligence of our public debate or the integrity of our public officials. It measures neither our wit nor our courage, neither our wisdom nor our learning, neither our compassion nor our devotion to our country. It measures everything in short, except that which makes life worthwhile."[8]

The best way to measure a country's growth is to start valuing and evaluating those things that matter and make life worthwhile like human dignity, national integrity, unity and equality, human development, inclusive social progress and prosperity, quality of education, health, housing, employment, and environment etc. After all, a country's success and its leadership will eventually be evaluated on whether it was able to make a difference in the lives of its citizens who have been deprived of the benefits of education, health, and housing.

However, facts and figures show that even after 70 years of independence, 26 years of economic reforms and being hailed as world's fastest growing economy with its GDP growing steadily over the years; the benefits of India's economic growth have not trickled down to the millions living at the bottom of the pyramid. The face of "shining India" has another hidden side of a "suffering Bharat" that shows a contradicting picture where on one hand India claims of everincreasing technology, space and nuclear programs and ever-growing billionaires; on the other hand, the majority of population (around 68-69%) still lives in villages with most of the rural poor surviving on low income, low quality health, education facilities, inadequate rural infrastructure and lack of better opportunities.

As we discussed earlier, such contrast indicates that there is something missing in our method and measure of inclusive growth and development. While India's performance in global competitiveness index improved in quite a few areas like innovation, efficiency in the goods market, business sophistication etc., the global indexes and indicators on human development and social progress are falling behind other developing nations. What is worse that in some crucial indicators like health, nutrition, and education, India's performance is dismally lower than the poorer and slower developing countries in the group.

The fact is disturbing as India is now being hailed as the next "Asian miracle" and is ready to overtake China to join the exclusive club of "Asian miracle" economies, such as Japan and South Korea and the four Asian Tigers (Hong Kong, Taiwan, Singapore South Korea). The point however remains, that all these countries have had phenomenal success in not only increasing per capita income and living standards of majority of their population but also in reducing poverty, improving educational standards, creating efficient infrastructure and making affordable health care services available to most of its citizens as well, a feat that India has failed to achieve so far!

Moreover, what's worth contemplating is that around 1950, after India became independent; most of these countries were dirt poor and had almost similar income levels as India but in the 1960s, several of them, including South Korea, Hong Kong, and Singapore, started to have accelerated growth, underwent rapid industrialization, high technological development, maintained exceptionally high growth rates till 1990 and developed into advanced, high-income economies in the 21st century. Their economic success stories are known as the "Asian miracle" and have inspired many developing countries, particularly, the Tiger Cub economies namely Indonesia, Malaysia, Philippines, and Thailand who followed their growth model. Even China followed their path albeit, partially. In fact, around 1980 China and India had almost the same GDP and China's per capita was lower than India around 1991, but today China's GDP and per capita is almost four times greater than us. Similarly, most of the tiger economies have per capita incomes more than 10 to 20 times of India.

What is worse that in another peer group that India shares with China - BRICS (Brazil, Russia, India, China and South Africa- known for their large populations), not only India is lagging behind in terms of per capita GDP (India's per capita GDP one third of Brazil's, and one-fourth of Russia's) but in many important social indicators and in quality of life too, India is an exception. In fact, while every other BRICS nation has achieved universal or near-universal literacy in the lower secondary enrolments and higher primary enrolments, India scores the lowest in the list on both dimensions. Similarly, on the dimension of Higher Education, quality of education, gender equality, health and childcare and immunization etc. also India remains a laggard. The poor performance on providing basic human needs like access to electricity; sanitation and piped water etc shows a contrasting picture of India's growth.

Most of the global indexes and reports on human development, social progress, sustainable development, shared prosperity and equality validate these findings and have categorized India as low social progress and low human development nation despite being an economic success while China and other neighboring Asian countries have outperformed India on many social and economic indices like poverty, education, health care, employment, social security, infrastructure and housing etc.

What is obvious from these indexes and reports that despite being a bright spot in a slowing global economy and fast economic growth; the growth story of India seems to be skewed and there is something terribly wrong in India's path of development.

So what went wrong?

The failure

"An imbalance between rich and poor is the oldest and most fatal ailment of all republics."- Plutarch

"Why is India proving such a failure?" asked noted journalist John Elliot in his book "Implosion," a question that needs to be retrospected and debated urgently within India. With the culture of jugaad (quick-fix) and chalta hai (let it be) rampant in the country, as an outsider he made an important observation when he wrote - **"India punches below its weight, failing to achieve what it could and should be doing."** [9]

No other sentence could better sum up India's journey so far! It explains the great unachieved potential of India not only from the perspective of other miracle economies but for a nation that is a study of contradictions. He further states- "perhaps the biggest and most important…is the failure to rise to the expectations that stem from the combination of a rich and deep culture with an apparent openness and accessibility, plus an unrealized potential in terms of people and natural resources" and "where politicians and bureaucrats link with businessmen to plunder the country's wealth, deprive the poor of sustenance and aid, steal natural resources that range from land and coal to wildlife, and secure future wealth through layers of political dynasties". [10]

The same question was raised by India's chief economic advisor Arvind Subramanian recently in an interview with regards to the IMF's prediction on India overtaking China this year. He said - "We are going to grow faster because we are poorer, so the fact that we are going to overtake China is good. But it is a reflection of how poorer we are than China in level terms. The flip puzzle for India is not that it is going to overtake China, but why it didn't do so earlier?"[11]

There are still many concerns and apprehensions about India making it to the "Miracle economy category. Any more delay would cost India dearly for, as a country, we have already missed the bus as far as the Asian miracle growth stories are concerned. In fact, we are 25 years far too late!

Before we celebrate our achievements, we must evaluate our progress in terms of missed opportunities or lessons learned and what must be done to catch up with others before we could claim to have arrived.

There was a comparative study of East Asian economic development in 1990 conducted by the World Bank to understand how these Asian economies achieved such rapid growth. The study concluded that some of the Main drivers behind the "East Asian Miracle "phenomenon were focused attention and investment in human and physical resources i.e. health, education and infrastructure during the early years of development, comprehensive land reforms for equitable and inclusive growth, choosing priority policies, areas or sectors for providing a stable macroeconomic environment that included a balanced relationship between governments and private sector with a large export orientation. What made their effort more remarkable was the factor that instead of focusing on the one-dimensional approach to economic development, these countries deliberately adopted "choose and focus" strategy until the desired results were achieved. Moreover, this strategy set the priority areas and became the fundamental principle of their development plans that was assessed and adjusted after every five years to accelerate growth and development.[12]

China too followed these principles closely though, partially, as their land reform policies resulted in less equitable distribution than the other successful countries like Korea or Taiwan but its focus on improving its human capital and keeping a stable macro-environment with a strong export orientation, made it keep the momentum going. In short, the miraculous transformation of these countries from dirt poor to high income was mostly due to their ability to set realistic goals and taking pragmatic approaches on "getting the basics right," according to the World Bank.[13]

India's economic performance, on the other hand, remained lackluster compared to its neighbors. Though India saw a boost in economic growth after 1990 trade liberalization, other economic reforms, the pace slowed down, the fiscal and current account deficits rose, and GDP growth fell. It failed to follow the "East Asian Miracle "principles, and as a result, its human capital and physical infrastructure lagged behind these economies. India's economy failed to build a robust manufacturing sector and remained largely closed and mostly service based. Income per capita and trade remained low, and on social indicators, also it lagged behind China, Korea or Taiwan and other peer group countries. Today China's GDP has grown to $11,008 billion from $59.7 in 1950 almost 184 times, but India's GDP grew at a slower pace in the same duration from $ 37.7 to 2,096 billion currently.[14] Result- China's per capita is four times and GDP is five times of India!

In 1980, the number of poor in India was half than China at 402 million against China's 785 million but today that has grown ten times to (268.3 million) against China's just 25.2 million. Moreover, India's middle class accounts for only 3.1% of globally (wealth of $10-100k) and has not changed much while China accounts for a huge 33% of middle-class people globally, almost ten times of ours which has doubled since 2000 and shows that China's growth has been able to lift millions out of poverty into a thriving middle class even if inequality is on rise in both the countries.[15]

There was another interesting observation that these miracle economies mostly had the authoritarian and socialist governments yet they promoted an open economy and advanced from "middle income" to "advanced status."[13] India on the other hand, despite being the largest democracy in the world somehow failed to deliver the promise of democracy to its stakeholders yet, the failure to develop its human capital, physical infrastructure and a successful socio-economic environment is not a democratic failure rather it is a failure of politics – of the promises and mandates of successive governments.

Moreover, it is a failure of management of policies and priorities to provide sustainable and inclusive development to all the citizens. After the economic reforms when other Asian economies took off, critical formative years of nation building were wasted in India by successive governments' misplaced priorities, communal politics, and massive corruption. The miserable and disastrous performance of India's huge public sector in providing basic services like health, education, and nutrition only made things worse. Instead of focusing on health, education and developing human and physical capital, the entire thrust of our policymakers was on economic growth that failed to achieve long term goals of our constitutional vision that is highly ironical, for the very vision of sustainable and inclusive growth and focus on human development have been the foundation and the goals of the National planning commission and successive five-year plans.

After getting freedom in 1947, our leaders swore to end poverty, ignorance, illness, social and economic differences and inequality of opportunity. They were greatly influenced by the vision of Democratic Socialism that was based on the idea that a nation should provide enough freedom to private sector to thrive but at the same time, should keep a check on one-dimensional approach and tendencies to ensure that they use this freedom to achieve the main objective of social gains rather than economic gains only.

Mahatma Gandhi too was greatly pained by the contrast between the rich and the poor. He said "The poor villagers are exploited by...their own countrymen, the city-dwellers. They produce the food and go hungry. They produce milk and their children have to go without it. It is disgraceful. "Today there is gross economic inequality. The basis of socialism is economic equality. There can be no Ramarajya in the present state of iniquitous inequalities in which a few rolls in riches and the masses do not get even enough to eat. Everyone must have a balanced diet, a decent house to live in, and facilities for the education of one's children and adequate medical relief."

He was sure that India would become truly independent only when the poorest of its people would be free from human suffering.

Ironically, his dream of Ramrajya has turned out a nightmare for India by successive governments!!

Consequently, based on these overwhelming concerns for the poor and equitable distribution of wealth, opportunities and other resources, the first National Planning Commission was set up In March 1950 and all successive plans thereafter. In fact, after 1991 economic reforms, the eighth five-year plan was made with human development as the ultimate goal. All major policies were focused on creating jobs, controlling population, universal primary education, poverty and illiteracy eradication, providing safe drinking water and primary health care facilities to all. Further plans re-emphasized the need for inclusive growth and self-reliance in agriculture, eliminating human deprivation with recently launched 12th plan and the planning commission (now known as NITI Ayog - National Institution for Transforming India) gearing up for the same.

Every successive government after independence based their election mandates on "Garibi Hatao," "Roti Kapada Aur Makan" etc. and made big promises to eliminate poverty and inequality. Unfortunately, even after having such strong concerns for eliminating poverty and deprivation, promises to focus on human development and wowing to follow constitutional directive principles, India has repeatedly failed to deliver.

Amartya Sen emphasizes that **"economic growth is just a mean…..human development is the goal. The purpose of development is to enrich human lives, not the richness of economy which is only a part of it."**

He further states – **"We have to recognize the importance of the two-way relationship between economic growth and the expansion of human capability, while also keeping in mind the basic understanding that the expansion of human freedom and capabilities is the goal for which the growth of GDP, among other factors, serves as important means. Growth generates resources with which public and private efforts can be systematically mobilized to expand education, health care, nutrition, social facilities, and other essentials of fuller and freer human life for all. And the expansion of human capability, in turn, allows a faster expansion of resources and production, on which** economic growth ultimately depends. This two-way relationship has been a central feature of the so-called 'Asian economic development.'[16]

The UNDP's Human Development Report that is based on Amartya sen's human capabilities- positive freedom theory and promotes development as a function of human potential rather than economic growth alone; suggested that for just four per cent of its GDP, India could provide "a basic and modest set of social security guarantees for all citizens with universal pension, basic health care, child benefits and employment schemes.[17] In the recent economic survey, Arvind Subramanian, the chief economic advisor, India has also emphasized that for 3% of GDP (that's what all the subsidies cost us), India can provide a universal income to all the deprived ones and wipe tears from every eye. The Survey said, it has been necessitated in India, all the more because there is weakness in existing welfare schemes that are plagued by misallocation, leakages and exclusion of the poor.The central government alone runs close to 950 central and centrally-sponsored sub-schemes, which cost about 5 per cent of GDP, clearly there is a rationale for many of them, but there may be intrinsic limitations in terms of the effectiveness of targeting."[18]

The UNDP (United Nation's development program) has also suggested a broad inclusive framework for national employment strategies, along with interactive policy formulation approaches to promote worker's rights and benefits and decent work practices for a more equitable, cohesive society where all citizens enjoy the freedom of association, equality, security and human dignity.

Similarly, in a recent World Economic Forum (WEF) "**Inclusive Development Index**," India has fared worse than other countries in the same income bracket, such as Egypt, Indonesia, Nigeria and Pakistan. India was ranked at the bottom 60 out of 69 countries on most of the parameters for inclusive growth and development even as it has performed much better globally on business and political ethics fronts. Even Pakistan at 52 is doing a better job than India when it comes to inclusive development governance. Two BRIC nations, Russia and Brazil, are at 13th and 30th places, respectively. Others in the top ten are Poland (4th),

Romania (5th), Uruguay (6th), Latvia (7th), Panama (8th), Costa Rica (9th) and Chile (10th).[19]

WEF has noted that while India fared well on finance for business development and investment and business and political ethics, corruption, large administrative processes and underdeveloped infrastructure hamper the scene. Huge disparity in income and wealth distribution and bottom ranking on most parameters like access to education, sanitation, health coverage and infrastructure show that India has yet to embrace inclusive growth and development for all its citizens.

WEF observed that India's poor performance is due to certain factors like regressive tax regime, low social spending and limited access to health care and basic services like sanitation that continues to be a problem. The focus must be to make the growth process more inclusive so that the share of the population living on less than $2 can be reduced and moved to middle class. India must encourage equality of education and employment as educational enrolments and labor force participation is low and informal sector is huge where many workers are vulnerable and susceptible to external shocks and market fluctuations.

An article in Wall Street Journal suggests China is doing a much better job of taking care of its population of more than one billion people as more Chinese are educated, covered by healthcare and there is a much larger middle class compared to India[20], and that's why China is an "upper middle income" economy while India is a "lower middle income" and has an economy more than four times the size of India's. The US has the largest number of affluent class and China has a bulk of middle class while India accounts for one of the largest numbers of poor population in the world.

Another report by Indiaspend shows that India's middle class accounts for only 3.1% of the global middle class bulk (wealth of $10-100k) and has not changed much over while China accounts for a huge 33% of middle-class people globally, almost ten times of ours which has doubled since 2000 that shows that China's growth has been able to lift almost 800 millions out of poverty into middle class ;even if inequality is on rise in both the countries; that is the highest feat a country ever achieved . Even as the growth of wealth has been the fastest in India after China in the last 15 years yet, more than 90% of the adult population falls into the bottom of the wealth pyramid (less than $10,000), indicating the uneven distribution of wealth in India.[21]

At the other end of the spectrum, there are around 230 million living below poverty line (officially) that is the most ridiculed and pathetic poverty line in the world and shows the lack of empathy and common sense of our policy makers. According to various estimation (from conservatives to liberals), the numbers of BPL people may vary from 20 to 50% of the population as there is a lack of consensus among states too. The issue is not only politically sensitive, but it has other complications too like a low threshold and acknowledging 240 or 600 million under BPL means a drastic change in the fiscal policies and priorities for governments! After all, the higher the number of BPL population, the greater subsidy spending for the government! The Rangarajan panel considered people living on less than Rs. 32 a day in rural areas and Rs. 47 a day in urban areas as poor.[14] Most economists and critics believe that the poverty line is deliberately kept low by policy makers to gain political mileage and show that many millions have been lifted out of poverty.

Moreover, huge sections of the population such as discriminated communities, minority ethnic tribes are not included in the official data. This kind of social exclusion or marginalization of large sections of the population is clearly a violation of basic human rights and the right to live a dignified life, and it's a known fact that a country that fails to provide protection and opportunities to its vulnerable or marginalized communities, face a higher risk of social disorder and conflicts. There are so many environmental concerns, consequences of mining and other disruptive activities on forests and there have been cases of secret MOUs signed between governments and big corporates/ industries resulting in lacs of poorest tribals being driven out of their lands and placed into camps that have led to Naxalism and violence within the states.

The refusal to acknowledge these issues will only delay solutions because how can we debate and tackle any issue if it officially does not exist? Ignoring these facts would create more problems as a direct effect of this poverty is rural migration that results in urban poverty that creates a plethora of problems like massive joblessness, underemployment, slums and crime etc. Urban poverty gives rise to a dangerous and unbalanced society as watching the privileged section enjoying the benefits of growth might stir discontentment, instability, and violence in the lower strata.

The global risk report [22] has already been warning nations that growing global wealth inequality and unemployment are becoming the fundamental risks to democracy and to economies around the world and these issues are really dangerous as more and more people think that governments favor the rich and the rules are rigged in favor of them, and if they are not able to succeed within the system, they will find other means and ways that break the system.

There are many experts and economists who repeatedly emphasize the need to tackle inequlity that can prove to be the greatest socio-economic challenge for any nation. The 2015 Nobel Prize winner in economics, **Angus Deaton** said in a recent interview "**Revisions that increase growth are more readily accepted than revisions that reduce growth. So I am more worried about growth being overstated than poverty being understated in India,**"[23]

The consequences of not tackling inequality result in the rich capturing more political power, and the state stoping serving the common people, a fact that is observed in the recent report by the **World Bank – inequality and shared prosperity**, [24] that while many countries, well almost 40 of them have been able to get income inequality down, but in India it is rising. That leads to various issues like crime rate going up, social conflicts, recession, depression and civil disturbance etc.

 World Bank researchers have found out that those countries who successfully reduced inequality recently (Brazil, Cambodia, Mali, Peru and Tanzania) used six high-impact strategies that rapidly produced results and they are- better nutrition and child care in the first 1,000 days of life, affordable public health care, access to quality school education, increase in earnings of poor families, roads and electricity in villages and a tax system that transfers resources to the poor. Moreover, the most significant factor that worked is the ability to choose and focus the tailor made policies and strategies to cut inequality and the World Bank said if countries could act strategically, they can also achieve the faster results.

According to the World Bank - though, India is the fastest growing economy; the income of the poorest is growing at a slower pace than the average.[24] Even Pakistan is better than India in this regard! One more common belief is that high inequality exists in most developing or developed countries like China, Russia, and the USA too yet, in these countries everyone has the basic needs covered like education or health while in India the level of deprivation is something else. What are we waiting for? We need not wait for even higher growth to provide basic health, education or infrastructure to all as many countries with lower growth rate and per capita income have shown excellent human development indicator than India. For sustainable and inclusive development , both higher growth and higher human development are needed.

What's more, the worst victims of poverty are children who have to bear the brunt of it as the parents fail to afford good education or health facilities, their chances to escape dim and they get trapped in this vicious cycle. In a recent noteworthy report, "Even It Up" Oxfam [25] showed 85 people own as much wealth as the poorest half of the global population put together. This is a "tiny elite whose numbers could all fit comfortably on a double-decker bus." They further said that "the growing inequality between men and within nations, continue to block chances for billions of the world's poor to improve their life situations as a child born to a rich family, even in the poorest countries, will go to the best school and will receive the highest quality care if they are sick. At the same time, poor families will see their children taken away from them, struck down by easily preventable diseases because they do not have the money to pay for treatment."

This inequality is more evident in our education system that is so extraordinarily diverse where while, a small section of our privileged class enjoys high-quality education, ample opportunities, and facilities to excel and rise up the ladder, the rest has to rely on the pathetic public system that is still deficient with inadequate resources and facilities; nipping their future prospects in the bud!

Similarly, while our bright students from the esteemed IIT and IIMs are highly successful and wowing the world, India remains the country with the highest number of illiterates – around 280 million according to a recent UNESCO report.[26] Despite implementing the fundamental right of right to education, around 50% of our children can't read or write properly while almost 70 % drop out before completing the full education cycle because of unavailability of seats and lack of resources at higher levels and though, the secondary and tertiary levels have seen some expansion, the higher education levels especially technical and vocational training systems remain inadequate. This dysfunctional educational division is not only unjust but is one of the biggest reasons for India's uneven growth and productivity. With about 600 million people below the age of 35, India has the largest demographic advantage - the largest young population in the world, but alas, we don't have the infrastructure and facilities to provide them enough opportunities to utilize their optimum potential!

"The World Economic Forum's Human Capital Report 2016"[27] that measures the human capital of 130 countries showed a disturbing picture of our dismal education and employment sector. The Index shows how countries are nurturing, developing and deploying skills, knowledge or experience of their people for economic growth. India (105) ranks very low in the index, almost at the bottom and manages to get ahead of only last ranking countries like (118) and Nepal (108) while most of the neighboring countries like Bangladesh (104), Bhutan (91) and Sri Lanka (50) have performed better than India. Among BRICS countries, India is ranked lowest as against Russia's 28th, China's 71st, Brazil's 83rd and South Africa's 88th.

WEF reported that India has optimized only 57 per cent of its human capital with youth literacy rate at only 90 percent (103rd in the world), well behind the rates of other leading emerging economies. India also ranks poorly on labor force participation with the largest employment gender gap and is ranked 121 among 130 countries. Finland, Norway and Switzerland hold the top three positions, utilizing around 85 per cent of their human capital.

No wonder India, despite being the fastest emerging economy, is still categorized as a "low income, low social progress and low human capital" country in the various global indexes and reports. In the Social Progress Index (SPI) 2016 [28] too regrettably, India does not perform very well and ranks 98th out of 143 countries. The report says there is a great scope for improvement for India. The SPI report defines social progress as the capacity of a country to meet basic human needs of its citizens, establish building blocks that allow citizens to improve their lives, and create the conditions for individuals and communities to meet their full potential.

The SPI offers a comprehensive framework for measuring social progress that is independent of commonly used economic measures like GDP and provides a holistic and systematic foundation to guide strategies and policies for inclusive growth and development. The indicators reveal a stark reality and show that a country's level of social progress is the result of collective and effective choices made by its governments, citizens and businesses about how to invest and integrate the limited resources for better outcomes.

In other words, GDP is not destiny or the end as widely believed, what matters is how we choose to invest our surplus GDP. Whether it is used for political ends or for developing our human, physical and environmental resources and capitals, that makes the difference. SPI measures inclusivity, equality and serves as a roadmap for guiding policy making and prioritizing our decisions and resource. It is a great tool to analyze and assess what really matters.

By shinning a light on where we're advancing social progress and where we're still falling short, the SPI helps us all be more effective agents of change."- Sally Osberg, CEO, Skoll Foundation.

GDP does matter to a great extent, and higher economic growth raises many out of poverty but social progress may not always relate to higher growth. Many areas of concern like environmental sustainability, human development and rights, political rights and freedom do not improve with economic growth as seen in many countries. Many smaller countries that have made substantial investments in their social safety nets perform better like Costa Rica, Uruguay, Nicaragua etc. over performed on social progress while some rich countries like Kuwait, Iraq, and Saudi Arabia fall significantly short on a number of progress measures.

After all, the true purpose of our global competitiveness and economic uprising will be fulfilled only when the fruits of our growth reach all and we achieve Sustainable Development Goals by eliminating hunger, diseases, malnutrition, illiteracy and uplift all, leaving no one behind. Yet, another report that shows how far India is from achieving these goals is, the index launched by the Sustainable Development Solutions Network (SDSN) and the Bertelsmann Stiftung that provides a report card for tracking Sustainable Development Goals (SDG) progress and ensuring accountability. India has ranked a low 110 out of 149 nations on 2016 country list.[29]

In 2015, the UN general assembly formally adopted 17 new development goals designed to end poverty and hunger by 2030 based on the three pillars of sustainable development: social, economic and environmental along with good governance. India is the worst BRICS performer on the UN SDSN list. The point to note here is that the countries that are closest to fulfilling the goals are not the biggest economies but comparably small, developed countries.

We need to have a reality check before we could claim to have arrived. We must find out the causes of India's low performance on the social front and explore all the possibilities and solutions for pushing India to become a world leader in economic as well as in social development.

Let us have a reality check with some facts and figures before proceeding to explore the causes and solutions…..

India- A reality Check

"The test of our progress is not whether we add more to the abundance of those who have much; it is whether we provide enough for those who have too little."

— Franklin D. Roosevelt

No society can surely be flourishing and happy of which by far the greater part of the numbers are poor and miserable.

--Adam Smith

Despite being hailed as the country with the 3rd largest numbers of ever-growing billionaires, India is still home to the 1/3rd of world's poor and deprived population. While a tiny section of emerging middle class is prospering and enjoying the fruits of increased growth and wealth, the greater part of India's 1.3 billion people remains disadvantaged and overall social indicators have hardly improved. As Amartya Sen and J Dreze' explained – the economic reforms based on Western capitalism that promoted "trickle down" economy failed as most of India's aggregate growth is occurring through a disproportionate rise in the incomes at the upper end of the income ladder, that has served to make the rich richer while the bulk of the Indian population is still overwhelmingly poor, remain disadvantaged and overall social indicators have hardly improved. In some cases, they seem to be going down. [30]

As for India's poverty line, it is the most mocked and disputed line and known as the starvation line in the world. According to the latest World Bank report, India is by far the country with the largest number of poor people living under the international US$1.90-a day poverty line, 224 million, more than 2.5 times as many as the 86 million in Nigeria, which has the second-largest population of the poor worldwide, Sub- Saharan Africa has one in two of the poor worldwide, while India accounts for one in three. [31]

But the recent Multidimensional Poverty Index (MPI) report of UK-based Oxford Poverty and Human Development Initiative (OPHI) 2016 and the United Nations Development Program (UNDP) say that according to the index that measures deprivation on six indicators, over half of India's population is multi-dimensionally poor, while a further 18 % are close to destitution line.[32]

According to the 2016 Report, India has the highest multidimensional poverty after Afghanistan in South Asia. Nearly 54% of the Indian population is multidimensionally poor compared to 66% in Afghanistan. The poorest region in South Asia is Bihar, followed by 'South' Afghanistan. The poorest 15 subnational regions in South Asia are all in India or Afghanistan, plus one region (Baluchistan) of Pakistan. There are more 'Multidimensional poor people (421 mn) in the eight poorest Indian states (Bihar, Chhattisgarh, Jharkhand, Madhya Pradesh, Orissa, Rajasthan, Uttar Pradesh, and West Bengal) than in 26 poorest African countries combined (410 mn).[33]

India tops the list with the most number of poor of the world. India's inability to ensure basic levels of nutrition is the greatest contributor to its poverty. Its recent analysis said the largest number of people classified as 'destitute' among developing countries was in India , the measure identifies a subset of poor people as destitute if they experience a number of extreme deprivations like severe malnutrition, losing two children, having all primary-aged school children out of school, and using open defecation.[32]

The fact became more evident in the recently released tax data that showed only 5-6 % of Indians have been working in formal sectors with an income of 2.5 lacs per annum and above. A staggering number of Indian household's i.e. 93% of the total population earn somewhere between $2 to $ 10 a day according to global reports. So while we go on chest thumping about India's GDP rating climbing to 3rd position in PPP (dollar exchange rate- purchasing power parity), by the same measure, 93% Indians would be considered below poverty line in US

and other developed countries where the poverty line is almost 12- 16 $ a day!!!
[34]

While a tiny affluent class has created a cozy cocoon and live an exciting urban life in ultra-luxurious high rises with world class amenities, credit cards, social media, holiday trips; more than half of India consisting of rural and urban poor who live below multidimensional poverty line, lack means to fulfill basic needs like food, energy, housing, drinking water, sanitation, health care, education, and social security. And millions of Indians, who are just above the basic poverty line, continue to struggle for a life of dignity, comfort, and security. The fact is that while India is one of the fasted growing economies in the world, it has also become one of the most unequal countries with the inequality levels at their highest since independence, which belies the cherished democratic rights of life to dignity, equality of opportunities and inclusive and sustainable development for all.

Moreover, the gap between the rich and poor is getting wider as the richest 1% own almost 58% of the country's wealth. According to the latest report from OXFAM,[35] only 57 billionaires own $ 216 billion that is equal to 70% population's share. The rich are becoming richer as the income of top 10% went up by 15% while the income of bottom fell by 15% over last 20 years. The richest 10% own 76.3% of India's wealth while at the other end of the spectrum, the poor at the bottom of pyramid struggle with only 4.1% of national wealth.[36]

The fruits of its massive economic gains are yet to reach rural poor, farmers and a vast number of deprived, marginalized people, Adivasis and other discriminated communities which make up to 25 percent of the population, that often leads to widespread social exclusion resulting in social disorder, violence and communal tensions in the country.

Moreover, India is increasingly going downhill with job creation as it has been a jobless growth for past few years. According to a new United Nations Development Program (UNDP), over 25 years of unprecedented economic growth could not get 43% Indians suitable jobs.[37] An example of this is that according to comparable data from the International Labor Organization, real wages in manufacturing in China grew at an astounding 12% per year in the last decade compared with about 2.5 % per year in India. In India, by contrast the growth rate of real wages has been much lower than that of per capita GDP over the same period showing a very large part of the Indian economy is suffering badly with acute under-employment and human underdevelopment.[38]

India today has the best demographic dividend in the world with almost 600 million of youth force (workforce) entering the job market in the coming years and to do so it needs to create at least 25 million jobs every year yet, in last three years, not even 1/3 rd. of the target is achieved. India's official employment data site – the labor bureau that shows a 7-year low employment generation in all eight key sectors in 2015. In fact, the unemployment rate has shot up to a 5-year high of 5 percent in 2015-16, and about 77 percent of Indian households do not have regular wage/salaried person. Out of 1.3 billion Indians, over 60% are of working age and out of 10 to 12 million Indians who enter the job market every year, only a few get employment opportunities. After demonetization, the scenario in SMS and MME has worsened. While big industry houses in various investor summits promised mega investments, few have fructified. [39]

Also, only 4 to 6% of them undergo skill training as compared to an average of more than 50% across the developed countries in the world. The fact is evident as India's skilled workforce is only 2-4% compared to other countries like Korea (96%), Japan (80%), Germany (75%), UK (68%) and China (40%).[40]

Not to forget that more than 90% of our workforce is in the informal or unorganized sector without any fixed income or social security, that is highly unstable and according to a recent report in Forbes[41] , around 18.7 million Indians are engaged in modern slavery even after the 70 years of independence!! Out of those working in the informal sector, as many as 60% do not find employment for the entire year showing ever spreading 'under-employment' and lack of temporary jobs. In the absence of any safety net, they live in a vulnerable state and prone to fall back into poverty due to health, sudden economic shocks or calamities as seen during recent demonetization drive.

On the education front, of those children who finish primary education, 83 percent transition to the next level. Enrolment rates for grades 9–12 are just 40 percent, and of those enrolled, approximately 15 percent drop out, and one-third fail their examinations.[42] While we have some of the best private schools and institutes for privileged urban population, our public education system is in a dismal state. Despite having one of the largest education systems in the world with more than 1.4 million schools with over 227 million students enrolled and more than 36,000 higher education institutes, millions of our students don't have the right skill sets. Of all the students entering the job market across the country, hardly 1/3rd meets the criteria of employment set by various employers (out of 97 percent graduating, only 3 percent have suitable skills to be employed in software or product market, and only 7 percent can handle core engineering tasks according to research agencies). According to UNESCO, India still accounts for one-third (over 250 million adult people) of the globe's illiterate people.[43]

According to a latest UN report (submitted in 2016 by Housing and Land Rights Network) [44] India has the world's largest number of urban poor and landless people, 31% of India's population (377 million people) lives in urban areas while 69 percent (833 million) is rural. India also has the largest number of landless persons (over 500 million) in the world. Fifty-six per cent (101.4 million) of rural households do not own land while 30 per cent (53.7 million) households consist of landless labourers, who face the worst deprivation. Though land ownership is highly inequitable, land reform is not a priority. The average land given to rural landless families fell from 0.95 acres in 2002 to 0.88 acres in 2015.The draft National Land Reforms Policy 2013 has not been finalized. Instead, land pooling policies are being promoted,which result in loss of tenure, and in many instances, increased marginalization of landless agricultural labourers.Despite the existence of a rural housing scheme operational since 1985, the national rural housing shortage was 40 million households; 90 per cent for 'below poverty line' houseOholds.ver 13 per cent (23.7 million) of rural households live in one room with kutcha (mud/temporary) walls and roof.

The report further said that " over the last few years, several new schemes have been announced/renamed. Pradhan Mantri Awas Yojana (PMAY; Housing for All–2022) proposes to construct 20 million houses in urban and 30 million houses in rural areas by 2022. Despite PMAY's existence for over a year, most projects are still under the approval stage. As of 17 August 2016, the Ministry of Housing and Urban Poverty Alleviation had sanctioned 891,346 dwelling units under PMAY but only 2776 dwelling units had been constructed. Almost 65-70 million Indians live in slums and footpath across the country. Thirty-six per cent of these houses does not have basic facilities of electricity, tap water, and sanitation within their premises. Around 8 million children under six years (mostly homeless children, street children, displaced children, and those living in low-income settlements, relief camps, resettlement sites, and other precarious locations) suffer from insecurity, malnutrition, adverse health, increased vulnerability to diseases, and the absence of secure places to play and grow. India, reportedly, has the highest number of street children in the world."

Mahatma Gandhi once said "India lives in villages" many years ago, ironically it still stands true as the data shows the majority of Indians still live in the villages. Though the migration from rural to urban areas is on rise, still, almost 69% of India continues to live in rural areas. As per the last census' report, (barring the rich farmer's community) in nearly 75 percent of rural poor households, the main earning family member makes less than Rs 5,000 per month (or Rs 60,000 annually). Just 8 to 10% of households have a salaried person while over half of all rural households derive their household income mainly from casual manual labor. Another 30 percent derive it from cultivation. Around 56% of rural people don't own any land while 30 per cent of them are laborers who face the worst deprivation. [45]

Up to 300,000 farmers have committed suicide since 1997 due to economic distress as per the Global research article [30], and many more have quit farming while 300,000 of the nation's poorest people being driven from their lands in tribal areas with thousands of them placed into 'camps' in the name of development by government and private companies. Rural wages are at the lowest in the decade, as agriculture sector, which employs more than half of India, is growing at snail's pace. More than half of India's farmers do not have access to formal credit. Only a tiny percent of farmers has access to crop insurance, and given the high dependence on weather, are exposed to the vagaries of nature. Poor people are highly vulnerable to health shocks with medical expenses contributing to household poverty.[46]

India's growth story has been driven by a services-led growth model with nearly 65 percent of GDP contributed by the service sector yet the sector provides employment to only 28% of Indians, a little better than our weak manufacturing sector which employs only 12% of Indians and contributes 16% to India's GDP while almost 50 percent of India's workforce is engaged in agriculture sector that contributes a mere 17 percent to the national productivity (GDP) with very low productivity levels.[47]

On the health front, we are a country that is the highest exporter of milk and has surplus wheat and rice production yet millions of our children are dying of hunger, malnutrition or lack of proper hygiene, sanitation. Almost a third of all children in our country are stunted and even after a dozen social welfare schemes launched in the last few decades to tackle malnourishment, it remains a primary health concern in India. 19.8% are wasted (underweight and short) and 36% are underweight according to the recent global reports India has a "serious" hunger problem and ranks 97th out of 118 countries, according to the Global Hunger Index that was released last year. The report by the International Food Policy Research Institute said 15.2% of the country's citizens are under-nourished, with 38.7% of children under five years being stunted because of lack of food. India was given a GHI score of 28.5, which is worse than the developing nation average score of 21.3. India's GHI score has fallen by 25.4% since 2000, according to the report. It also ranks worst among its Asian neighbours with the exception of Pakistan, which ranked 107 on the Index. China was placed at the 29th position, while Nepal ranked 72nd, Myanmar was 75th, Sri Lanka 84th and Bangladesh at 90th place.[48]

According to Unicef, stunting and other forms of under-nutrition are thought to be responsible for nearly half of all child deaths globally. Stunting is associated with an underdeveloped brain, with long-lasting harmful consequences, including diminished mental ability and learning capacity, poor school performance in childhood, reduced earnings and increased risks of nutrition-related chronic diseases, such as diabetes, hypertension, and obesity in future. A lack of adequate food is a primary cause of death, under-nutrition, and stunting; but the story of child mortality and malnutrition in India is not just one of poor diets. The lack of water, sanitation and hygiene practices - which leads to illnesses and life-threatening diseases like diarrhea - is thought to cause of up to 50 percent of all child malnourishment. 2.5 billion Cases of diarrhea in children under-five are recorded worldwide every year.[49]

According to the social progress index 2016, some other basic human needs indicators also show a contrasting picture of India's growth as only 28.1 % population has access to piped water compared to 73% in China and 87% in Russia. Similarly, only 39 % of total population has access to improved sanitation facilities while the ratio in Russia and China is over 72% and around 78 % Indians have electricity while Russia, China, and other developed countries have 100% population having access to electricity. India still has one of the highest open defecation rates in the world.

Increased investment in infrastructure is critical for India to improve its manufacturing competitiveness and achieve higher growth. A failure to bridge this infrastructure deficit—particularly in the power and transport sub-sectors—could dampen expected economic growth in the years to come, according to a recent report.[50] The Indian government expects it will need $1.15 trillion in infrastructure investments over the next 10 years, but according to the report, this figure will only help India meet the existing infrastructure shortfall "rather than create room for more growth in future." With private investment down after demonetisation and public banks suffering from bad loans, NPAs and twin balance sheet problems, the infrastructure growth in India still remain too low compared to its peer group countries.

So where are the benefits of India's meteoric GDP growth going?

Where are we going wrong?

"In a country well governed, poverty is something to be ashamed of. In a country badly governed, wealth is something to be ashamed of."

— Confucius, Chinese teacher and philosopher.

As long as poverty, injustice and gross inequality persist in our world, none of us can truly rest.

-Nelson Mandela.

The question is despite numerous policies and programs, massive amounts of aids and spending to alleviate poverty and malnutrition in the country, every 3rd poor person in the world an Indian, one in every 15 Indians hungry and starving and around 30% of our below 5 years of age children malnourished and stunted, what GDP growth numbers and super economy are we talking about? We have the highest number of hungry and poor people in the world. What does being the citizens of the world's fastest growing economy mean to them? How can we become a superpower when little, undernourished, unclothed children live in pathetic conditions on the streets of our cities or sleep on the footpaths? How do we have a section having access to world-class schools and institutes like IITs and IIMs and yet the majority of our children go without the basic quality education? How do we claim to be the new rising global superpower when we cannot provide sufficient skills and job opportunities to our ever-growing young population?

No doubt, India has achieved partial success in improving its performance on these issues yet the missing urgency to eliminate hunger and poverty from the country and provide jobs to the ever-increasing young population; that is predicated as an explosive situation by all global experts and economic pundits, makes one wonder what else should be the priority of the nation!!

Many global researches and a recent report by OXFAM[51], suggest that contrary to the common belief that inequality is an inevitable outcome of high economic growth and globalization, the fact is that inequality is the result of poor economic and political choices and policies. When governments encourage market fundamentalism and favor the rich elite in the guise of privatization and freeing up the markets for higher growth, public investment suffers. That pretty much explains the situation in India today. In fact, this is the biggest cause of low social development in India after the reforms since last 25 years. India's successive governments pursued market fundamentalism rigorously while human and physical capital took a back seat.

Higher economic growth is always good for a country but not at the cost of it social growth as encouraging market fundamentalism opposes public investments in crucial social sector like education, nutrition and health, and progressive taxation, and demands dilutions of labor protections and acquisition of people's lands and forests, all of which further increase inequality. 25

Though, there is nothing wrong with encouraging market liberalization itself as all countries aspire to have higher economic growth yet in a developing country it can be disastrous because market forces will only invest in profitable areas and the role of states is reduced that is of empowering citizens and making sure they can participate in the economy and growth of the country which triggers further exclusion. That is why it is very crucial for countries to keep a healthy balance between both social and economic growth and unfortunately, in India since last 25 years, this has not happened and we have not learned from other miracle economies that thrived on this principal. On the contrary, there are plenty of examples of how liberalization led to more poverty and aggravated inequalities in India.

OXFAM emphasized that the high inequality not only undermines the productivity and morale of the working class but limits the workers" participation in the market too that is bad for a robust and lasting growth. It over-rides the commonly propagated belief that fighting inequality would damage the pace of economic growth.

OXFAM further states - "The ways to dam the surging tides of inequality are today well known: raising and enforcing statutory wages, expanding taxation of the rich, enhancing public investments in education, health and the small farm agriculture, enlarging social protection for the aged, infirm and disabled, enhancing maternity and child benefits, protecting indigenous and socially disadvantaged groups, ensuring water, sanitation and basic utilities to the rural poor and urban slums, and protecting the rights of workers. But in India, as in much of the world today, market fundamentalism, the political class and a section of powerful economic elites still determine state priorities and resist policies for a more equal world. The world, therefore, remains one in which however hard poor people, women and socially disadvantaged communities toil, to survive with dignity remains distant, often impossible dream. Such inequalities create a vicious cycle as growing disparities in income level also inflict direct costs such as low life expectancy, higher crime rates, growing violence and property offenses, poorer health, as well as social degradation like family breakdowns, vices and drug use. Unequal societies are affected by various diseases that are born out of poverty, poor nutrition and hygiene, inadequate housing, and a lack of sanitation and access to timely health services."

Oxfam report quoted Thomas Piketty who demonstrated in 'Capital in the Twenty First century', without government's intervention, the market economy tends to concentrate wealth in the hands of a small minority, causing inequality to rise. Despite the fact market fundamentalism played a strong role in causing the recent global economic crisis, it remains the dominant ideological worldview and continues to drive inequality'. The study, released by Oxfam in 2017 showed that just 57 billionaires in India now have same wealth (USD 216 billion) as that of the bottom 70 percent population of the country and while over the last two decades, the richest 10% of the population in India have seen their share of income increase by more than 15%, the poorest 10% saw their share of income fall by more than 15%.[52]

According to OXFAM, the major cause of inequality 'is the influence and interests of economic and political elites. Elites in rich and poor countries alike use their heightened political influence to curry government's favors – tax exemptions, sweetheart contracts, land concessions and subsidies – while blocking policies that may strengthen the rights of the many'.

Oxfam also asked the Indian government to end the extreme concentration of wealth to end poverty, introduce inheritance tax and increase wealth tax as the proportion of this tax in total tax revenue is one of the lowest in India. "Indian government must eliminate tax exemptions and not further reduce corporate tax rates. Governments must support companies that benefit their workers and society rather than just their shareholders," Oxfam said. "Indian governments must crack down on tax dodging by corporations and rich individuals to end the era of tax havens. Governments must generate funds needed to invest in healthcare and education. The governments must increase its public expenditure on health and education," it added. The recent economic survey also asked the Indian government to increase public spending on human capital yet it remains low. For instance, in 2017, the public health expenditure has risen just a little over 1 % of GDP but still remain below the world average of 5.99%. Similarly, with almost 600 to 700 million Indians entering the job market in coming years, the education expenditure at 3.7 % of GDP too is far below the world average of 6% (as seen in many developing countries).

India's chief economic adviser Arvind Subramanian in the economic survey has been emphasizing on the need for "double-digit growth" investments in health, education and delivery of services. He says "If India has to reap the benefits of this 'demographic dividend' in the years ahead, it is imperative that investments in social infrastructure are made in an appropriate measure to achieve the desired education and health outcomes," The 'sweet spot' created by a strong political mandate is still "beckoningly there" for now but "not indefinitely", improve investments in education and health, where India fares the worst among BRICS nations, the survey says to realise the potential.[53]

India has already missed the bus as far as the "miracle of social and economic growth" in the Asian region is concerned. Now with the highest number of young population in the world, still neglecting these crucial sectors will cost us much more than those lost 25 years!

The high contrast in our private and public health and education show the need for urgent actions to upscale the public infrastructure and services for facilitating inclusive and sustainable development that has been the success mantra of all major Asian economies.

The healthcare system in India validates this contrast as on one hand, India's healthcare sector is growing at a rapid pace around 17% per annum and is expected to become a US $280 billion industry by 2020 yet, nearly one million Indians die every year due to inadequate healthcare facilities and close to 700 million people have no access to specialized care. There are wide gaps between the rural and urban population in its health care system. A shocking 69% of the population still lives in rural areas and has no or limited access to quality hospitals and clinics. Around 80 % specialists live in urban areas. There is a huge shortage of doctors and other skilled staff at primary health care centers in rural areas yet, public spending remains low and results in inadequate infrastructure and manpower in public health facilities.[54]

India continues to have the largest number of infant deaths, maternal deaths and other diseases related deaths (India has high tuberculosis cases in the world). Our public health systems are in a dismal state as a high number of doctor positions at primary health centers are lying vacant, and thousands of community health centers do not have even a single obstetrician. Our health sector continues to be among the countries with the lowest relative public expenditure on healthcare at around 2% of GDP that is far below the world average of 6.5 percent. Even South Africa and Nepal spends a higher proportion. On the other hand, our private health sector, with its state-of-art infrastructure and specialties, is recognized as one of the best in the world.[55]

India ranks 143 among 190 countries as per the World Bank's Universal Health Coverage index on per capita expenditure on health, and 157 positions according to per capita government spending on health. Health insurance coverage is low and India has one of the world's highest rates of out-of-pocket spending in health care. Per-capita health care spending according to World Health Organization (WHO) in India is around $61 compared to Australia $6,110, China $367, Japan $3,966 and Southeast Asia (Singapore) $2,507.[56]

The 2016 Global Hunger Index report shows that although the level of hunger in the developing world has declined by 29 percent since 2000, we still have a long way to go. India ranks 97th out of 118 countries with over 15 percent of its population undernourished while China is ranked 29th with 9 percent of its population undernourished. India scored a 28.5, while China scored 7.7. According to the index, "Scores between 20.0 and 34.9 points are considered serious." [57]

The report also highlights that around 40% percent Indian children below five years of age are stunted, with 15.1 percent suffering from wasting. The report is an eye-opener and a wake-up call for us as at this rate we would not be able to achieve the UN's Sustainable Development health Goals in 2030. The reports show that we need to rethink and relocate our priorities and take necessary and effective steps to improve gender equality and address malnutrition and stunting, especially among young children if India aspires to outpace china and other Asian countries in sustainable and inclusive social development.[57]

Another report the *Lancet's* Global Burden of Disease study, which is a comprehensive global research program that assesses mortality and disability from major diseases, injuries, and risk factors, ranked India 143rd out of 188 countries in meeting its health care goals. India came at the bottom among the BRICS Nations health related goals and lagged behind other smaller developing countries too like Malaysia, Indonesia, Thailand, and Myanmar. [57]

In 2016, public social spending averages an estimated 21% of GDP across the 35 OECD countries (the Organization for Economic Co-operation and Development).[58] Public social spending-to-GDP ratios are highest in France, at 32% of GDP, followed by Finland, at over 30% of GDP. Belgium, Italy, Denmark, Austria, Sweden, and Greece devote more than a quarter of their GDP to public social spending. At the other end of the spectrum are non-European countries such as Latvia, Turkey, Korea, Chile and Mexico, which spend less than 15% of GDP on social support. Social spending in India in 2017 is around 7% still very much lower than the average.

There is also a debate on how much should India spend on education? The Kothari Commission (1964-66 based on Education Policy of 1968) had instructed then government that Indian public expenditure on education must be 6% of gross domestic product (GDP) that is a global norm across the world.[59] Since then every elected government reemphasized this goal during elections yet never could fulfill the promise. The average Public expenditure on education in the OECD countries (Organization for Economic Co-operation and Development) is 5.4% and in Brazil 5.8% while India has the highest number of population (29%) under 6 to 21 age group which need to be taken care of against OECD average 18%. Clearly, if India wishes to reap the fruits of its demographic dividend advantage, with such low budget our youth potential could not be realized!

India is lagging behind China and other countries in efficiency ratio too. Efficiency ratio shows the innovation output of a country and what it is getting for its inputs, which again reminds us that though we have a huge demographic advantage, we have not been able to nurture, develop or deploy our human capital to optimum use as China did. In spite of recent initiatives for skill development, the results are poor. In ICT and export, India is supposedly doing well yet the World Development Report 2016 recently, ICT's employment share falls to only 0.87% of the total employment pool.[60]

According to the study, the number of patent applications by residents in India is much lower than the numbers for comparable economies such as China and

Russia. In addition, the study finds only 3.84 percent of graduates qualify for start-up technology jobs. The World Development Indicators also show that India has consistently performed poorly as compared to the world average as well as against its peers in the case of researchers in R&D per million people. Yet our R&D and research expenditure remains low and neglected.

The global reports suggest that to become an innovation powerhouse, India needs to converge public and private sectors to participate actively in research and development related work and skill, re-skill and up-skill its people urgently. What is certain, that public investment in education and health remains distinctly inadequate and undermines India's development model. It is high time that our policy makers and governments took firm and focused action to tackle these issues as many international organizations like Oxfam, World Bank and International Monetary Fund (IMF) are warning India about the social risk of growing inequality.

The lackluster half measure in elementary education or in health through insurance schemes cannot tackle the main issues of poor quality of services delivery. Most of the allocation goes into infrastructure and salaries while quality and service issues are neglected. Moreover, the lack of concrete measures and the massive gap between expenditures and outcomes in India remains the most problematic issue not to forget the leaks, corruption and non-spending as there is no transparency or accountability in these processes. In this era of stiff competition where most countries such as BRICS, spend a much higher proportion of their GDP on health (ranging from 3.5% to 8.5%) to keep their people and workforce in good health that in turn increase the national productivity, India must pull up its socks and match the allocations to fuel and sustain high growth. It must walk the talks as there are huge commitments and initiatives launched every now and then, but the concrete results in terms of targets achieved and increased quality levels show a different picture.[55]

Considering the fact, that inequalities in education, skill training, and health are the main factors for increasing productivity, empowering and securing the workforce, in other words securing higher, inclusive and sustainable growth; India's public spending in GDP's share puts a big question on the intention and objectives of successive governments' promises to its stakeholders. Even after repeated election mandates, intents and political consensus to eradicate poverty and inequality, the unwillingness and inertia to change or increase the GDP share of public spending shows displaced concerns and misplaced priorities of our policy makers and governments.

It is not that India does not have the means or resources. Among the 77 OECD countries, India has the fiscal capacity to spend on healthcare and others, "contrary to popular perception that India has a low fiscal capacity, India has the capacity to wipe tears from every eye" according to the economic survey. [61]Still, our public spending on social Infrastructure that includes crucial sectors like education, health and delivery of essential services remains below average as we explored earlier.

This continued disregard for the interests of the underprivileged in public policy and failure to acknowledge the urgency and importance of a vibrant social infrastructure in the country leads to further exclusion and inequalities. The neglect of school education, health care, social security and related matters in our policies and planning is only one aspect of our policy makers' biased approach, the other aspects of it manifests as the neglect of agriculture and rural development, exploiting the natural resources for private gains and the showering of public subsidies and freebies on privileged groups.[6]

The privileged class in India -known as "Aam Admi-common man," varies from businessmen to educated ordinary people who are somewhere in between the "have all'and "have nots" as they are not rich enough yet have higher levels of the living standard than those deprived ones living at the bottom. This class is usually manipulated by the political parties for vote banks and showered with subsidies and freebies to survive in elections. The consequences of that is a colossal wastage of national wealth and resources which could be used for promoting inclusive development, developing social infrastructure or effective safety nets for the bottom 40% of those who are really deprived and need help. The biggest gainers of such subsidies are those affluent landowners, rich farmers, fertilizer companies or rich businessmen who drive in SUVs with subsidized diesel and enjoy free electricity according to the economic survey.

In fact, Arvind Subramanian calls this the 'Bounties for the Well-off and says that there are a fair amount of government's interventions that help the relatively better-off in society. Commodities that are primarily consumed by the rich have a low tax rate like gold or aviation fuel. For the rich, India is as good as a tax haven.[62] According to the survey, subsidies to the rich are hurting the capacity of the governments to spend more on essential sectors such as health, nutrition and education as the share of the top 1% it almost doubled in the past 15 years. The fact is disturbing according to many experts, that while the rich are able to amass considerable wealth, the failure to tax them more leads to a fiscal imbalance in the country. The fact has been emphasized in the economic survey that India's rich feed off subsidies worth over Rs. 1 lakh crore a year that are meant for the poor, citing the subsidies on six commodities, two public utilities, the Railways and electricity and one small savings scheme, the Public Provident Fund.

The economic survey has suggested some urgent reforms to address these problem that are decreasing income tax, reduce leakage subsidies and tax exemption and build a robust property tax regime.

International Monetary Fund (IMF) too has warned that Neoliberalism, a term used for the dominant economic ideology since the 1980s that advocates a free market approach to policymaking- promoting measures such as privatization, public spending cuts, and deregulation is the main cause of inequality and exclusive growth. It is generally antipathetic to the public sector and believes the private sector should play a greater role in the economy. [63]

As prevalent in every sector, our private sector too is a study of contrast though. There is one section that is hardworking, honest, has high business ethics, compassion, and national integrity believes in sharing profits and works towards fulfilling the aspiration of the fellow countrymen. On the other hand, there is another section that is self-centered, unethical, self-serving and is driven mainly by self-interest and profit at any cost. It hoards and hogs and does not believe is sharing the booty. It suppresses and exploits workers, manipulates the rules and regulations and influences politicians by sponsoring elections, financing rallies and arranging vote banks. This section lacks moral and social ethics and has a huge political clout. This political clout controls the nation, buys them tax exemptions, land concessions, cheap credit, and subsidies. The rising influence of this in the policy making, form a nexus of politicians-bureaucrats-business that is growing bigger and so are the favors for them warns OXFAM.

This fact is quite evident in our system where policies are being written to serve some of these elites while mere lip servicing is provided to the poor as our public spending still remain one of the lowest in the world even after many global warnings and recommendations and the incentives to the rich are increasing in the disguise of tax exemptions, cheap credits and subsidies on electricity, air fuel and water!

According to OXFAM, not only some of these elites are being benefited by these tax rates and exemptions, but manage to get favors back in disguised payoffs like subsidized credit and loan write-offs that resulted in a crumbling banking sector which was on the verge of collapse with piled up debts and NPAs (non-performing assets) again last year. What is amazing that using their political influence across political parties, most of them manage to get huge amounts of loans on fake and inflated assets without proper due diligence while majority of our landless farmers and poor workers who badly need the money for survival are turned down for measly loans of thousands and lacs loans due to the financial limitations and inadequacies of our rural banks!

Moreover, instead of reforming the legal and institutional framework to identify and penalize defaulters, Banks resort to distress sale of publicly owned assets to foreign capital leading to further financial inequalities. Banks are instructed to be lenient and help the defaulters by restructuring and rearranging their loans. As seen in the recent budget, public sector bank NPAs and problem loans worth several lakh crores are written off even after the Economic Survey complaining about the twin balance sheets syndrome that Indian banks and corporate community are suffering from. While on the other hand, even after two consequent droughts and demonetization hit, the debt-ridden farmers in many states like Maharashtra are still waiting for relief, as their loans are not waived off apparently due to lack of funds! All they are given is peanuts (interest waivers for 60 days) while the big corporates get the cake! No wonder India today has the largest number of debt-ridden, distressed farmers committing suicides!

This dichotomy of our government protecting the rich while penalizing the poor is perplexing. Instead of concrete policies and strategic reforms to tackle inequality and poverty, the incentives and protection of the rich and powerful while lip servicing the poor shows the insensitivity of our power brokers. The problem of bad loans has emerged largely because of the nexus of corrupt businessmen, negligent bankers and inefficient auditors and instead of bringing them to book and penalize them, the RBI has allowed huge amounts of debt to be restructured over the years, which has amplified the loss.[64] All successive governments have; in the name of globalization, allowed huge amounts of debt to be restructured over the years that has taken a toll on the banks that led to the near collapse of the banking sector.

Ex-RBI governor Raghuram Rajan repeatedly emphasized the need for a pro-market policy framework instead of a pro-business policy for proper and even distribution of benefits that he felt was a continuing problem with the Indian policy regime. In other words, India's economic policies are customized and tailored to cater to big business houses under liberalization garbs that would promote development and employment. He called it riskless capitalism flirted by the rich and powerful who in good times enjoy profits and in bad times are bailed out by the banks!! Many research agencies and Credit Suisse India has been listing these top business houses who owe huge amounts (more than 7.5 lac crores) to the banks and most of them are on the verge of being defaulters.[65]

Last year, the Bank's piled up debts and stressed advances were estimated around 6 lac crores that put a huge dent in the private investment sector; just got saved by demonetization! According to the latest report from RBI, the gross NPA may rise from 7.6% to 8.5% in 2017.

While demonetization saved the banking sector from collapsing and big business from failing, it created an irreparable loss to the underprivileged section of our society as it hit them hard. It shows the exclusion and apathy of our system towards the downtrodden! The farmers were already quietly suffering from last 2 years of consequent droughts and received nothing substantial from the government. Just when they were looking forward to a normal year, the shock of demonetization blew away the chances to recover losses. In the areas where there were bumper crops, poor policy choices like importing the surplus produces further made the situation worse. While those who amassed insane amounts of black money and unaccounted wealth invested in gold and properties or stored it in offshore banks and tax heavens escaped unscathed; the axe fell on the most economically deprived ones and daily wagers who suffered pitifully and were pulled back into poverty. Unharvested crops, rotting vegetables, falling prices-raising debts, loss of wages and work do not count in our national balance sheets as our policymakers need to keep the fiscal balance to keep macroeconomic stability to cheer up the global capital and stock market!

Of course, India needs global capital flow and for that macro stability and fiscal balance, both are important but not at the cost of India's poor and hungry who lost their livelihood and jobs. After all, the higher growth must translate into uplifting those who are most needy, not for the rich to get richer but alas, that's exactly what is happening in India since the economic reforms. As a democratic nation, our first priority should be micro stability to provide Roti, Kapda, and Makan to all the citizens especially, to the most vulnerable ones. Yet, all the policies like globalization, digitization, and demonetization are always made at the cost of our lowest strata. The hungry and unemployed need to be taken care of first as they don't have any other back up, unlike our market forces who have access to all the facilities and are in a better position to handle any shocks or fluctuations. Any policy that affects the most vulnerable ones without providing any alternate solution or social security needs to be debated and confronted, as that is a violation of their fundamental rights and states' welfare duties and provisions.

India has the potential to achieve 8 to 9 even 10 % GDP growth and for that, it needs private investments that in turn need a proper fiscal balance; at the same time, in order to have higher and sustainable growth, India needs to review, revise and prioritize its policy and implementation system so the twin objectives of raising public investment and maintaining fiscal deficit can be achieved without disturbing the balance.[66] It is no rocket science! Everyone knows that if populist subsidies, favorable credits and exemptions to corporates are removed and the tax system is rationalized, there would be enough revenue to invest in crucial sectors like agriculture, health, education and employment.

Now, when the global economy is down and private investment is low, the focus should be to revive the domestic economy. The issues like large NPAs, crony capitalism and political interference should be resolved to boost trust in private investments. Even as the corporate tax is reduced, they must be supported by increasing direct taxes, reduction in exemptions and revenue forgone should be brought down so that the revenue saved could be invested in infrastructure, agriculture and social sectors that are most crucial for achieving sustainable development goals and need urgent attention.

But it so happens that in India where votes bank politics is rampant and politicians have to keep everyone happy with populist measures and crony capitalism; there is always a revenue deficit and as a result, the axe of misplaced policies and priorities invariably falls on the most vulnerable sectors! A better and wider tax infrastructure with simpler processes, a better information system with citizens' data cloud, satellite and GPS-based data tools, tougher and smarter law enforcement and a tighter and more efficient administration could yield better results if implemented in a proper manner and generate enough revenue to meet the demand. Better services and transparent processes would also produce better results and generate more trust that is, unfortunately, lacking in our system and is a major setback.

To top it all, limited revenue and budget allocations are hijacked and siphoned off, shipped out of the country in black or leaked through the complex layers of our corrupt public system. Moreover, the black economy in our country is not a parallel economy; it is an inside job! The whole system is infected by corruption, the booty is circulated within the system amongst the politicians- bureaucrats along with the rich and powerful who amass it as black wealth (gold, real estate, bonds etc.) within and outside India. 90% Indians earn somewhere between 2 to 10$ a day according to global reports as we explored earlier. Top 10%, who own over 70% of national wealth, hardly store it in cash! Where is the massive black money? Most of the deposits in the bank are the hard-earned money and savings of public.

Also, as we all know that only low-level corruption is in cash, the high-level corruption uses e-cash, bank notes, Hawala route, tax evasions and other forms of cash like property deals or equities etc. that are huge in comparison. Then there are huge leakages in the funds allocated towards social welfare huge amount where the money doesn't reach the beneficiary but is siphoned off inside only to resurface in foreign banks and tax heavens as black money or come back (round tripping) via the FDI route disguised as white money to avail a plethora of tax exemptions! And not to forget, most of the unspent funds by various departments going back to the black hole called the consolidated fund only to be repackaged as new schemes or increased allocations.

These are the main causes and drivers of the black economy prevalent in our country today and they will continue unless the whole system is dismantled and reformed. As far as the fake money is concerned, it is already in circulation and terrorism and corruption are far from over. The gains of demonetization are debatable but the demons of it will plague the nation for long - slowdown growth, job losses, the collapse of the supply network, reverse migration of informal workforce have caused such irreparable and irreversible damage that cannot be estimated in terms of mere percentage of GDP growth.

Many renowned economists around the world have been questioning the need and effect of demonetization that is not actually understood even by the educated classes of India leave aside the uneducated masses who welcomed the move thinking it would punish big scamsters, black money holders and address the issue of corruption which unfortunately is not really true. Like Nobel Prize winner and Bharat Ratna economist Amartya Sen said -demonetization is as much of a failure as the promise to bring back black money stacked in the foreign countries! He said that the people who are best equipped to avoid the intended trap of demonetization are precisely the ones who are seasoned dealers in black money- not the high-interest people and small traders who are undergoing one more misery in addition to all the deprivation and indignities from which they suffer![67]

The same thoughts were echoed by the former US treasury secretary Larry Summers when he said- "petty fortunes and not the hugest and problematic ones are being targeted. He further added- "most societies would rather let several criminals go free than convict an innocent man". Yet in India innocents had to bear the cross of demonetization while the criminals got scot-free and yet the general perception is that, the move is for the common man's benefit that is sadly far from the truth.[68]

Similarly, former chief economic advisor of India and chief economist, World Bank Kaushik Basu said- "Demonetization was ostensibly implemented to combat corruption, terrorism financing and inflation but it was poorly designed, with scant attention paid to the laws of the market, and is likely to fail. So far its effect on middle, lower and poor class has been disastrous and the worst may be yet to come. While the intention in tackling the black money is commendable, it will only make a minor dent in corruption. It is, however, likely to rock the economy.[69]

"Demonetization cannot weed out black money as the owners of black money have already intelligently covered all the money into tangible and intangible assets- this is not a strike on black money as those who hold black money or black assets they do not keep them in cash. 1% of top rich own 53% of the total assets and 10% own almost over 85% of India's wealth. Now, these rich fellows cannot put all the money under mattresses! They are holding it abroad- and there also it is not in gunny bags, its property! Maybe jewelry, maybe other assets, maybe stock markets"- economists Arun Shourie explained.[70]

About demonetization promoting a cashless economy, as suggested by experts; is a premature baby as we simply do not have the infrastructure in place. Daily wage earners cannot use credit cards or online transactions as they earn just enough to buy food daily! Why not go and catch them who are supposed to amass massive black wealth. There are already names floating around of these black money holders by global agencies and WikiLeaks etc. Yet, instead of going behind them, or naming and shaming those listed in various reports and expose', the axe fell on those living at the bottom of the pyramid. Meanwhile, the remaining black money escaped through various routes to untaxed donations like temples and hospitals of which a certain amount would be returned to the donors as white money. A small amount of this has been written off but for now, the remaining black cash has been successfully laundered.

It is not about criticizing or condemning the government as there may have been strong reasons behind the decision. It is about going above party loyalties or preferences and debating the effects and gains as a nation to find out whether it served the collective good or not. What has it achieved? What are the gains or losses?

Moreover, the most important question is whether it was worth it? A country like India where over 90% manpower is in the unorganized and informal sector without any security net or fallback option, we must ask ourselves what should come first? The massive loss of jobs and livelihood when the country is already suffering from underemployment and unemployment; which is the most critical and explosive issue it is facing today; makes one wonder what else should be the priority of the nation? At a time, when India was poised to take on the world with the highest growth rate predicted to cross 8% , pulling it down to 6.1 % (Jan to march -2017) brought it back to square one! To fulfill the needs and aspiration of all the citizens, India needs to maintain atleast 8% growth rate; all miracle economies achieved this feat that we already missed post-economic reform. Unfortunately, we have not learned our lessons and India once again lost its miracle time due to poor policy choices.

Where there is no doubt that demonetization is an excellent tool to address corruption and improve digitization, we must ask ourselves do we have the bandwidth to lose any more jobs when the government has already failed to create a decent number in the last 3 years ? Do we have the proper infrastructure to support these moves without harming the ones who are most vulnerable? As a nation today, the need of the hour is to provide Roti, Kapda aur Makan and suitable jobs to all, especially those who have nothing. After the bad weather years, when things were looking up, a step like this derailed them again and hit them hard. To top it all, the bumper crops were mostly ruined by some ill–planned and ill-timed import policy decisions that lead to price crisis and massive wastage.

Ironically, the fiscal cushion (the promised fruit of demonetization) that was supposed to stabilize and support them in this hour of need instead is used to make the already rich and powerful more comfy!

We need to understand that all the credit schemes, bima yojanas etc. cannot substitute the pathetic social security and need for a steady income to survive. The increased allocations or random schemes cannot fulfill the urgent need for a comprehensive policy framework with improved monitoring and evaluating processes and definite time bound outcomes. We must ask ourselves whether just a tiny percent of GDP allocation for agriculture sector is enough to neutralize the effect of droughts and demonetization and provide income security to those working in the informal sector that is most affected by it? Is it enough to create much needed rural infrastructure or double the income of the farmers being promised year after year?

The integrated & sustainable rural development program designed by APJ Kalam in 2000 is by far one of the most comprehensive and effective plans ever introduced but unfortunately, it has been ignored by all successive governments. It would have changed the rural scenario by now with a thriving rural sector and increased per capita income of the rural people. Instead, every time a plethora of old schemes in new garbs are launched which never get translated into targeted outcomes.

Moreover, the obsession to keep the fiscal deficit down by cutting down social expenditure on health, education and agriculture to make the markets happy is something that we need to take a call on as a nation. Instead of implementing comprehensive, integrated, sustainable development strategies and plans; the focus is on random, short term gains or misplaced priorities like creating AIIMs hospitals while the country needs a basic primary healthcare system badly or a basic physical infrastructure or a bullet train while our railways need a massive infusion of funds to augment safety urgently. Sadly, the fundamental issues are being ignored that low revenue generation or tax fatigue are not because of the black cash in the economy, but the results of poorly designed, implemented and enforced tax policies.

Digitization also does not require drastic steps like these. It requires well-planned processes, focused, and well-monitored outcomes. Moreover, it requires a basic infrastructure on which the digital process can work. Ironically, globally India already ranks too low as far as the digital Infrastructure and e-governance are concerned. Only 1/ 3 rd. of our 1.3 billion populations has access to the internet. In rural and tribal areas there is scarce or no electricity or network even offline app would not be of any help. A large number of Indians including women have no bank account and only a few ATMs are deployed in rural India. Out of millions of debit cards, many are idle or have low value. A large percentage of PMJDY accounts lie empty. Out of a billion mobile phones, only a few have smartphones.

Moreover, most of the rural population would not even know how to make digital transaction even with a simple application as BHIM. There is still a huge section that is out of internet or banking services.

The fact is that the required infrastructure for a cashless economy in rural areas is critically inadequate. Power cuts, no electricity in almost half the villages, negligible or scant ATMs facilities, low literacy and awareness, lack of any formal training for rural and tribal citizens, make digitization- cashless economy premature policy choices that unfortunately, have brought more pains than gains. The logical decision would be to first have a basic infrastructure in place and then go for it. Those who hardly can meet their basic needs cannot afford to do banking and are dependent on cash and save it for rainy days. For years they have been taken for a ride with big promises of their income doubling and better days ahead yet nothing substantial is done to address their problems.

Of course, they are given record MNREGA funds and credit sops, which are supposed to double their income as promised though, someone must tell the nation how that feat would be accomplished as most of the marginal farmers (40%) who do not own land or any asset, do not even get the loans! So whom does the credit money go to? As seen in Maharashtra, most of the credit goes to Mumbai and to big agro-business chains and big rich farmers or farm businesses.

As far MNREGA is concerned, it is a demand based program and the expenditure for last year was already more than the allocation; with pending wages and the demonetization blow that pushed millions of informal workers out of their jobs and livelihood back to villages, how would the "record allocation" provide any job security to all of them? Also, it provides only 100 days job guarantee, but the national average is around 50 days, what about the remaining period? For almost a decade, the program was in bad shape and has been dragged by the previous governments. This year, the expectations ran high as the agriculture and informal sector are still reeling from the aftershocks of drought and job losses, yet, the amount allocated remains inadequate to stabilize them or fulfill increased demand.

Moreover, though it has been highly politicized, the increase in amount for MNREGA and SC ST funds is not the political will but the result of the Supreme Court's directive to the center and state governments to release the outstanding and necessary funds immediately, pay compensation for the delayed funds and meet the demand as per the directive. The court also pulled up the governments saying 50% success rate is nothing to be proud of. The average days of employment provided per household are around 46 days in drought-affected areas. The apex court said while issuing a slew of directions last May 2016 that Governments cannot hide behind a smokescreen for lack of finance.

It said if the state governments maintain an ostrich like attitude towards disasters like drought when millions are affected then the center cannot wash off its hands from the constitutional responsibility as the "buck stops" with a matter concerning common people. When the rights of thousands of people are affected by delayed payments of their legitimate dues, there is a clear constitutional breach committed by the governments; social justice has been thrown out of the window.[71]

According to the recent National Crime Record Bureau (NCRB) annual report, around 12,602 farmers committed suicide, an increase of 2% over the death toll recorded in 2014. Between 1995 and 2015, in a period of 21 years, more than 3.18 lakh farmers have committed suicide due to debts, poverty, health expenses and other various disturbing reasons. [72]

The farmers account for more than 50% of our informal workforce and the average income of a small farmer is almost below the poverty line. Half of our poor farmers are ridden with debts, most marginal and landless farmers work as contract labors on the farms owned by rich landlords or others agro-business owners. There is a section of rich farmers who are landowners and enjoy tax-free income and get most of the subsidies like credit, electricity and fertilizers that never reach those who are most needy. More than 50% of loans are from private lenders with high-interest rates as farmers do not get loans from banks. Those, who do own some lands and manage to get some credit, are still vulnerable to the whims of the weather. A bad monsoon can make or break them. On top of it, they have multiple challenges like low selling prices, no proper storage facilities, low water levels, adverse climatic conditions, poor infrastructure or transport facilities, no proper markets or Mandis. Moreover, they have no alternate income source so any natural calamity like a bad monsoon, droughts etc. or manmade calamity like corruption - irrigation scams, political nexus, demonetization etc. push them into despair. They not only lose their livelihood but the debt can take away everything they own.

There are cases where a nexus of land sharks, politicians and bureaucrats create artificial calamities like a drought to drive them out of their lands. Millions allotted for water irrigation and soil cultivation never see the light of the day! The land booty is distributed amongst the high and powerful to make their fortunes while the farmers go for distress sells to repay the debts! With no political or financial backup or lobby, they, therefore, lose everything and hopelessly, quietly choose the noose.

Since independence, rural development and agricultural growth have been the focus of every budget speech by every successive government. Yet, even after 70 years, so many of our poor farmers are still driven to end their lives due to poverty, corruption, debts, depression and other various reasons or live a life of utter deprivation and misery. In fact, the rural and agriculture worker is far poorer today than his urban or industrial counterpart than at the time of independence.

Sadly, this is a political failure in a democracy where all successive states and central governments; that are constitutionally supposed to be welfare states and provide them their basic fundamental rights i e right to work and right to life with dignity; have not been able to provide substantial resources and support to a sector that employs half of our workforce and is home to 69% of our entire population. Even after the work demand has multiplied and thousands are homeless and jobless, the allocations remain inadequate. The governments, of course, do not have the means as the big NPAs, tax exceptions and subsidies costing almost 3 to 4% of the GDP are needed to keep the vote banks and the sponsors happy while the entire allocation for agriculture sector remain below 1% of GDP this year also, even after creating so much hype about being a pro-farmer and pro-poor budget! Even the hyped loan waivers to farmers are not going to solve their lively hood issues unless there are concrete plans to double their income at the earliest!

It is not about the current or previous governments being better or worse or budget sops. It is about the largest democracy in the world and its promise to its most needy and deprived ones. Unfortunately, as a nation, we have failed to take care of those hands that feed us, clothe us, clean our homes...cities and build our houses. Our system has not been able to utilize capital to develop our human capital and infrastructure to facilitate inclusive and sustainable growth and development. The failure to divert adequate capital to modernize agriculture, improve productivity, promote supporting industries and to provide a sustainable urban infrastructure to rural people who migrate in millions per month for better opportunities; is a big letdown to the lofty ideals and dreams of our founding fathers. Instead, the revenue generated is used for buying popular votes through various subsidies to the privileged ones or maintaining fiscal balance and keeping the markets happy at the cost of our human development that again puts a big question mark on our national priorities and policies.

Mahatma Gandhi always emphasized that the policymakers must focus on the unprivileged section first. He said- I will give you a talisman. Whenever you are in doubt, or when the self becomes too much with you, apply the following test. Recall the face of the poorest and the weakest man whom you may have seen, and ask yourself if the step you contemplate is going to be of any use to him. Will he gain anything by it? Will it restore him to a control over his own life and destiny? In other words, will it lead to Swaraj for the hungry and spiritually starving millions then you will find your doubts and yourself melting away.

Yet, even after all the warnings and recommendations, the neglect of such crucial issues falls on deaf ears of those sitting in power as seen in our subsequent budget sessions. Year after year, governments after governments, budgets after budgets, same speeches full of rhetoric on pro-poor, pro-farmer and pro-rural propaganda; barring some marginal changes here and there; agriculture and social spendings remain low. Instead of walking the talk, the urgency of a clear vision; focused policies, strategies and concrete actions for improving social infrastructure especially in crucial areas like health and education are brushed under the carpet after the performances are over! Moreover, social spending in the budget tests the governments' commitment, vision and intention, which is sadly lacking in India as all successive parties, cohesive vision for basic social policy. It is time for our policymakers to take a step back and think as to where we are going wrong.

Every year many new innovative schemes are launched to deliver targeted benefits but they do not substitute for basic pillars of social policy like health and education. Even a scheme like MNREGA cannot double the income of farmers as it provides only 100 days job guarantee. For those over 300 million informal workers and farmers, these schemes cannot fulfill the need of a secured job or a basic security net.

Unfortunately, every successive government milked the poor to come into power. In fact many owe their political career to endlessly talking about the poor and eliminating poverty from the country yet poverty and deprivation still exist, social indicators keep going down and worse, the trend still continues. In fact, according to OXFAM, dramatic reductions in public investments in the social sector, weakening of labor protection and the land acquisition law, are still prevalent in the current political regime.

This is saddening. After independence, India inherited poverty by being looted of its wealth and resources by various outside invaders for ages and it was considered destiny but afterward, the loot is continued in the country by the ones who are supposed to serve the nation. It became a ticket to power and Garibi Hatao became the most popular game of electoral politics. Every election, the politicians line up at the doors of the poor and beg for votes with the promises to eliminate their suffering and provide jobs to all but once in power, they serve the rich by granting them all sorts of favors in the guise of tax exception and freebies at the cost of social welfare!

All international organizations stress the need for broadening access to health, education, promoting financial inclusion and reducing inequality of opportunities to bring down overall inequality levels. They also stress on the need for effective fiscal policy that broadens the coverage of social spending but at the same time moves towards a progressive taxation system that taxes the rich more. French economist Thomas Piketty, who has been repeatedly emphasizing the need of tax reform in India said in a recent interview that if you use the extra tax revenue to invest in the health system, in the education of the bottom 50% or bottom 70% of the country, then, yes, increased tax of the rich in India would be actually good for growth. It would reduce inequality and at the same time increase growth. [73]

According to OXFAM, [74] this is the dark side of globalization and market fundamentalism as a section of wealthy elites often use their power and position to get huge political favors and economic gains for themselves by manipulating policy changes. Deregulation, privatization, financial secrecy and globalization, banks and other financial institute help them further. This is the main cause and significant driver of inequality. According to IMF, the economic system is rigged in favor of the rich and powerful with a huge network of tax heavens and an industry of tax avoidance, which is helped and maintained, by highly paid banking, legal, accounting - investment consultants and professionals. This system is made intellectually legitimate by dominant market fundamentalists with the intellectual argument that low taxes for rich individuals and companies are necessary to drive economic growth and are good for the country's future! The result is that big companies and individuals; and those at the top- the wealthiest; who should be paying highest tax, go scot free. To offset this, governments rely more on indirect taxes and cut down on social spending thus affecting the poorest of the poor!![75]

Paying as little tax as possible is a key strategy for many of the super-rich. To do this they make active use of the secretive global network of tax havens, as revealed by the Panama Papers and other exposés. Oxfam further explains - even a tax as little as 1.5% imposed on the wealth of all the world's billionaires, could get every child into school and deliver health services in all the poorest countries of the world, saving an estimated 23 million lives and if India strategically just stops inequality from rising, it could end extreme poverty for 90 million people by 2019.

Thomas Piketty explained the scenario during his visit to India some time back that while Inequality is widening in India, tax-to-gross domestic product (GDP) ratio is abysmally low and the Indian state spends too little on health and education. Furthermore, India taxes its citizens much lower in proportion to its GDP compared to other competitor economies and a substantive portion of such taxes are collected through largely regressive and distorting indirect rather than direct means.

The same fact has been stressed by the Organization for Economic Cooperation and Development (OECD) and India's ministry of finance that India's tax-to-GDP ratio (both central and state tax revenues) is too low and the tax system has little redistributive impact. Few people pay income taxes and property taxes are low. Meeting social and development needs will require raising more revenue from property and personal income taxes.[76]

The ratio of direct and indirect taxes that are around 35:65 while other OECD economies the ratio is opposite i.e. 67:33 which has been constant through 50 years. This is bizarre because according to the economists, direct taxes such as income, wealth, property and capital gains taxes are considered progressive for developing countries as they function better both in terms of efficiency and fair play; while indirect taxes are considered regressive and inferior as they impact economically weaker sections of society much more. And most progressive countries prefer direct taxes complemented by indirect and capital taxes to optimize their potential. Surprisingly, post –reform, the policy focus on reducing budget deficit has been primarily centered on curbing government spending rather than aiming for a more balanced approach (enhancing tax revenues and broadening tax base). Though, Goods and Services Tax (GST) is expected to the base of indirect taxes,(economists suggest that the introduction of GST would boost the tax-to-GDP ratio by 1-2% points by bringing the unorganized sector under the purview of taxation), massive tax reforms to arrest evasion of direct taxes in India are needed according to the global experts.

Although due to demonetization, advanced tax payments, black money amnesty schemes etc., this year's revenue has jumped up, India needs to sustain a higher ratio in coming years as only 3-4 % Indians pay the income tax so without simplifying the personal income tax structure and expanding the tax base; the exercise would not yield desired results. We still are a country where many billionaires having ridiculous wealth, frequently declare bankruptcy to avoid paying their dues! Then there is the twin balance sheet syndrome, corrupt bankers and wily financial consultants who make the job easier. That's why economists and experts around the world prefer wealth tax. But the issue in India is that it relies on indirect and income tax to generate revenue against the more progressive forms of direct taxes like capital and wealth tax that are more tangible and measurable than income.

Moreover, in developing countries, as experts suggest, by taxing productive capital that is investments profits while shielding wealth and capital investment; in a way means subsidizing the unproductive capital that results in income dodging or overburdening the domestic investment. It, in turn, affects job creation that is bad for a healthy, growing economy while the productive use of this unproductive capital – wealth can serve as a key driver of economic growth.

This is perhaps, the reason that India's richest have rapidly become richer since the 2000s according to the OXFAM and Credit Suisse report. In India, the richest 1% own 58% of the country's wealth, while the top 10% have 76.3%. At the other end of the pyramid, the poorer half struggles for a measly 4.1% of national wealth. Moreover, India is becoming a tax haven for the rich and a hell for the poor as indians make up a chunk of the world's poorest population, while China accounts for a bulk of the middle class, and the United States has a majority of the richest people in the world.[77]

Oxfam believes that this sharp rise in inequality in India must be curbed with focused effort as it is damaging, and will lead to slower poverty reduction, undermine the sustainability of economic growth, compound the inequalities between men and women, and drive Kuala Lumpur in health, education and life chances. The warning from World Economic Forum's Global Risks Report 2016 is clear that says severe income disparity is one of the top global risks in the coming decade and would lead to many social and health issues like violence, crime and mental illness.[78]

Even World Bank and other international organization have joined the chorus and feel that India has to scale up its efforts as ordinary measures will not work. India must strive to have a balanced growth with new approaches with increased vigilance to ensure that privatization does not equal exclusion of the poor and marginalized. "For a country to prosper, the urgency of making more and more effective investment in people cannot be overstated and it will determine the very future of nation states while failing to invest in health, education and skills could leave a large number of people unable to compete in the job market – a problem that could "sow the seeds of future crises," World Bank stressed.[79]

As World Bank President Jim Kim said last year- "the era of trickle-down is over. Elites have done what they can to ensure they do not have to share growth. Wealth creators have been exposed as wealth hoarders, and the poor are written out of the game. When it comes to inequality, political power and voice is everything. While rich lobby for their rights, the poor are too busy surviving. For them, even $4 a day is not enough. Not enough to have any real choices or fear of debt. And yet they were in a world that counts them as being out of poverty because they are living on well over a $1.90 a day. No one who really had to live on $1.90 a day would decide that that was enough to be above the poverty line. But no one on $1.90 a day has had the chance to make those decisions."[80]

The World Bank is clear that without redoubling their efforts to tackle inequality, world leaders will miss their goal of ending extreme poverty by 2030.

"Businesses are the lifeblood of a market economy, and when they work to the benefit of everyone, they are vital to building fair and prosperous societies. But when corporations increasingly work for the rich, the benefits of economic growth are denied to those who need them most. In pursuit of delivering high returns to those at the top, corporations are driven to squeeze their workers and producers ever harder and to avoid paying taxes which would benefit everyone and the poorest people in particular."
- Oxfam

In the recent report titled 'An economy for the 99 percent', Oxfam said it is time to build a human economy that benefits everyone, not just the privileged few. The same findings have echoed in the recent economic survey that showed that India spends almost 3- 5 % GDP on various subsidies, exemptions and bad loans that mostly helps the privileged section, and then there are leakages, corruption etc that divert the flow. It suggested that at the same cost, there can be a basic income for all those living at the bottom.

OXFAM says - "It doesn't have to be this way! The popular responses to inequality do not have to increase divisions. An Economy for the 99% looks at how large corporations and the super-rich are driving the inequality crisis and what can be done to change this and shows how we can create a fairer world based on a more human economy – one in which people, not profit, are the bottom line and which prioritizes the most vulnerable."

According to World Economic Forum – "this is another side of globalization that has driven rapidly rising inequality in country after country, based on an economic system that has benefited the few at the expense of the many. Oxfam aptly calls it the economy of 1%. For Oxfam, there is no doubt that globalization has delivered tremendous progress in terms of reducing extreme poverty, but at a very high cost in terms of rapidly increasing inequality, and the neoliberal economic system that underpins it is deeply inefficient and ultimately unsustainable." [81]

OXFAM suggests that – "together we need to create a new common sense and turn things on their head to design an economy whose primary purpose is to benefit the 99%, not the 1%. The group that should benefit disproportionately from our economies is people in poverty. Humanity has incredible talent, huge wealth and infinite imagination. We need to put this to work to create a more human economy that benefits everyone, not just the privileged few. It promotes a human economy that would create fairer, better societies. It would ensure secure jobs paying decent wages. It would treat women and men equally. No one would live in fear of the cost of falling sick. Every child would have the chance to fulfill its potential. Our economy would thrive within the limits of our planet, and hand a better, more sustainable world to every new generation. Markets are a vital engine for growth and prosperity, but we cannot continue to accept the presence that it is the engine that steers the car or decides on the best direction to take. Markets need careful management in the interests of everyone so that the proceeds of growth are distributed fairly, and to ensure an adequate response to climate change or to deliver healthcare and education to many – particularly, but not exclusively, in the poorest countries." [82]

The bottom line is that the continued rise of economic inequality in India is not destiny anymore; it is not the inevitable outcome of liberalization either; rather it is the result of displaced concerns, misplaced priorities and policy choices. It would need deep reforms, rejecting market fundamentalism, stop protecting special interests of the powerful elite and changing rules and system that include taxation and public investment to provide proper distribution of wealth and power and level the playing field. In fact, much will depend on how much the government is committed to spend on education, health and social protection and how progressive are the spending and taxes. Unfortunately, in both the key indicators i.e. taxation and social spending, India performs relatively below par as we discussed earlier. India's tax-to-GDP is still too low - about 53% of its potential and on social sector spending (budget -2017) too, India performs poorly. Even South Africa spends more than twice on education (6.1%) and health (3.7%) that shows its commitment to reducing inequality and if India does not step up fast; our goal of ending extreme poverty by 2030 will remain a distant dream![83]

Oxfam further states in its " An economy for the % report– "there is no getting away from the fact that the big winners of globalization are those at the top. Once there, an ever more elaborate system of tax havens and an industry of wealth managers ensure that it stays there, far from the reach of ordinary citizens and their governments. Instead of an economy that works for the prosperity of all, for future generations and for the planet, we have instead created an economy for the 1%. Our economic system is heavily skewed in their favor (the rich), and arguably increasingly so". It warns further- "Far from trickling down, income and wealth are instead being sucked upwards at an alarming rate. Once there, an ever more elaborate system of tax havens and an industry of wealth managers ensure that it stays there, far from the reach of ordinary citizens and their governments."[84]

Worse, our tax system and the nexus of corrupt politicians –bureaucrats-rich elites make the task easier and protect that loot. Before independence, there was a wealth drain that bankrupted India and after independence, the brown sahibs and their army of corrupt bureaucrats, bankers and politicians have replaced the Gora sahibs (British) and wealth drain continues to bleed India.

Between six and seven trillion dollars' worth of black wealth lies hidden in tax havens across the world, according to a fresh estimate by a trio of senior economists from the Bank of Italy. Indians' share in this is estimated at $152-181 billion invested in shares and debt securities or held in bank deposits. Black assets like real estate, gold or art etc. are impossible to measure.[85] Most of the black money is invested in real estate abroad or laundered in tax heavens by crony capitalists and finds home again in India via FDI route (round tripping) as seen when 50 % of the FDI came to India from a small building in Mauritius some years back. There are around 100 tax heavens around the world so how this issue is going to be addressed, we will have to wait and watch.

Oxfam says the huge gap in wealth and incomes is due to increased returns on capital through interest payments, dividends, retained profits as well as tax avoidance and exemptions given by governments as seen in many developing countries while the share of national income going to workers is falling and they are unable to enjoy the gain. In India, the gap between top and bottom workers is rapidly widening as there is a huge difference in salaries of top CEOs and management while workers find their wages stagnant. The CEO of India's top information technology firms make about 400 times the salary of a typical employee there.

In 2014, French economist Thomas Piketty in his popular book "***Capital in the Twenty-First Century***" wrote that economic inequality was worsening and proposed wealth taxes as a solution. [86]He explained with examples that inequality is not an accident, but an outcome of capitalism, and can only be reversed through state interventionism. He argued that unless capitalism and market fundamentalism is resolved, the very democratic order would be threatened. According to his thesis, when the rate of return on capital is greater than the rate of economic growth over the long term, the result is a concentration of wealth, and this unequal distribution of wealth causes social and economic instability.

In India, uneven distribution of wealth is the main cause of growing inequality that is bad for long-term growth and it can be addressed if the rich - Indian elites behave responsibly and play an active role in ending social inequalities. Piketty proposed a global system of progressive wealth taxes to help reduce inequality and avoid the vast majority of wealth getting concentrated in the hands of a tiny section. As per him, India has zero wealth tax and the tax-to-GDP ratio is a too less. If the rich agree to pay more taxes and the ratio can be brought up to at 30-35 %, India can bridge the inequalities between the rich and poor.

He compared India to 19th or 20th century Europe as the level of taxation and public funding into health, education, and infrastructure is highly inadequate and hoped that Indian elite would take a call on that as China did. He said, "The Chinese Communist Party has been much more successful than the democratic and parliamentary Indian elite in mobilizing significant resources to finance a strategy of social investment and public services,". He proposed a properly structured annual wealth tax that could equalize effective tax rates between labor and capital, while simultaneously stimulating more productive capital allocations and job creation. He said structural preferences aimed at wealth have, in effect, made tax avoidance and valuation manipulation more profitable than productive enterprise. Repealing the inefficient, highly variable, often contradictory, and much-abused taxes currently imposed on investment income and replacing them with an assessment directly upon accumulated net wealth would remove the distorted incentives that are undermining our productive economy. [87]

One of the factors that explain this concentration of wealth is that inherited wealth and invested capital in the stock market, in real estate will grow faster than income, Picketty explained in a recent interview. According to him, Inequality is a matter of policies and institutions, our tax laws are not really designed to reach those who have used human capital to amass great fortunes. An investor can borrow against the value of his stock and avoid taxes on capital gains, dividends or high salaries, as his borrowing would not show any income. A wealthy person will have a large amount of unearned income from stocks, bonds, property, land, patents etc., that must be taxed. Moreover, wealth grows faster than annual income and unless one sells it, it is not taxed that incidentally, the rich mostly never do yet get the interest lifelong. Even a tiny 1% of capital tax would be equivalent to 20% on income.[88]

As we discussed before, the tax base in India is one of the lowest in the world at only 3-4% taxpayers (some sources say it's below even 3%) out of 1.3 billion Indians belying the common belief of the governments that lowering the tax rates will lead to better tax collections. In fact, a recent report in times of India showed that as the tax exemptions went up, the number of taxpayers from 1.2 crores in 2003 came down to just 2.5 lacs even though revenue has increased.(Demonetisation effect) . The failure of India's tax system is again a policy failure as most of the developing country around the world has a high tax rate, especially post-war Europe and other developed countries who had more than 60% tax rate during the time their economies were being built after the war. On the contrary, India continued to lower the tax in personal and corporate tax as companies making larger profits are now paying a lower rate of effective tax, and the trend is still continuing with a further cut down in the corporate tax rates to 25% from the existing 30%. Indeed, for higher growth we have to lower corporate tax and encourage more investments as it gets quite competitive yet, there has to be a fine balance between direct (wealth tax) and indirect taxes if we plan to have sustainable and inclusive growth.

But the issue is not that very few Indians pay the tax; the question is why don't they pay?

But first, why do we have tax?

The states are supposed to provide certain public services like health, education, employment opportunities, roads and other civic amenities etc. and for that they need revenue and tax the citizens but in India, it so happens, that the quality of public services is so poor that most people have to rely on the private sector for basic necessities like education, health, infrastructure etc. and that creates a tax fatigue. It then becomes a vicious cycle as those, who can afford to pay tax exit the tax system and those who cannot; get stuck in the lower income cycle due to inadequate opportunities and poor quality of education.

When the focus is more on redistribution of wealth rather than providing quality essential public services, then the consequence would be that upper-middle class and rich will exit the public system. This explains why only 3-4 % citizens are taxpayers in India compared to about 90% in Norway Sweden and Netherlands. This also explains why India has lower fiscal capacity compared to other democracies like USA and UK. These countries have an excellent public infrastructure and their citizens are happy to pay the higher taxes, sometimes up to 60-70%, as they get value for money given in taxes.

Another factor is the lack of transparency and accountability, that somehow disconnects the citizens from their obligations as they feel their money will be sucked off into the black hole and high-level corruption that our public institutions are known for! Even an honest taxpayer feels apprehensive as he thinks his money would go down the drain or worse, fill the pockets of corrupt bureaucrats and politicians. No wonder those honest, compassionate, wealthy people and business houses who really believe in philanthropy, often have their own trusts and organizations, as they do not trust the system to utilize their money ethically and efficiently!

This massive failure of our public sector is perhaps the biggest reason that India has not been able to widen its tax base, as unless the citizens get their value for money or transparency in tracking down their tax money, they would not be motivated to share their hard-earned money. That is why in India, only those pay taxes who have no option (tax at source deduction), for the rest; it will take more than force or regulations. The states have to earn the trust and cooperation of the citizen by improving the system and processes. It is by serving them only the bridge will be formed; not by punishing or using force!

Moreover, the inability to get a large section of rich & privileged pay their share in nation building; is the failure of our system, that could not get them involved or motivated. For that matter, globalization, capitalism and our private sector are not to be blamed for poor taxes, lack of revenue or inequalities; as they were the very factors that saved the sinking ship and made India an emerging super economy today. Yes, there is a section of self-centered capitalists who along with corrupt politicians and financial institutions have formed a mutually beneficial arrangement, managed to steal the country's wealth and resources and still are doing it but by and large, our private sector's contribution is tremendous in nation building. They have shown remarkable grit, determination, enterprise, discipline, integrity, efficiency and professionalism that sadly, our public sector is lacking. There are many entrepreneurs and industrialists who have set examples of excellence and integrity for many to follow. Many of them work with high ethical values and in their own capacity have pioneered various initiatives, strategies and philanthropic activities for improving the socio-economic environment in the country and have put India on the global map. In fact, to a large extent, India owes its economic success to them.

The failure is of our system that could not manage to keep a healthy balance between capitalism and socialism that leads us to another perplexing paradox that exists in our country between our public and private sectors.

In a recent policy analysis, "Twenty-Five Years of Indian Economic Reform: A Story of Private-Sector Success, Government Failure, and Institutional Weakness" eminent economist ,expert Swaminathan S. Aiyar has described the gains of post-reform liberalization as a contradicting picture of private-sector success and public sector failure.[89]

He writes – "Twenty-five years later, the outcome has been an outstanding economic success. India has gone from being a poor, slow-growing country to the fastest-growing major economy in the world in 2016. Once an object of pity, India has become an object of envy among developing countries; it is often called a potential superpower and is backed by the United States for a seat on the UN Security Council. Yet those successes have been accompanied by significant failures and weaknesses in policies and institutions. The past 25 years of liberalization are largely a story of private-sector success and government failure and of successful economic reform tarnished by institutional erosion. Even as old controls have been abolished, new ones have been created, so what leftist critics call an era of neoliberalism could more accurately be called neo-illiberalism."

He further states: The quality of government services remains abysmal, and social indicators have improved much too slowly. The provision of public goods—police, judiciary, general administration, basic health and education, and basic infrastructure—has seriously lagged improvements in economic performance. Political appointees and government interference erode the independence and quality of institutions ranging from the courts and universities to health and cultural organizations. India's economic reforms have been highly successful in moving the country from low-income to middle-income status, despite little improvement in its institutions and quality of public goods. To sustain rapid growth and to become a high-income country, India will need major reforms to deepen liberalization and build high-quality institutions."

The Fraser Institute's index of economic freedom ranks India at 114th of 157 countries. Successful economic reforms are tainted by institutional failures as many old controls like the license raj were abolished but many continued and many more new controls introduced in various sectors i.e. Environment, health, tribal areas, and land and in new areas like retail, telecom, and Internet-related activities. Many state governments have failed to liberalize sufficiently and corruption and red tape are still rampant. The World Bank's 2016 Doing Business report also ranks India at 130th of 189 countries in the ease of doing business in the country. Though there is a welcome improvement from the last position (142) but the fact cannot be ignored that India still is in the bottom half of countries. India ranks especially low in the ease of getting construction permits (183rd), enforcing contracts (178th), paying taxes (157th), and starting a business (155th).[89]

The point is that the achievements of India's rapid economic progress somehow have been unable to fulfill the goals of socio-economic freedom and equality for all that form the foundation of our democracy as not only the increasing wealth is unequally shared and the gap between rich and poor is widening but also the resources created with this growth have not been utilized adequately to remove widespread social deprivation and uplifting the living standards of millions living in the bottom of economic pyramid. Social indicators on education, health, and nutrition are alarming while the delivery of all governments' services remains pathetic. Poor governance, massive corruption and political interference have eroded the quality and freedom of crucial institutions varying from judiciary, police to educational and cultural institutions. In short, the objective of inclusive and sustainable growth and development have gone askew in the pursuit of one-dimensional effort to increase and maintain GDP growth that should have been just a part of the larger comprehensive plan.[89]

The success of private sector in India is a big lesson that unfortunately our governments and public sector tend to overlook and undermine. In their highly informative book "Why Nations Fail: The Origins of Power, Prosperity and Poverty by Daron Acemoglu and James Robinson, through a wide range of historical case studies analyzed the socio-economic and political policies of developed and developing nations to understand why nations develop differently, with some succeeding in the accumulation of power and prosperity and others failing. [90]The book offers some valuable insights which are highly relevant to India in today's times. They emphasized the need to improve institutions as the quality of a country's institutions ultimately determines whether a nation would succeed or fail. Though there are examples of many poor nations succeeding rapidly initially, despite having weak institutions but as the countries advance to the middle-income group; the need to improve their institutions becomes the main requirement lest they suffer an economic slowdown. According to them, the future of productivity depends not just on technology but also on the creation of strong, reliable, meritocratic institutions that are not easily subverted by money, muscle, and influence.[89]

The example of China is significant as it developed inclusive institutions, incentivized agriculture and industry, adopted advanced technology and focused physical and human infrastructure development made it grow by leaps and bounds. In fact, all tiger economies transitioned to higher income group with highly efficient and competent public sector that propelled higher growth and a successful private sector. Based on these models, not only they proposed a mix, with public sector involvement in areas such as education, healthcare and nutrition but also emphasized that success depends on the public sector becoming transparent and accountable. On the other hand, India failed to reform and transform its political and economic institutions that remained the biggest obstruction to the sustainable economic development of the country. No country can prosper without good governance and better institutions. These governance and public sector service delivery failures along with weak Indian institutions pretty much sum up the last 26 years of economic reforms. In fact, if India is scaling the height of economic growth today, the credit must go to India's robust private sector mainly IT, Auto and pharma sectors that have performed exceptionally well and made up for what our ruling system could not provide i.e. jobs and income to the millions of Indians and India's transition from lower to lower middle-income group. This in spite of the fact, that though, globalization made the markets more competitive yet, many areas still remained largely unreformed with new regulations and limitations. India has also become a global hub for R&D and for frugal engineering.

As S. Aiyer concludes - " India has also witnessed several private-sector failures, notably of companies in public– private partnerships in infrastructure. Crony capitalism has become a problem in many areas where political discretion flourishes. However, both cronyism and public–private partnerships could be called examples of government failure rather than private-sector failure. On balance, India's private sector has done a world-class job of transforming India. By contrast, government failure has been widespread. All tiger economies witnessed a big improvement in the provision of public goods, which was needed to encourage private dynamism and sustain growth. But in India, the provision of all government services remains poor, and so India has slipped in social indicators compared with its slower-growing neighbors in South Asia. Even remote Indian villages have an adequate supply of shops providing cigarettes and tea. But they have no adequate supply of education, health, public safety, or judicial redress. Why? Because the sellers of tea and cigarettes are accountable to the consumers they serve, and their income depends on satisfactory service provision. But government services are provided by salaried, unsackable staff, who are not accountable to those they serve, and who are justly notorious for corruption and callousness. They are accountable only to ministers in state capitals, where powerful trade unions ensure that there is no penalty for nonperformance. India needs new laws and institutions to ensure accountability of government servants of all consumers: this alone will raise the quality of government services.

He further writes– "THE INFRASTRUCTURE IS A MESS. Poor infrastructure is India's Achilles' heel. Any time economic growth takes off, it runs into an infrastructure constraint. From 2004 to 2014, the government aimed to overcome the problem through a massive expansion of public–private partnerships and boasted that India had more such partnerships than any other country. Alas, many of them are now bust, and many others have been abandoned. The 12th five-year plan (2012–17) envisaged $1 trillion of investment in infrastructure, of which half was to come from the private sector. That goal now sounds like a pathetic joke. The gargantuan losses of many infrastructure companies now threaten to sink the banks that lent to them. About 10–20 percent of the loans of public-sector banks have been restructured or are under some form of stress."[91]

After the world war, while other developed countries successfully built a healthy and vibrant social and economic infrastructure; the failed state of our public infrastructure is worrisome. Even other Asian countries who started their growth story with India like Japan, South Korea, Singapore, Malaysia including China have made great leaps in improving their social and economic environment and other essential services from health, education to electricity, water, sanitation etc. lifting not only the income per capita of their citizens but the standards of living too along with an enabling physical infrastructure.

If we compare the states of our leading metros with Shanghai, Kuala Lumpur, Singapore and Beijing, the failure of India to match the growth pattern of these countries pose a big question on our public sector. While our private sector has made great strides in providing world-class education and health services to privileged sections of the society; the quality of our public schools, hospitals and civic infrastructure remains pathetic and unexplainable. The situation is so bad that even the poor people prefer to use private schools and hospitals even if they have to forego free treatment! Haphazard urban growth with failing sewage & garbage disposal facilities, killer roads and chaotic traffic still persist. Pitifully, for an emerging super economy, we still have some of the most dirtiest, congested and ill-planned cities in the world!

Today, saying our public sector is in a big mess would not be an exaggeration. The question is not that it has improved or there are some corrective measures being taken now, but why have we failed to get basic essential services and proper infrastructure even after 70 years of independence? The point is why India has failed to reform the biggest and most important sector that is the lifeline of the nation? What are our excuses? Given the sheer abundance of resources and manpower, the condition of our public sector and services leaves much to be desired. Why such indifference and tolerance to this suffering and Chalta hai attitude that we Indians have mastered over the years?

It need not be this way! India, today, has all the resources and manpower to provide an excellent socio-economic infrastructure and essential services to its citizens. In fact, India has everything that is required for it to become a developed nation now and here! We do not have to wait for anything else as even the poorer countries have successfully created better facilities and amenities than us. We just need to plan and utilize our resources wisely.

India needs to dismantle the old systems and processes that are no longer serving and create new laws, processes and institutions to ensure transparency and accountability of public servants to its citizens. This only can improve the quality of public services as the condition of our public institutions is still dismal even after seven decades of independence! Not only the physical infrastructure is a mess but the processes and methods are also out-dated and inefficient.

That is what S. Aiyer further warns about – "Markets cannot function without good governance. With almost no exceptions, the delivery of government services in India is pathetic, from the police and judiary to education and health. Unsackable government staff members have no accountability to the people they are supposed to serve, and so callousness, corruption, and waste are common. Politicians like a patron–client system in which they earn gratitude by helping constituents and sundry groups through the many controls and permits, rather than abolishing the controls and permits, which would level the playing field but also leave them less powerful. THE JUDICIAL SYSTEM IS A MESS. Justice is supposed to be blind. In India, it is also lame. India holds the world record for legal case backlogs (31.5 million), which will take 320 years to clear, The current sanctioned judicial strength is just 17 per million, and unfilled vacancies are as high as 23 percent in the lower courts, 44 percent in high courts, and 19 percent in the Supreme Court. No wonder the staggering backlog of cases does not diminish, and most people are reluctant to litigate to redress their grievances. THE POLICE SYSTEM IS A MESS. India has 123 policemen per 100,000 population, almost half the UN recommended level of 220 and far below the levels in the United States (352) and Germany (296). Huge unfilled vacancies are common in all states. In Uttar Pradesh, a state of 200 million people, the overall shortage is 43 percent, with the shortage of head constables being 82 percent and inspectors 73 percent."[1]

The Association of for Democratic Reforms found 186 MPs with criminal records elected in 2014 out of which 112 had serious charges like murder, kidnapping, and crimes against women while in the 2009 elections, the number was 158. Though, we do have some honest and clean leaders; the same cannot be said about their parties. Most of them join politics in the lure of power, position and money that give them a huge clout and immunity against prosecution.[2]

Our electoral sector is also highly ineffective as the election process is not free and fair. In fact, it is the fountainhead of all political corruption in the country as there are no checks and balances on selection and election processes. It allows politicians with the criminal records contest and encourages the use of money and muscle power that, in turn, creates a vicious cycle of cronyism and public – private nexus leading to further moral degradation of politics. Today, the state of

---

[1]

Pradeep Thakur, "Vacancies in Judiciary Hit Judge-People Ratio," *Times of India*, April 17, 2016. Swaminathan S. A. Aiyar, "Strong Lokpal, Weak Judiciary Recipe for Failure," *Times of India*, December 25, 2011. Deepak Gudwani, "World Largest Police UP Has Half the Strength," *DNA India*, April 4, 2013

[2] *mediaindia.eu/issues/corruption-needs-to-be-weeded-out/*

our electoral sector is such that any honest or middle-class citizen cannot even dream of contesting the election, forget winning the one! Elections have become an arena of wealthy and criminals. Leaving a few good men, most of our politicians are tainted. As many as 82% of the newly elected MPs have assets over 1 crore and the average assets per winner is approximate 15 crores![92] No wonder politics today has become a ticket to power, insane wealth and insulation from the law of the land. Instead of serving the nation, the system has become a shelter for looters who along with corrupt bureaucrats and businesses create a wealth and resource drain of the country!

Our bureaucratic system too is disreputably corrupt and sluggish with increasing social apathy and inertia. Un-accountable, un-impeachable, inadequate and inefficient staff lacking required skills and motivation further brings the chips down. Dust gathering files, pervasive absenteeism, huge backlogs, widespread corruption, non-performances mark the most important sector in our country. No wonder, government jobs are highly sought-after, from peons to clerks to inspectors and even lowly positions like municipal cleaners are auctioned at the highest bidding price as there is a guaranteed return on investment!! The general belief is that if one gets a government job, his life is set forever. In fact, government employees are much sought after for matrimonial alliances.

Over 2 million applied for 368 government's peon positions and around 20,000 for 114 sweepers post in UP recently.[93] For the jobs that require minimum basic qualification; there are thousands of Ph.Ds, MBAs, engineers and overqualified people vying and dying to get through. This not only shows the pathetic level of unemployment in the country that has the highest number of youth, but also the reputation of our public sector. These jobs, after all, come with lifelong security, no accountability, no fear of being sacked, no performance criteria or pressure, unlimited holidays and a great scope of extra income read bribe that is not possible in private jobs even at a higher scale!

The public sector that is supposed to be the lifeline of the nation, unfortunately, has become a system that has sucked the nation off its wealth and resources. For any developed nation, a strong and efficient public infrastructure creates a solid foundation that is of utmost importance for sustainable growth and development and that can really make or break a nation. Such is the power of the public sector institutions and services. On this foundation, the pillars of freedom, justice and development are erected. If the foundation is weak and crippled with corruption, it will corrupt the whole nation.

Ironically, our bright and enthusiastic minds that join the services with idealistic dreams and intentions have to serve an army of corrupt bosses that drain them of their zest and drive. Their zeal and dedication are sidetracked or they are transferred frequently. Some of them succumb to pressure; some brave ones don't give up and continue to fight their way up. Since corruption is rife from top to bottom, their time, energy and ideals get lost in the game and fail to bring the changes they so dream of. Some get lucky and are able to make some innovative changes here and there but mostly fall victim to a ruthless system that does not care for change, does not appreciate their efforts. On the contrary, there are many cases where such innovative and courageous officers are penalized, removed or transferred to other insignificant positions or sectors.

This is a stark reality of India today and the biggest reason of public sector failure. Our institutions are weak and not independent. For a nation to thrive, the quality of strong and independent institutions can make a huge difference, especially in educational and regulatory institutions but alas, political interference and favoritism have eroded their values and ethics. Lack of proper vision, subjective and technical expertise, analysis, transparency, and accountability results in poor project planning and outcomes. Inefficient financial planning, misused and ill-used funds, slow decision making, low capacity building, under-utilization of resources, low productivity, no proper assessment or review mechanism, no regular up-gradations, out-dated data management and information system, inefficient use of technology and information, poor administration management, ineffective leadership and complete lack of accountability in terms of cost and quality consciousness, mark our public sector. There is almost no pressure for performances or time-bound outcomes unlike private sector and hasty, huge spending or massive unspent funds towards the year-end are quite common that triggers off corruption and swindles.

It is quite perplexing, that in a country like India where governments are always complaining about limited resources and funds; such misuse and mismanagement of funds create a huge setback and a criminal wastage. What's more appalling is that it is not the lack of resources or funds but misplaced policies and priorities, poor planning of the projects, lack of comprehensive and integrated plans, poor review and revise mechanisms and under-utilization and mis-utilisation of funds; that create a bottleneck. Some of it does trickle down to target beneficiaries, but most of it is sucked off at the top and lower layers of our intricate hierarchy in the public system. The examples are many - in some departments like SCST and many welfare schemes funds allocations, where the deep-rooted corruption eats away the major chunk of the welfare budget and the unspent amount that is sometimes over 50 to 80% goes unnoticed and unchecked. There are also huge chunks of international aid and funds that are mostly distributed within the system itself in the guise of paper NGOs and trusts owned by close confidants or relatives of the power holders and bureaucrats and never reach their optimum utilization and conclusion.

Furthermore, irregular, unreliable audits, inadequate disciplinary checks, neglect in monitoring huge gaps in expenditure and outcomes and sluggish; half-measured actions against the culprits, provide a free field of play for all. If only we could have a balance sheet of India's budget allocations and targeted outcomes monitored monthly and annually and track the flow of money in the public sector, India will crack the code of corruption, black money and missed revenue! Till then, no outer exercise can put an end to it. Chasing wealth drain once flown overseas and getting it back is like a wild-goose chase as we know there are over 100 tax heavens in the world. Plugging the gaps and loopholes at the source level can only address the issue in a definite and substantial manner otherwise, the rest is just political games to divert nation's attention!

Our municipalities too are a mess. There is a sense of despondency and an utter lack of confidence in the capacity of the local bodies to handle urban issues and deliver services. In most cases, there is a nexus of unqualified, semi-literate corrupt politicians & corporators who use money and power to get elected and lack any moral obligation or spirit of service towards their electorate and constituencies. The municipalities today have become money-making institutions for parties without any performance deadlines, transparency or accountability. The out-dated systems, incompetent processes, and structures that were inherited from the British are still being followed in many institutions. There is a resistance to adopt better and more transparent monitoring and review system for fear of losing power and control over funds.

There is no effective interface between the citizens and the public employees. A lack of effective feedback or grievances redressal system further mars the effectiveness of the services. A lethargic and corrupt administration, absenteeism, lack of innovation and motivation is common in even essential service agencies like health, education, water, electricity, sanitation, sewage etc. that are inefficiently organized and badly managed. Never ending road and infrastructure projects without any time-bound limits, clogged sewage lines, pathetic schools, poor quality teachers and doctors, unhygienic conditions, unskilled workers make the dream of having proper basic services delivered to its citizens remain an unlikely possibility.

Instead of experts leading our most important projects, most often, we have political lobbies appointing their proxies who serve their masters instead of the nation. Corruption and leakages in various schemes and projects are widespread in our public sector. Just a certain percentage reaches the targeted, designated beneficiaries, Most of the times it is diverted to fake beneficiaries while the real needy ones are ignored and since there are no checks and balances, no transparency and accountability, the booty keeps the whole bureaucracy well-oiled at the cost of poor and needy. No wonder there is no hurry to privatize ailing public sector units and services as they continue to be such convenient cash cows.

There are some areas that have been privatized, but cronyism and politics of mutual benefits dominate the scenario there.[89]

Unlike many developing and advanced developed countries where most of the public services are privatized, and the citizens are given high-quality services and infrastructure, in India the possibility looks bleak and unless there are massive reforms and dismantling of the obsolete and inefficient systems and processes, things will not look too bright.

The huge Public-sector units and corporations have become like white elephants that are a big criminal waste of national resources unless reformed urgently. The public sector banks still control the bulk of bank lending (almost 70%), are notoriously known for the worst record of bad loans and financial losses, and still, there is no hurry to reform or privatize them as they prove to be such convenient cash source for politicians and crony capitalists.Those areas that have been privatized are not been able to thrive either as many public - private infrastructure partnership projects failed to take off due to massive corruption and cronyism. Some of those saw the light of the day but many of the projects went kaput or had been cast off that resulted in many public sector banks and financial institutes pushing on the verge of bankruptcy. There were many reasons like too much political interference and delays in land acquisition or environmental clearances. The loss of power sector also ran in trillions. Even today, a number of investments pledges are made yet how many get translated on the ground, is questionable. Infrastructure-wise India's still growing at a snail's pace compared to high infrastructure growth of Asian tigers and china.[89]

One more example of large scale wastage of nation's wealth and resources is the number of organizations employed to do the same job without any coordination or comprehensive plan. A multitude of local authorities and boards and fragmentation of administrative responsibilities create a confused state of things where no one can be held accountable for service failures! Like in Delhi, there are over 100 government agencies-public sector units and departments to monitor weather and pollution yet every monsoon the capital is in chaos and smog never really clears. The state and central governments keep playing passing the buck while the citizens suffer. The same thing happens in other metros and towns. The traffic is increasingly getting horrible; pollution levels are going from bad to worse, haphazard urban development is unable to keep pace with the ever-growing population and rural migration.

The lackluster and lackadaisical approach, utter public apathy, inertia, and a lack of any personal, professional stake or motivation make our public institution's such massive losers. Moreover, complete lack of a comprehensive, integrated national vision and plan; national integrity, obligations, clear-cut social policies and objectives; has created a socially apathetic and inert system that is slowly bleeding the nation. Instead of serving the public, barring a few, brave and honest ones; a large number of public servants are using the nation's resources to serve themselves and their masters.

It took almost 26 years for India to make a slow transition from low-income to middle-income status and to get into the high-income club, India would need to make urgent and radical institutional reforms and create a more honest, accountable, transparent institutional infrastructure. It must strive to become a country with better governance, empowered citizens, efficient and improved public services and infrastructure, better police and justice system and a fair and just electoral system. Failing which, the potential of becoming a superpower would remain a far-fetched one.[66]

Today, India crucially needs to reform its public sector and service delivery. The efficiency of the public sector, focused policies and priorities based on choose-run-review-revise strategy have been the game-changer for all miracle and developed economies and we must learn from them. We still have a long way to go as compared to the Asian miracle experience; India seems to be heading in the opposite direction. There are a plethora of new schemes launched every now and then. Some of them are good, innovative; some are like the old wine in new bottle. There is an urgency to cover as many sectors as possible and develop every corner of the economy but the focus and clarity of vision and capacity to manage and successfully implement these schemes are lacking. Moreover, the goals and objectives of many schemes are too idealistic and far-fetched and with somewhat skewed priorities. For instance, a bullet train for the privileged section at a cost that would put more burdens on the fragile fiscal health of the states; while the pathetic rundown railway stations across the country urgently need a facelift, does not really make sense![94]

What India really needs today, is fully functional cities with proper provision of basic services like sanitary sewage and waste system, sufficient water -power supply, and health care system, not futuristic smart cities. The same goes for the recent demonetization drive. What India needs is more job creations and social security for the already suffering population, not another shock that pulls them back into poverty and job losses! While demonetization and cashless economy are excellent tools for economic reforms, a lack of having a proper infrastructure in place, inefficient staff, and unplanned implementation marred the effect. On the contrary, it made some irreparable losses to our economy and to weaker sections.

Similarly, instead of opting for a comprehensive and sustainable rural development program; as suggested by former president Abdul Kalam to develop facilities such as educational institutes, colleges, hospitals, along with agro-based industries in the villages and at the block level that would create opportunities within rural areas and will drastically reduce migration to urban areas; various random and haphazard schemes are launched without any planned or focused outcomes. The examples are our irrigation, dairy development, credit schemes and subsidies that help the rich farmers and big agro businesses instead of reaching to the needy. Poor monitoring, inadequate evaluation and almost no accountability make the task harder. Though India has more arable land than China, yet our productivity is way behind it. There is not enough investment in increasing the technology and R&D output as other countries have done in recent past.

The bottom line is that unless we learn to prioritize our policies and dismantle the old leaky system and faulty processes to create a new system that is efficient, transparent and accountable, the dream of inclusive and sustainable growth and a new India that works for all will remain in the pipeline only.

It is high time that India acknowledged this fact, as unless we admit something is wrong, there can be no rectification. The great Indian growth story is stained by the country's dismal performance in social and physical infrastructure development, which is mostly due to the mismanagement of its economy and misplaced priorities. After all, the success of a country's and the outcome of its higher growth would eventually be judged by the difference it makes on the lives and living standards of the people in the country.

To recap, the miserable performance of India in every area of social sector i.e. poverty and inequality eradication, healthcare, education or gender justice even after 7 decades of democracy shows that something has gone awfully wrong in the path of development in India. Moreover, the rosy picture of India's achievements on the economic front does not give a balanced account of the multitude of failures and shortcomings to deliver the promise of democracy to its citizens, that is being lost amongst the hype and euphoria of celebrating India's growth by the media, governments and privileged section of society. It is alarming since ignoring these failures or brushing them off as the by-products of rapid growth has already cost us heavily as the crucial years of nation's development have been lost in the game of communal politics, corruption and public ignorance.

Another failure is the neglect to bring these issues out on the public platform, in public understanding to be discussed, debated and rectified; that has given rise to an apathetic society with democratic failure to address the serious issues that are critical to the national and social fabric of our country.

This brings us to another major paradox that exists in our media and society. The culture of trivia, sensationalism, negativism, TRP and reality shows that overtake crucial issues like poverty, inequality, lack of national vision, corruption, communalism, misplaced concerns and priorities of our power holders. On the one hand, we have Bollywood, elite, the rich and powerful and their interesting lives and on the other hand, there are those unprivileged ones who lead boring, insignificant existence and hardly anyone is interested in knowing their plights and woes. Though, there are some highly motivated, uncompromising, idealistic media professionals who play fair and take great pains to keep the spirit and ethics of unbiased journalism alive; the majority ignores the facts and is dictated by TRP and sensationalism. The poor and their plight have no place in our media space or even in our collective awareness space.

The media, barring some exceptions, serves the politicians, rich, powerful, influential ones and caters to the privileged sections that are obvious in the coverage of headlines, analyses and programs displayed on the channels today. This is perhaps, due to the "political and elite capture" as known in the world. It may be because media today is an expensive field and needs massive financial backup and advertisements to run the show. Most of the channels and papers are owned by the rich and powerful that uses money and power to influence the elected and the electoral. It has become a dangerous game as the power of media can be a game changer and the power brokers know how to make use of it to their benefit. No wonder so many crucial news stories and analyses go unnoticed where insignificant, trivial issues are blown out of proportion to divert the nation's attention.

An example of this is the recent job losses and slow down growth-rate which are the most explosive and crucial challenges our country is facing today, unfortunately, could not find place in some so called nation's highest TRP channels while insignificant, communal issues or scandals occupied the prime time debates.

The fact remains that India that is shown in our media today, by and large, is the India of the affluent and privileged! We are a nation of pretending and sensational reality shows who is ashamed to acknowledge its own reality. We are a nation where a large section is more interested in watching celebrity scandals, pretentious family soaps while the real cries of a huge section and their plights are ignored. We, as a society, are ashamed to acknowledge this suffering Bharat as the other hidden part of the shining India.

The champagne glass economic structure[95] of India as it is called by experts is an interesting yet somewhat disgusting observation for its peculiarities and weirdness. The top ultra-rich elite has an exciting, happening, shining India that is full of wealth, fun, luxury and opportunities. They live too high in their ultra-lux mansions and high-rises, travel in private jets and yachts, and are largely disconnected from ground realities. This section is diverse though, where some are hardworking, full of ethics and compassion; socially aware and responsible. They do whatever they can for society and the country. On the other end, we have a society full of Marie Antoinettes' who in their ivory towers do not look down on lowly, crawling, starving poor and slums don't exist for them. They have invested heavily abroad and are least interested in what is happening in India except for the gossip on Bollywood or page 3 sections. This India is well connected and has a big clout too and sometimes manipulates things in their favor using the power of wealth.

Then there is another section that is not so rich yet a little richer than the rest. This India has created a virtual universe of their own and lives in a bubble with all those social media, WhatsApp groups, TV soaps, foreign trips, kitty parties and gossip sessions occupying their time and energy. This section is also out of the public system as they have access to quality education, health and enjoy other services provided by the private sector. Though, there is a section that is socially aware, responsible and eager to see changes in the society and quietly works towards that yet, a large section of this India has no time or inclination to learn about or empathize how the other India survives. It is largely protected from political and market fluctuations as it is given enough subsidies, freebies and sops to be occupied and interested in the great India rising and shining saga.

Not that they are at fault and should not enjoy their privileges for they have worked hard for it. The problem is that the ignorance and lack of awareness of this section cost our democracy heavily as they are used as pawns in the highly politicized games of votes. They are known as "Aam Admis or common men" and create a barrier between "have all's and "have not's as the focus is to keep them engaged in the game. This India is manipulated by various parties using minority or majority cards, party ideologies; resulting in a highly diverse and fragmented society that has divided and polarized the nation. The real issues like poverty, inequality, unhygienic condition, corruption, pathetic public services and overall public sector failures are sidetracked as trivial matters while high political dramas and tactics occupy nation's attention and precious time.

This India is blissfully ignorant and insulated from outside realities. It does not bother that on the other end of the spectrum, there is a suffering Bharat[96] - the bottom 40 % as they are called by the World Bank[97]- that has no access to quality education, basic health and other facilities and that is kept trapped in a vicious cycle that goes on for generations. They have no lobby, are not organized as they are busy surviving and suffer quietly.

As seen during demonetization, this India living in its happy bubble was not really affected as it had access to credit cards, e-cash, e-stores etc. and was blissfully ignorant and insulated from the outside fires and fumes. They had minimum inconvenience, so there were hardly any complaints, their jobs were secured and homes well stocked. Since they have their own virtual universe of Facebook and social media, their opinions are taken as the common sentiments of the whole Nation. However, those who lived at the bottom rung of the pyramid were severely affected as millions of daily wagers lost their jobs and lively hood and were thrown back into poverty. They had no money to eat and suffered quietly. They were not counted, as they did not have the energy or time to protest or demonstrate.

Without raising any hue and cry, they are quietly busy surviving, waiting for promised better days to come and take things at face value. They took the blow of demonetization as a promise for better days ahead even as it damaged their lives.

They are used to it you see.

They have been ruled and exploited by outer and inner invaders, kings, Zamindars, Gora, Brown sahibs and Netas for too long to stand up for their rights. Their passive resilience has become a weakness that is being routinely taken advantage of by those in power. Their ignorance and unawareness of their own rights and power make them easy game for crooked politicians to manipulate and maneuver them for their selfish motives. Every election, every party tries to get their vote by misleading them, bribing in cash or kind or showing big dreams only to abandon them later.

They are being used as pawns by political parties, most of whom having no real empathy or compassion for their suffering or proposing any substantial long-term reforms; make their issues a game of passing the buck or gaining political mileage. But then it is nothing new as it is an old game, played in turn by all successive parties, some win, some lose but the real India pays the price!

The point is not about political parties manipulating the priorities and resources of the nation as per their whims and fancies that have been happening for years by all successive parties in the power. The point here is that in a nation where majority of electorate is ignorant and easily manipulated by false promises, money power, emotional or communal issues, the role and responsibility of its socially aware and educated citizenry to question and confront the misplaced motives and priorities through social accountability and participation; that are the some of the most effective democratic tools that can bring the desired change in the country; are ignored or rendered useless.

Unfortunately, in a large democracy like India, where the citizens are the primary stakeholder and have the power to elect or reject, there is no move or effort to exercise that power and change the system. Those who are educated and aware, choose to look the other way or get caught in the never-ending petty party politics or communal fundamentalism while those who are ignorant and unaware have no clue or support to stand for themselves and end up being used by various parties for their personal agendas. Regrettably, the potent power of voters is wasted and fails to bring any substantial change in the system. Instead, it becomes an impotent society that is ruled and manipulated by a few smart minds in power or religious miscreants.

In any democracy, the power of its educated, intellectual and socially aware citizens' contribution is invaluable as they form the critical mass that can create a phase transition as seen time and again in various parts of the world. It happened in our country during British rule when some aware, compassionate and educated minds united and created a revolution to turn India's destiny around.

Thus, the success of a democracy depends on its stakeholders and their opinion, awareness and votes. In any democracy, the real power lies in the hands of those who vote as they have the power to either elect or reject their governments. Yet, this power is a double-edged sword that can be misused or manipulated by power mongers to suit their ends. Moreover, the power of democracy is wasted when there is widespread ignorance in society about their rights and roles. As the extent that the electorate/voter is informed and aware of its rights and roles in national issues, policies and priorities; determines the role its governments and allied sector would play in a nation. Otherwise, an ignorant electorate will only play in the hands of power brokers and will be repeatedly taken for a ride. Like seen usually during election time, when votes are bought with cash or kind from gullible, naive rural and urban poor vote banks. Free dinners, drinks, gifts and false promises are used as carrots to bring them to polling booths. This results in highly flawed electoral outcomes as a large section of educated and aware citizens don't feel the need to participate in the process for the sheer lack of motivation, lack of a deserving candidate or out of hopelessness about the state of things in the country; rendering the power of democracy useless.

Getting elected is only a first step for any government. Making a big list of promises during election campaigns that is used to lure voters and cure all ills is an art that our successive governments have already mastered over the years-but carrying them out and living up to Nation's expectation is a task that they need to master in order to sustain and survive.

Most governments start with great ideologies and plans; some genuine idealists try and bring fresh dynamic ideas to the table but soon lose their way and vision due to the loopholes in our system and present day politics. Most policies and strategies get caught in the haze of our political maze and rarely get translated into groundwork successes. Hundreds of reports, schemes and action plans have been launched regularly by successive governments with much hoopla and fanfare, but very few see the light of the day. Most of them gather dust or thrown into the cold storage just within a short period. Those that get implemented are rarely monitored or analyzed and found to have huge gaps in expenditures and outcomes.

Every party uses great, elaborated mandates and promises to come in power and every five years India is taken on a hope ride only to come back on earth later to find little or no significant changes around except big high-level corruption, leakages and large amounts of nation's wealth and resources gone as black money is siphoned off and stacked away in other countries!!! There are some steps taken to curb or show yet nothing substantial comes out of it. The leaked lists of culprits and names given by global agencies are never put out in the public domain and brushed under the carpet, no real long term actions are taken against the powerful ones. There are over 100 tax heavens in the world so plugging the loopholes can never really work yet, the broken system that creates leakages and pilferage possible never actually gets reformed or cured.

And if that's not enough, we find our country increasingly broken and divided over caste and communal politics, which are used to divert attention from real burning issues and problems we are facing today. Parliament is alarmingly becoming the place for playing blame games and passing the buck for missed opportunities and actions, inadequate development, vote bank politics and cover up of scams and corruption. Political parties, instead of playing a constructive role in nation building by debating and finding solutions for prevalent critical issues like massive unemployment, inequality, communalism, poor infrastructure or services; are increasingly indulging in ever stooping games of accusation, mudslinging, name calling and eroding the sanctity of parliament. All the crucial issues are hijacked by the politicians, gullible and naive voters play into the hands of few smart people in power; the media along with the nation too gets distracted and instead of questioning and asking for accountability, get caught in the political dramas and the show goes on.....

Sadly, this is not a cynical take but a reality check on the state of our nation today. No matter how much we choose to ignore or brush it under the carpet to project a happy shining and growing India, we will have to face and address these issues sooner or later if we need real reforms and transformation.

The role of media and citizens, therefore, is of the utmost important and catalytic in the future of India. We need to be awake, alert and proactive after all governments and bureaucracy are just parts of the system but we- the people of India, are the system! In a true democracy that is of the people, by the people and for the people, we all are the primary stakeholders and must play our roles in nation building. We need to make sure that the objectives of vibrant democracy and inclusive & sustainable development are met successfully and most importantly, we need to contemplate why has it not happened until now? What is missing? What lessons should we learn? As a nation, what are our strengths and weaknesses; opportunities and threats? It is time we took stock of things in our country as our ignorance and negligence have already cost us crucial years of nation building lost in petty politics, massive corruption and communalism.

The fact is evident as while all other Asian miracle countries including China who started from almost the same ground levels as India; were busy building their nations and writing their growth miracle stories, India was burning with riots, communal politics, party clashes, massive corruption, scams, abuse and misuse of power and resources that put its growth behind by 26 years! The result is that we are way behind these countries in economic and social development. Today, as we discussed earlier, these nations have a per capita income more than 10 to 20 times of India and their living standards and infrastructure are at par with the most developed countries in the world. Even China who had a lower per capita income than us during the 90's today has a per capita and GDP that is almost 4 times that of India. What's most obvious and worth contemplating is, that the loss of missed opportunities and resources was definitely not borne by politicians as they had their fill in terms of money and power but it was the citizens and the country that had to pay the price!

That makes one wonder whether it all was worth it? Those wasted crucial years of nation building and the glorious opportunity for miraculous growth and development that India had after the economic reforms in 1991 like other miracle economies, should make us sit and think hard! It is high time we accepted that there is something terribly wrong in the models of democracy and politics being followed in our country today. It is high time we woke up, rejected the politics of divide and rule and moved beyond silly trivial communalism and fundamentalist issues that have already created so much damage in our country and focus on the real issues for a change! We cannot afford to lose any more time as these crucial issues of poverty, education, health, unemployment, infrastructure and communalism etc. demand urgent action and we need all the resources to counter and overcome them as soon as possible. The first step towards that would be to accept and acknowledge those unconscious, old destructive patterns and paradigms that created these issues and replace them with new, vibrant systems and frameworks that would put India on the path of peace, progress and prosperity (inclusive and sustainable development). That is what we need today first and for most, to counter and overcome all ills that exist in our society today.

Let us identify those misguided beliefs and destructive patterns that are pulling India down and making it unable to reach its full potential.

What Are We Doing?

The purpose of life is to obey the hidden command, which ensures harmony among all and creates an ever better world. We are not created only to enjoy the world, we are created in order to evolve the cosmos.

- Maria Montessori

Today, India is divided into various states, sects, cities, parties, organizations, ideologies, castes, creeds, communities, classes alas, there is no nation! We have built so many barriers, divisions and narrowed down our circles so much that we have turned our great country into weak, misaligned cells instead of a strong, well-organised and synchronized body. And we all know what happens when the cells of a body start acting as stand-alone entities, paying no heed to the whole body's well-being or creative intelligence - they create cancers and havoc - destroying it eventually into a heap of the disorganized matter!

Today, it is all about my land-your land....my city- your city...... my party – your party.....my state- your state........ my religion -your religion......my language-your language.......my food- your food..... my way- your way but where is India? A whole India exists only in textbooks and maps for namesake! Every political, state, social or religious body caters to their own fragmented ideas of India. It is like that proverbial elephant in the room that is felt in parts by blindfolded people. We too have blindfolded our eyes with different perspectives, divisions, and discriminations and have reduced our great nation into pieces and then we go on blaming everyone and everything else for burdening our life with lack, struggle, violence and misery! Nobody divided us – we did! Nature has bestowed upon us everything in abundance……enough land, enough air, enough water, enough resources but we built all sorts of barriers and are totally oblivious and ignorant about the repercussions and consequences!

We need to answer the basic question life is asking today. Are we playing our role as assigned by life and fulfilling our purpose individually and collectively? Life means the ever-increasing joy of creation but are we enjoying? Are we creating perfect health, wealth and peace for ourselves and for all? For a certain percentage of the human population it could be somewhat true – they seem to have created enough resources, enough wealth, luxuries and pleasures to enjoy life however narrow their frame maybe. But can we be really happy if other parts of our human collective body are decaying, suffering or lacking basic facilities?

The general attitude today is to hell with all-let me stuff my stomach-stock my bank- stack my barn! We don't even know what is going on in our surroundings! It is like living in a nucleus blissfully ignorant about that a lone nucleus cannot survive on its own when the whole cell goes astray and for the matter, the whole organs, systems and eventually the body collapses due to the sheer imbalance of its powers and resources. How long do we think it will be before the impact of this imbalance hits us? Is this real happiness? Today, almost half of India is living without basic facilities of food, shelter, education...millions are without jobs.....hundreds of farmer's still committing suicides ....is this development? Is this success? Is it economic growth?

Whose economy is it anyway? OXFAM aptly calls it the economy of 1% and calls for changing it to the economy for 99%. Economy means making the best from the lot, for all. Today the Indian economy is manipulated, maneuvered to such an extent that the gap between rich and poor is widening. From Nature's point of view, it is sheer imbalance. There is nothing wrong in making one's life happy and fulfilled but as long as there is an imbalance in the body.......no part, no cell can be expected to be healthy or happy as the body will collapse anyway!!!

Let us not forget that this is the same land where civilization after civilization, generation after generation, great Avatars, kings, leaders and poets like Krishna, Buddha, Tagore, to Gandhi fought, struggled to teach us the lessons of unity and oneness. They all encouraged us to know ourselves, to overcome duality and find the unity in all that is....where the great sages and Rishis sang the song of the soul......TAT, TVAM, ASI - I am THAT, you are THAT and all is THAT.

That is one, which is called many. It does not matter what we call it - Brahma, Shiva, Allah, Christ, Jehovah, the unified field or the singularity. What matters is the truth. History has witnessed that the truth always triumphs, no matter how much it is misused or distorted. So how long are we going to deny the truth?

Where should we go and seek the omnipresent Brahma if we cannot worship the living God, his supreme creation- our fellow humans??

Which temple should we go to offer gallons of milk to Shiva when his children are dying of hunger or shower him with tons of gold when his creations are wandering without clothes or shelter??

Which mosques should we go and hail Allah when his children are killing their brothers just because they call Him by some other name??

Which church should we go and sing the praises of lord when his children are being crucified every day??

What a mockery of religions we have made! We have divided not only our beautiful planet and our great civilization into pieces but have reduced that one great almighty omnipresent, omnipotent and omniscient power into your God, my God or their God and then fight over which one is greater??

We have allowed our so-called leaders and keepers of religions to distort, skew the truth and brainwash millions of our fellow Indians to serve their selfish ends. We keep feeding this communal poison to our children and suffer all kinds of violence and discrimination in the name of religion without telling them the truth. Have we really forgotten who we actually are?

It is high time we accepted the truth and rejected the lies. It is high time we told our children the truth as they are the ones who are going to take it forward. It is high time we broke the old, outdated dogmas and biases that have created such a divided and dysfunctional society and embrace our highest truth to unite and create a better tomorrow for our children and for all.

It is high time when the enlightened minds from all religions came forward to reject the religions of hate and divisions and create the **"temples of humanity"** where the truth is taught in its true glory and pure form without any distortion, misinterpretations, and misperceptions. Where the **"book of humanity"** or **"Scripture of love"** becomes the most sacred scripture of new generation with an account of all great religions conveying the same universal truth in different hues and perspectives. Where the universal unity behind diversity is taught to every child in their formative years, so that they grow up being better human being with the light of truth igniting their minds and love and compassion illuminating their hearts.

It is high time that aware citizens from all walks of life stood up, rejected those self-appointed, so-called keepers and leaders of religions, and created an enlightened and cohesive society where all work towards the same goals- creating happiness, health, peace and prosperity for all. An empowered and evolved society, where those who are aware and resourceful, help out those who are ignorant or less privileged and enlighten and empower them. It is time to overcome all petty communal differences and focus on real issues that are plaguing our society and work towards creating a new India that cares and works for all.

As Vivekananda said – "let us hang our scriptures and doctrines for a while and focus on living Gods, every creation is a living temple of God. "For now, this alone shall be our keynote- this great mother India. Let all other vain God disappear for the time from our minds. This is the only god that is awake, our own race- everywhere his hands, everywhere his feet, everywhere his ears, He covers everything. All other Gods are sleeping. What vain Gods shall we go after and yet cannot worship the God that we see all around us, the Virat? When we have worshiped this, we shall be able to worship all other Gods."[98]

He wrote- "I accept all religions that were in the past and worship them all; I worship God with every one of them, in whatever form they worship Him. I shall go the mosque and kneel before the crucifix; I shall enter the Buddhist temple, where I shall take the refuge in Buddha and his law. I shall go into the forest and sit down in the meditation with the Hindu, who is trying to see the light that enlightens the heart of everyone. Not only shall I do all these, but I shall keep my heart open for all that may come in the future."

He warned- "Religion is not talk, or doctrines, or theories; nor is it sectarianism. Religion cannot live in sects and societies. It is the relation between the soul and God; how can it be made into a society? It would then degenerate into business, and wherever there are business and business principles in religion, spirituality dies. Religion does not consist in erecting temples, or building churches, or attending public worship. It is not to be found in books, or in words, or in lectures, or in organizations. Religion consists in realization".

All the religions in the world teach this universal truth of our oneness and embrace all religious people without barriers. A truly religious person is the spiritual one who sees the same God in every being but ignorant and selfish men take them to be the exclusive privileges of one group only and create various sects and dogmas. These sects become the centers of fanaticism' based on very petty issues like minor doctrinal differences or organization, cults or myths and create lifeless mockeries of great religions. They fight with each other holding they are right and others are wrong. He would call these sects, fanaticism, bigotry and violence the "Demons of religions".

Today, in India, these demons have eroded the true secularism of its spiritual and universal values and have made a mockery of it. In fact, in our country today, secularism has become a much-hated, four-lettered word as it has been misused and abused by various political parties and religious clerics to suit their selfish agendas and motives. The whole country has been divided and polarized into various sects and creeds who without knowing the real truth play in the hands of power hungry miscreants, ill-informed and misled minds who manipulate the classes and masses for their sick power games.

Years of vote bank politics based on pseudo-secularism and on the age old strategy of "divide and rule" used by the British, have created such a big chasm, social tensions and divisions in our society where instead of fighting against such dangerous anti-social elements, misguided beliefs and eliminating them from society; the people of India are pitted against each other and are fighting within themselves. True secularism means not supporting or favoring any particular religion but accepting and respecting all religions within a vibrant democratic framework and under a fair rule of law. Many countries operate through a sound uniform civil code to maintain peace and harmony in their society yet, after 7 decades of independence such a code has not found priority in our political landscape for reasons not difficult to guess - as such initiatives would put an end to their vote bank politics or pro-minority /pro-majority appeasement policies! The nexus of religious clerics and politicians use every possible loophole in our constitutional framework to yield power and control over gullible and ignorant people. What is more alarming that even Media and educated sections of society get into such mindless debates that are mostly created to divert nation's attention from critical & crucial issues.

The onset of social media, internet, and mobile phones has aggravated the herd mentality where most of the time insane, mindless forwards and posts on such petty, unverified facts and issues are blown out of proportion and keep the nation occupied in trivia while burning issues are sidetracked or brushed under the carpet!

While a tiny, enlightened section of educated intellectuals and Media struggle to keep the balance and use their power of discernment over such issues, majority in our Media and society fail to distinguish between pseudo secularism; that is characterized by selective compassion and selective activism; and true secularism, that is based on eternal truth and universal wisdom. This twisted, selective compassion, intolerance or condemnation of certain groups, practices or organizations as against a uniform consensus that stands for every social ill or assault on any part or section of India regardless of its religion, caste or color; has resulted in deterioration of the moral and social fabric of the country.

Moreover, it eventually results in propelling a chain of events where minorities or majority feeling exploited, are pitted against each other, getting locked in a never-ending, senseless tug of war. That's exactly what is happening in our country since last seven decades where oppression and exploitation in the name of pseudo-intellectualism and pseudo-secularism by politicians and religious clerics have resulted in several sections of society, even the most tolerant and liberal ones; uniting and uprising, demanding justice and asserting their fundamental rights. Unfortunately, they fail to get any substantial results in terms of definite policies and law enforcement or worse, mostly end up being used or manipulated by politicians and power mongers for serving their twisted agendas and motives to be in power.

It is high time that we woke up and put a stop on these mindless and senseless games and focused on the real burning issues that are threatening the future of our country. It is the time we rejected the old, obsolete beliefs and paradigms and accepted our highest truth. It is time to remind ourselves who we really are!

Who Are We?

A human being is a part of the whole, called by us, "Universe," a part limited in time and space. He experiences himself, his thoughts and feelings as something separated from the rest -- a kind of optical delusion of his consciousness. This delusion is a kind of prison for us, restricting us to our personal desires and to affection for a few persons nearest to us. Our task must be to free ourselves from this prison by widening our circle of compassion to embrace all living creatures and the whole of nature in its beauty.

- Albert Einstein

We must remember the great heritage and values on which the foundation of world's greatest enlightened civilization was laid. The country of great wisdom that was called the light house of the world and illuminated the world with teachings of love, compassion and peace. This mother land of ours is the same land where the most advanced and ancient civilization was built on the mighty pillars of Karma and Dharma. Where Dharma did not mean any particular religion but the duty towards one's countrymen, mother land and environment. Where sarvadharama (duty towards all) was the only dharma up and above any svadharma (personal dharma) and was built on the principals of sarvahitay (well-being of all), sarva sukhay (happiness for all) and sarva sampannay (prosperity for all).

This is the same land, which saw so many wars and revolutions for freedom and equality, where people from all castes and creeds rose above their differences to unite and strive for freedom and self-reliance.

This is the same land, which was called the land of wisdom, where so many wise men were born and gave world the gift of love, compassion and wisdom. Where no religion, caste or creed existed....where the caste system was based on merit; not on hierarchy -on division and dignity of labor; not on birth. Everything coexisted in great peace and harmony. The whole creation was one living body and look what have we done today?

We have broken our civilization, our country and our society into numerous pieces....there is no harmony, no synchronization. We hate and kill each other in the name of religion and caste..... destroying our country for selfish motives............cutting forests to create concrete jungles.....depleting its resources without thinking of consequences..... creating all sorts of social, economical inequalities.....creating so much imbalance and chaos and blaming everyone and everything else but ourselves for our follies!

Is this the free India, which our forefathers gave life and blood for? A nation broken into pieces by communal, social, economic, financial inequalities and divisions! A Nation where stones, mortars and animals are revered and showered with gold, milk and honey when millions of living temples of God - his children are dying of hunger and poverty!

This is the same land where many died, sacrificed so that future generations could have all the freedom and privileges that they could not see in their lifetime. They gave us this great legacy, a free India to transform their dream into reality. The leaders who ushered India into the dawn of freedom after years of struggles, conflicts and humiliation were so full of hope and enthusiasm that their children and next generation would honor their efforts and sacrifices and continue the legacy. Now, as the only link between our last generation and their rightful inheritors , what are we going to gift our children? What are we going to tell them....what legacy, vision or dream are we going to pass on them? Is this the fruit of our father's struggle and sacrifices?? A nation where half of Indians are still living without essential social services, facilities and livelihood opportunities? Where millions of Indians are still struggling to make both ends meet and are not able to get a decent meal to fill their stomach......enough clothes to protect their bodies or roof to provide shelter to their family??

A nation where millions of children are uneducated, laboring to survive...where millions of youth are in dire needs of skills and employment opportunities.....where child mortality rate is still so high .....Where millions of Indians are living without health security....where every day a girl child is being killed or a woman raped ....where millions are still waiting for justice??

A nation where people are fighting over petty political, religious and communal issues when the monsters of poverty, illiteracy, unemployment, unhygienic conditions, corruption, poor development and uneven growth are tearing the country apart?

Where tons of food is wasted while millions are dying of hunger …..millions are still being socially discriminated , humiliated and forced to live a life of modern slavery??

Where trillions of rupees are stacked away in foreign bank and nation's wealth and resources are being squandered away due to poor policy choices, systemic corruption and mismanagement while honest, loyal citizens have to pay the price or beg for better infrastructure and basic facilities?

Where millions of national revenue is wasted or written off as NPAs, exemptions, and subsidies in favors of the rich and powerful while the poor and needy farmers struggle for getting measly waivers on their loans?

Where thousands of crores allocated for water& irrigation and other rural development schemes go unaccounted or fill the pockets of corrupt netas while thousands of debt-ridden, poverty-stricken farmers are committing suicides?

Where millions are spent on foreign jaunts of our politicians, while our sportsmen are denied better facilities and opportunities?? No wonder we are the only country with the highest number of youth and abundant talent that could manage only single digit Olympic medals while neighboring countries like China, Russia and Japan won over 70, 56 and 41!

Where mudslinging, name calling, blame games and passing the buck are the favorite activities of our leaders and communal politics is used to divide and polarize the society while the burning issues like poverty, unemployment, health, education , policy reforms are sidetracked or ignored

Where billions are allotted in the name of infrastructure development and maintenance, yet, the pathetic conditions of our roads, poor traffic, sewage and sanitation conditions still drive citizens mad and frustrated?

Where power hungry politicians with deep pockets enjoying subsidized facilities without any accountability or performance parameters and those who are supposed to serve the nation are being served as masters while millions are living without basic facilities, sanitation, electricity or water supply?

Where the national revenue is being mismanaged or misused by politicians to keep the rich and influential class happy and buying votes while millions of our children are wasted due to malnourishment , stunting and millions are trapped in low-quality education, opportunities and health cycles without any prospects of escaping?

Where ultra-luxurious high-rise pent-houses and million dollar mansions adorn the skyline of our metros while millions are still living worse than worms in the dingy, dreadful slums? Where millions of begging children sleep without a roof over their heads, proper clothing or beddings on footpaths?

How can a mother ever be happy if even one of her children is sleeping without food, shelter or clothes? How can India make real progress when such extreme inequality and apathy still persist in our society? How can we envision a healthy and happy growth for India when the foundation is so feeble and laden with tears and cries for help from such a large number of the lower unprivileged sections of our society?

Is this the India we are going to pass on to our children? How long are we going to play ostrich and refuse to see the writing on the wall and pay heed to the need of the hour?

How long are we going to pretend that India is growing and shining when such gross economical, structural and social inequalities persist in our society? Is this the growth we expect from this great country with the brightest brains, the largest number of hands and illuminated souls on the earth?

Is that all??

If we could imagine India as a body with 1.3 billion cells, it would look like a beauteous face with weak limbs and dysfunctional organs plagued with cancers like poverty, ill health, unemployment, corruption, communalism, un-hygiene etc. In fact, the state of our country today evokes an image of an amazing, powerful horse whose caretaker has left it fastened to a rotten wooden chair but years of slavery, bondage, and oppression have conditioned its mind so much that it is unaware of its own potential and power to break free!!

Today this great amazing country of over a billion people is chained and ruled by a handful of people in power and rendered helpless over the conditions. Years of slavery and oppression have taken a toll on our minds and turned us into such an impotent society that we turn a blind eye to so many atrocities around and shrug helplessly. The dismal state of the public sector, pathetic roads, drainage or sewage problems, traffic jams, poor infrastructure, unhygienic conditions, pollution, farmer suicides, women being raped & killed, no health, food or shelter for millions, illiteracy, unemployment, corruption, mismanagement and wastage of national resources, missed revenue, messed up social infrastructure, communal politics, nothing seems enough to shake or make us wake up and protest!!

Like that tied horse, we have given our power into few hands and never bother to see how they are using it. Unless we wake up and realize our full power and potential, there is no real hope for us. As world's largest democracy, India's destiny that seems to be enslaved to a handful of people in power is shameful, worse than those of monarchies and dictatorships. Or have we forgotten what democracy means?? Isn't it of the people, by the people and for the people? Governments are just the representatives of the people of India, to serve India not to rule or dictate. Unless we take the collective responsibility for the growth and development for all of us, nothing would change.

The point is not what this or that government did or how they are doing better or worse than the others. The point is, how is India doing or rather what India can and must do with all her resources, huge skilled and unskilled manpower pool, largest wisdom pool, largest land area and bio and mineral resources? Why has India not been able to achieve its highest potential as other countries have already done that? And most importantly, what it should and must do to achieve that?

Why haven't we been able to utilize our resources to create overall prosperity and development that so many smaller and less resourceful countries like Japan, South Korea, Malaysia or even Vietnam and Turkey have done? Today, resources wise, India is on par with most of the advanced developed countries in the world. We need not wait for 2030 or 2050 to become a super power as we already have all that needs to become a super power. If we cannot make it now, the time will beat us again as we have seen after the economic reforms. We are already lagging behind those who outpaced us. We cannot afford to lose any more time or ignore the explosive crises like unemployment, communalism, corruption or inequalities that are threatening and weakening the socio-economic foundation of our country.

It doesn't have to be this way!

It is high time we rejected what does not serve us anymore. We must reject those " Chalta hai and this-is-the-way-things-are" attitudes and pessimistic or fatalistic views prevalent in our country today. This is not the natural evolution or destiny of India. India's destiny is in our hands. We, the citizens of India must play our role in shaping our country the way we wish it to be. As Mahatma said - we must be the change we wish to see in our country!

We need to wake up and take charge of things. We need to break those old paradigms and patterns that are not working anymore and pulling the potential of India's highest optimum growth down. We need to dismantle all those old methods and out-dated processes that have created a chaotic and highly inefficient system that is unable to deliver. We need to weed out those moral, social and economic corrupt practices and methods that are eroding the very roots of our country.

Most importantly, we need to take the collective responsibility for the state our nation is in today. We cannot go on blaming governments, bureaucrats, and politicians. After all, we only have chosen them! They are just a part of the system but we, the people of India, are the system itself! Governments may come and go but until and unless we dismantle the leaky, faulty systems and processes, reform and design new, vibrant and effective structures and processes; the goals of creating peace, progress and prosperity for all would remain a pipe-dream with no scope for any real, sustaining reform and transformation!

Let us ask ourselves- is this the GDP or per capita income a country of 1.3 billion with its brightest brains, large manpower, technology, bio and mineral resources can manage to achieve? Anyone can have a look at our agriculture productivity, demand VS supply ratio and tell the gross mismanagement and mis-utilization of India's potential and resources. Despite having a large reserve of bio-resources, enough arable land, and huge rural workforce, our agriculture sector is unable to achieve a higher and sustainable growth rate! In fact, this supply vs. demand mismatch is baffling in our country and shows a pathetic picture of underutilization and mismanagement of our resources and potential. We have the largest number of youth still unemployed and unskilled while there is a huge demand for skilled and unskilled workforce in almost every sector especially manufacturing, IT and services. We have the brightest brains on earth yet we haven't been able to utilize them to optimize the use of technology and information in various sectors. We have one of the most vibrant and thriving private sectors in the world yet have not been able to integrate their expertise and resources for a comprehensive sustainable growth and development plan for the country.

A comprehensive framework for inclusive growth is no rocket science! It is simple as the most important elements of sustained, inclusive growth in any country are based on the three pillars of social, economic and environmental development; in short, it is all about, people, planet and profit. A perfect multidimensional and multifaceted development program based on poverty reduction- employment generation with improved quality and volume of employment- focused agriculture and industrial development along with equal thrust on social Sector development- reduction of inequalities- protecting the environment and providing basic essential services to all is what we need today.

The question is why have we not been able to utilize and optimize India's huge potential and resources? Why is India still punching too below its weight?

What are we missing?

What are we missing?

Growth is never by mere chance; it is the result of forces working together.- James Cash Penney

Democracy must be built through open societies that share information. When there is information, there is enlightenment. When there is a debate, there are solutions. When there is no sharing of power, no rule of law, no accountability, there is abuse, corruption, subjugation and indignation. - Atifete Jahjaga

Nelson Mandela said- "We must realize that it is not merely the lack of income, which defines poverty. An enormous proportion of very basic needs are to be met.... eliminating hunger, housing and jobs for all , providing access to clean water and sanitation for all, ensuring the availability of affordable and sustainable energy sources, eliminating illiteracy, raising the quality of education and training , protecting the environment, and improving health services and making them accessible to all."[99]

Moreover, we must accept that developing and following such a framework is not a complex or impossible task, given the resources, means, and tools we have. The fact that it has not been achieved, should make us sit and ask why?

The alarming indicators in the global indexes and reports should prompt us to review the existing schemes, policies and plans and come up with a better coordinated and improved plan. What lessons do the past decades offer or what will it take the country to sustain progress and bring about deeper changes that would make its citizens happy, healthy and prosperous? What methodology and action plans are required for sustainable poverty reduction and shared prosperity in India? And most importantly what is India lacking today?

This is the million-dollar question! We must ask ourselves what is it lacking? What does India missing? It is not the resources as we have plenty. It is not the plans and policies as we have plenty. In fact, we have plenty of everything. It is the gross mismanagement of national revenue and resources, misplaced policies and priorities and poor public service delivery that is making India unable to reach its full potential and provide inclusive and sustainable development to its people.

A lack of national integrity, proper transparency and accountability infrastructure and mechanisms to hold governments and public sector accountable for these shortcomings makes matter worse. The concepts of transparency, participation, accountability and integrity are deeply intertwined, as they form an interactive accountable platform where informed citizens can stand up for their rights and hold their leaders accountable for their actions, decisions and management of public resources.

Globally, misuse of national resources and revenue, misplace policies and priorities and poor public service delivery are considered the worst kind of corruption. It undermines democratic, sustainable and inclusive development, inhibiting the performance of public institutions and the optimal use of resources, denies increased quality of life to the most vulnerable members of society.

The global agency for corruption watch - Transparency International (TI) has recently reported in their March 2017 Global Corruption barometer report, India came across as the country with the highest bribery rate in Asia Pacific region with 69% Indians reported to pay bribes for most basic public services like government's healthcare, public schools, police, court and other utilities or for getting identification documents etc. Comparatively, the bribery rate is only 2-4% in the countries like Japan, Hong Kong and South Korea or Australia against India's 69%. **India**'s ongoing poor performance with a score of 40 reiterates the state's inability to effectively deal with petty corruption as well as large-scale corruption scandals. The impact of corruption on poverty, illiteracy and police brutality shows that not only the economy is growing but also inequality.[100]

Even as things have improved recently, in the World Bank's 2017 report on ease of doing business, India still ranks too low compared to other competitive economies. It ranked 130 out of 190 countries while top countries were New

Zealand (1st), Singapore (2nd), Denmark (3rd), Hong Kong (4th), South Korea (5th), Norway (6th), UK (7th), US (8th), and Sweden (9th). India ranked lowest among the BRICS nations. Russia (40), South Africa (74), China (78), Brazil (123) too. Even the smaller and less resourceful neighboring countries Bhutan (73), Nepal (107), Sri Lanka (110) are ahead of us.[101]

The countries that have topped the least corrupt list are the ones who have also topped various happiness and human development indexes (New Zealand, Denmark, Finland and Sweden, Norway etc.) They not only are considered the least corrupt countries but are also known for an enabling environment that makes their citizens thrive and prosper. They all have high GDP per capita, low inequality rates, literacy rates close to 100 %, and prioritized human right issues like gender equality, social security, freedom of information etc. Significantly, they all perform well in terms of government's openness and effectiveness. There is one thing common in all these countries that they have a highly developed "national integrity system" that is based on some key principles like a strong commitment to anti-corruption, public participation and transparency and accountability. Even developing countries like Indonesia and Malaysia are following their examples and have introduced many innovative and effective initiatives like national integrity university and plans.[102]

There are many initiatives and processes by global organizations like TI and OECD etc that have created a win-win environment in these countries where governments, citizens and other non-state actors together operate through various participatory approaches aiming at empowering beneficiaries to participate at all stages of the decision-making, implementation and monitoring processes as means to promote vertical forms of accountability, using tools such as participatory budget processes, social audit, and citizens' report cards. Against the top down model that some countries like Singapore follow, this bottom-up model is based on public trust, transparency and social capital that provides an inspirational and adaptable framework model that many countries can replicate to enhance the national integrity and good governance.

Globally these T& I (transparency, accountability and integrity) and anti-corruption initiatives are helping countries to democratize their governments and deliver the goods in terms of material outcomes. Countries must strive to meet the expectations and demands of its citizens by promoting Citizens' participation and empowerment within a national integrity framework based on transparency and accountability initiatives that are keys to address development and democratic failures like leakages, corruption, inefficiency, misuse and abuse of power and funds etc. As accountability increases, aid, public spending and development processes will get channelized effectively and yield better and visible results.

Let us have a look at some of these effective tools and strategies, learn from these successful countries and try to adopt the tools and strategies practiced by them.

Means and Tools

We shape our tools and afterwards our tools shape us.

-Marshall McLuhan

There are various guidelines, comprehensive programs, workshops, initiatives and tools provided by global agencies like United Nations (UN global programs against corruption), Transparency International (TI source book -2000), World Bank and Open Government Partnership Forum (OGP), UNDP, OECD etc. These are being used in many countries and have effectively improved good governance, integrity and accountability in the system. For example- anti-corruption programs and reforms, National Integrity System, Integrity Pledges, National Action Plans, social accountability tools etc. Though, most of the tools and processes are developed for the international donor agencies yet they are highly relevant and effective to be adopted as the basic national strategies and action plan to counter corruption in every form and develop a vibrant national integrity system based on the pillars of enhanced transparency and accountability.

These tools and strategies provide an effective, comprehensive framework for national reforms with multi-stakeholder approaches (governments, public sector private sector, citizens, NGOs and other agencies etc.). Here are some excerpts, guidelines and tools from their anti-corruption and integrity workshops and conferences conducted over the years (UN's prevention –an effective tool to reduce corruption and TI source book.)[103]:

The all-pervasive, monstrous corruption spreads its roots in every area of the country and manifests itself in various subtle forms. The nature and scope of corruption is described in four broader perspectives by Transparency International (TI) based on some authors and experts -

Bureaucratic corruption, *which* involves secluded transactions by public officials who misuse their authority to solicit bribes and kickbacks, pilfering and the award of favors in return for individual gains;

Grand corruption, that involves gargantuan amounts of public resources, which are either mismanaged or stolen by public employees or politicians

State or regulatory capture involves a situation where public officials and political elites get ensnared by the global capitalists or buoyant private sector that through their financial prowess are able to influence public decision-making, mostly to the detriment of the general public interest

Patronage or clientelism involves public officials portraying favoritism tendencies and exhibit exceptional interest in people whom they have some form of affiliation to public officials. This may influence public service delivery, decisions and recruitment skewed towards the 'known' thereby sidestepping professionalism, due process and neutrality principles. (Shah (2007)

Some other forms are described as use of public resources for personal gains, abuse of power for personal advantage; bribery, theft, embezzlement; fraud and receipt of kickbacks; rent-seeking; tax evasion; extortion and soliciting 'free rides'; demanding sexual or other favors; the practice of discrimination, of 'clientelism', patronage and cronyism; failure to speak the truth; distortion of reality or 'doctoring' of evidence in disingenuous ways in order to curry favor with the rich and powerful". (Argyriades (2006) [104]

Causes of Corruption

It is seen that when faced with temptation, officials normally engage in corruption, and the public often join the club due to various factors identified that include:

High-level corruption refers to misconduct at the top and by leading politicians. Since these people are generally well off and have a lot of privileges associated with their high offices, their corrupt behavior is not attributable to low pay and out of necessity to meet the living expenses of their families. Instead, greed is considered a main motivating factor.

Low-level corruption – such as the underhand payment that has to be made to traffic police officers, a clerk to expedite the issue of a driving license – has its peculiar set of problems. In this case the general
Perception is that civil servants with insufficient salaries to meet the living expenses of their families
Are driven by necessity to engage in corrupt practices. Raising their pay, it is argued, will mean less need to depend on illegal activities to earn a living while they have more to lose if they get caught.

Passive Judiciary partly caused by handpicked judges who owe their position to the executive are often
Willing collaborators in the obfuscation around allegations of wrongdoing; Businesses and individuals have been indoctrinated and conditioned into accepting and giving bribes as being a necessary benefit and cost of doing business. The system has a tendency to derail major corruption cases, in many ways protecting the culprits, who happen to be senior civil servants and politicians. Without the risk of being removed out of office and prosecuted, there is little incentive for those who engage in corrupt transactions to change their behavior.

Judicial corruption is attributable to factors such as "delays in the disposal of cases, shortage of judges and complex procedures, Emergence of the political elite who believe In Interest-oriented rather than nation-oriented programs and policies.

Corruption is caused as well as increased because of the change in the value system and ethical qualities of men who administer. The old ideals of morality, service and honesty are regarded as achronistic.
Tolerance of people towards corruption, complete lack of intense public outcry against corruption instead people are jubilating when the Anti-corruption agencies loose cases.

The absence of strong public forum to oppose corruption allow corruption to reign over people; the growing population coupled with widespread illiteracy and the poor economic infrastructure lead to
endemic corruption in public life.

Election time is a time when corruption is at its peak level. Big fund politicians to meet the high cost of the election and ultimately to seek personal favor. Bribery to politicians buys influence, and bribery by
Politicians buy votes. In order to get elected, politicians bribe poor illiterate people, who are slogging for two times' meal.

The pressure of a society in which material success is admired and even adulated and where material
failure is ruthlessly mocked drive people to go for more through corrupt practices Public officers are involved in both the demand and supply side of corruption, not minding the principle of conflict of interest.[105]

While corruption might, at least in theory, be tamed in an autocratic and dictatorial manner using a "big stick", the inexorable decline into corruption and other abuses of power on the part of totalitarian administrations suggests that this can only be temporary. The promotion of national integrity across the board is crucial to any process of sustainable reform. By raising levels of national integrity, corruption can be reduced; and this approach is vital if other efforts to promote sustainable and equitable development are not to be undermined.[106]

Most anti-corruption programs and actions end up making cosmetic changes in the socio-economic fabric of nation's and have not been able to root out the real issues. The failure to bring sustainable, positive changes in terms of institutional reforms and better services has much to do with the complexity, dynamism and pervasiveness of the corruption. Where corruption is choking development, a few with access systematically distort political and economic decisions, which might be made with conflict of interest at play. Largely unaccountable, small groups with huge political clouts seize new opportunities, from banking schemes to drug trafficking as swiftly as they develop. Development assistance and other reform plans are more likely to become hostage to corruption than to provide the 'cure' for it. Corruption is certainly one of the greatest obstacles to development and demand for good governance is increasing worldwide.[107]

Corruption is defined globally as "the misuse of public office for private gain." As such, it involves the improper and unlawful behavior of public-service officials, both politicians and civil servants, whose positions create opportunities for the diversion of money and assets from governments to themselves and their accomplices. Corruption distorts resource allocation and governments' performance. Among the contributing factors are policies, programs and activities that are poorly conceived and managed, failing Institutions, poverty, income disparities, inadequate monitoring, and a lack of accountability and transparency.

Evidence of corruption is becoming "accepted behavior" in the society with a fatalistic view or "this is the way things work here". In fact, this is a common, daily and open practice, so that we think the government has legalized the payment of bribes in the country. Public servants, lacking a service mentality, become more interested in serving themselves than serving the public. Public servants should realize that they are there to serve the public. That can only be done when government listens and implements community decisions.

It is a cause of reduced investment and even disinvestment with its many downstream effects including an increase in social polarization. Combating corruption is instrumental to the broader goal of achieving more effective, fair, and efficient governments. When there is inadequate transparency, accountability, and probity in the use of public resources, the state fails to generate credibility and authority. Systemic corruption undermines the credibility of democratic institutions and counteracts good governance. There is a high correlation between corruption and an absence of respect for human rights, and between corruption and undemocratic practices. Corruption alienates citizens from their governments.

The harmful effect corruption has on economic development, the emergence of an enabling environment for the private sector, and its role in deepening poverty in the developing countries is a worrisome situation that demands better methods and tools to counter these issues. There is considerable evidence that a strong negative relationship exists between the extent of corruption and economic performance. Pervasive corruption reduces the efficiency of governments in general and in particular reduces the effectiveness of private investment and domestic or foreign aid.

The negative impacts of corruption have served as the impetus for citizens and international institutions around the world to demand the establishment of good governance measures to improve integrity, transparency, and accountability in governments and private administrative transactions, to achieve sustainable growth and improved service delivery to the public. Transparency, combined with the empowerment of the civil society, helps governments ensure the efficient use of resources and manage a change process that results in increased accountability and improved service delivery, two elements that assist in the creation of an enabling environment for private-sector development and economic growth.

A comprehensive strategy must be based on four pillars: (a) economic development; (b) democratic reform; (c) a strong civil society with access to information and a mandate to oversee the state; and (d) the presence of rule of law.

(Excerpts from UN's global programagainst corruptionand TI source book)[103, 108]

SUGGESTED FORMULATION OF THE STRATEGY

The strategy should aim at tackling corruption through a multi-pronged balanced approach and combination of actions on three mutually reinforcing fronts

Prevention – systemic, institutional, legislative, administrative reforms and public education and
awareness raising, aimed at building democracy, create political competition, poverty reduction,
and delivery of public goods and services

Enforcement – improvement in the legal and institutional arrangements for the detection,
investigation and prosecution of corruption.
Suppression – the regular and systematic measuring of the nature, causes and extent of corruption
through reliable and verifiable data collection, analysis and co-ordination;
Political Will and leadership: demonstrations by a range of key leaders of commitment to change; setting the tone at the top
Transparency: openness in dealing with the public and public opinion
Accountability: responsibility for the performance of public duties and being answerable for all
acts and omissions
Meritocracy: promotion of the most talented and able to perform
Deregulation: systematic removal of unnecessary regulations, processes and procedures
Standardization and automation: simplification and widespread use of technology
Efficiency of service delivery: progressive performance improvement
Professionalism and competence: investment in recruitment and training
Public participation: active engagement of civil society and the media
Change management: measures which facilitate change, for example, capacity building and
awareness raising . [108] (Guidelines from TI Source Book , UN tools, excerpts from Jeremy pope and country strategy- Sierra Leone)

A good government is defined by some major characteristics. It must be accountable, transparent, participatory, effective and efficient, consensus oriented, responsive, equitable and inclusive, and lead the country by example by following the rule of law and a high level of national integrity.

Studies and researches suggest that well performing countries characteristically have a long tradition of government's openness, civic activism and social trust, with strong transparency and accountability mechanism in place allowing citizens to monitor their governments and hold them accountable for their actions and decisions. [109]

Accountability and transparency are fundamental requirements of good governance. In a democracy, the principle of accountability holds that government is responsible to the citizen of the country who elected it; for their decisions and actions.[110] The government has an obligation to report, explain and be answerable for the consequences of decisions it has made on behalf of the community it represents. Transparency means that public has a right to access all the information about the decisions and actions of those in governments and it should be freely available and directly accessible to those who will be affected by governance policies and practices, as well as outcomes. Government has to make sure that information should be provided in easily understandable forms so that people should be able to follow and understand the decision-making process. [111]Thus, accountability and transparency both form the very foundation of sound democratic governance. In a country, where the government is self- serving and is not providing enough transparency or accountability democracy has no meaning and merely makes a mockery of the will of the people and the entire election process.[112]

A good democratic government should keep the concept of transparency & accountability at the center of all its activities. It must ensure that the processes and policies implemented produce desired results and meet the needs and are in the best interests of all stakeholders especially of the poorest and most marginalized groups in society while making the best use of its resources – human, technological, financial, natural and environmental resources.

Some of the major initiatives are disclosure of budget information as well as encouraging citizens' participation that streamlines the revenue and addresses waste and misappropriation of public funds. The Open Budget Index shows that Sweden allows citizens to assess how their government is managing public funds. Similarly, Denmark has set up codes of conduct for public servants. It compels ministers to monthly publish information on their spending travel and gifts. They also have a strong legal framework criminalizing a wide range of corruption related abuses and an independent and efficient judiciary.

Though there are many ways and means through which governments can maintain or enhance its accountability, there is an increasing recognition worldwide that citizens' involvement is the most critical factor for a successful democratic government to operate in an efficient and responsive manner and live up to their obligations. In fact, in a democracy where people are the ultimate stakeholders, it is the social responsibility of citizens and civil society to hold the governments accountable and make it responsive to needs of citizens and beneficiaries with help from other sectors i.e. private sector, media and local players (NGOs, SHGs, Cooperatives, local authorities and municipalities, communities etc.). This initiative is known as social accountability throughout the world, provides extra sets of checks, balances on the governments in the interest of the people of the country, and offers a rich set of approaches and tools for applying the principles of transparency & accountability into practice.

Demand side accountability, also known as social accountability, refers to a broad range of actions and mechanisms beyond voting that citizens can use to hold the state and providers of public services accountable. Demand side measures for financial accountability include publicly accessible local governments financial information(including budgets, end-of-year financial statements and periodic implementation progress reports during fiscal year); public involvement in budgetary process through participatory budgeting practices; gender-sensitive planning, budgeting, and resource allocation, reinforced by gender audits; independent budget analysis and participatory public expenditure tracking programs that monitor budget execution and leakage of funds. - (Schaeffer ,Yilmaz)[113]

As seen quite often, so many well-intentioned schemes and development programs have been launched regularly by successive governments but very few see the light of the day due to inefficiency, misplaced priorities, and outright lethargy and apathy of office holders and of those in power. It is crucial to enhance the effectiveness of the public funds on social goals. The role of citizens along with media, social organizations and private sector is thereby catalytic and critical to maintain pressure, play a watchdog, and ferociously guard the budgets and policies to prevent any misuse, misappropriation or manipulation.

There are democratic, development and empowerment outcomes of social accountability as outlined by transparency and accountability organisation:

A) Social accountability improves the quality of governance: Citizens' disillusionment with the quality of governance moves them beyond electoral participation 'toward engaging with bureaucrats and politicians in a more informed, organised, constructive and systematic manner' (often referred to often as the 'democratic outcomes' case.

B) Social accountability contributes to increased development effectiveness: Given the difficulty, inability or unwillingness of governments to deliver essential services, service delivery effectiveness and policy design are improved by citizens' clearer articulation of their demands and more transparent public decision-making (often referred to as the 'developmental outcomes' case).

C) Social accountability initiatives can lead to empowerment: By providing information on rights and soliciting feedback from poor people, 'social accountability mechanisms provide a means to increase and aggregate the voice of disadvantaged and vulnerable groups' - sometimes referred to as the 'empowerment case'. - (Malena, 2004)[114]

These initiatives are providing tools to citizens for democratic empowerment that has been obstructed by various accountability failures across the public sector. The out-dated, obsolete, traditional ways of delivering political and bureaucratic transparency and accountability, like internal government's controls or elections, known as state-side, supply-side or institutional are more and more found to be limited and inadequate in scope. According to the World Bank, administrative bottlenecks, weak incentives or corruption in state-centered political and bureaucratic accountability mechanisms restrict their effectiveness, particularly from the perspective of the poor and marginalized people who need accountability most, but who lack the means to work round such obstacles.

Another initiative that adds to the growing global momentum in increased national integrity, transparency, accountability and civic participation in governance is Open Government Partnership (OGP). It is a new multi-stakeholder coalition of governments, civil society and private sector actors working towards the shared objectives and goals of enhanced open governance by increasing public sector responsiveness to citizens, countering corruption, promoting economic efficiencies, harnessing innovation and improving the delivery of services.

A research by a team at the Institute of Development Studies in the UK with participation of researchers in the US, South Africa, Brazil and India did a review of Impact and Effectiveness of Transparency and Accountability Initiatives.[115] A general review of the literature was carried out, plus reviews of five priority sectors: public service delivery; budget processes; freedom of information; natural resource governance; and aid transparency.

Public service delivery- In the area of service delivery, an array of strategies, often grouped together under the label 'social accountability', include complaints mechanisms, public information/transparency campaigns, citizen report cards and scorecards, community monitoring and social audits.

Budget processes - Budget transparency and accountability strategies include the now well-known 'participatory budget approach', as well as public expenditure monitoring (including, for instance, gender budgeting), participatory auditing, the Open Budget Index, and other forms of budget advocacy.

Freedom of information - Many of these initiatives are underpinned by initiatives to secure freedom of information and transparency, including right to know campaigns, strengthening the media, new legislative frameworks and voluntary disclosure mechanisms.

Natural resource governance - In the area of natural resources, initiatives such as the Extractive Industries Transparency Initiative and the Publish What you Pay campaign among others have focused on making revenues from natural resources more transparent, often through multi-stakeholder agreements and review.

Aid Transparency - Similar strategies are now being adopted in the area of aid transparency, through such initiatives as the International Aid Transparency Initiative, Publish What You Fund, and the longer-standing World Bank Inspection

Panel and various downward accountability mechanisms applied within large non-governmental organizations (NGOs).

It is suggested that for transparency to have more substantial impact on anti-corruption and development, deeper reforms are needed. For instance, though, publishing official statistics and general budget data online can be a good step but one should not take it for granted and declare premature victory as the real battle would be the proper implementation of freedom of information laws and well disseminated budgetary and procurement details at the project and municipal level that will ensure the final results. Other larger payoffs of such reforms could be transparency in the drafting of laws and in policymaking, campaign finance, lobbying, the disclosure of officials' assets, and public scrutiny on liasioning between governments, private sector and media executives. [116]

The National Integrity System – Strategies and tools [117]

The national integrity system is perhaps the most effective tool required to advance anti-corruption Reforms. Economic and social progress, the rule of law under good governance, democratic values, and strong civil society are some of the basic prerequisites to building the national integrity system to sustain a fight against corruption in various forms and at various levels. The concomitant values, institutions and comprehensive, integrative, inclusive and coordinated approach within this framework facilitate the process of building national integrity systems. The process is based on some basic concepts like Successful reform requires a country to integrate and harmonize all reforms in to a National Reform Program, including sector reforms, financial reforms, economic reforms, constitutional reforms, civil-service reform, decentralization, privatization, and legal reforms. The process must be continuous where attitudes and conduct must be examined and reevaluated for effectiveness at all levels. Reforms must focus on the areas like that can show credible impact on issues important to key stakeholders; where the return on investment is greatest; that are discrete and where reformers can control implementation, that are within the budget; and that can have some short-term positive impact. The process of and commitment to reform must be visibly supported from the top.

PREVENTION AND INTEGRITY TOOLS AND ACTIVITIES

The process of building a National Integrity System begins with a national dialogue on national integrity system assessment followed by national action plan. To promote national reform, the following prevention and integrity tools have been developed

- Online /offline Surveys focusing on service delivery
- Integrity or corruption Surveys
- Municipal and Sub-national Integrity Workshops
- External oversight in tender process
- Enforce code of conduct including declaration and monitoring of assets
- National and Integrity Workshops (NIWs) (broad based action planning)
- The Integrity Pledge
- Islands of Integrity
- National Integrity Steering Committee (NISC)
- National Integrity Unit (NIU)

The National Integrity System

The National Integrity System (NIS) comprises the principle governance institutions in a country that are responsible for the fight against corruption. When these governance institutions function properly, they constitute a healthy and robust National Integrity System, one that is effective in combating corruption as part of the larger struggle against abuse of power, malfeasance and misappropriation in all its forms. However, when these institutions are characterized by a lack of appropriate regulations and by unaccountable behavior, corruption is likely to thrive, with negative ripple effects for the societal goals of equitable growth, sustainable development and social cohesion. Therefore, strengthening the NIS promotes better governance in a country, and, ultimately, contributes to a more just society overall. [118]

To ensure that there is an enabling environment that is supportive of private- and public sector contributions to sustainable development, a National Integrity System needs to be built with mutually supportive pillars. The "pillars of integrity" in a society include actors outside the executive and outside government itself. The collection of stakeholder groups is referred to as "pillars of integrity" because it is incumbent on them to support and uphold practices that promote public integrity. A National Integrity System is based on eight pillars of integrity: (1) executive, (2) parliament, (3) judiciary, (4) watchdog agencies, (5) media, (6) private sector (Chambers of Commerce, etc.), (7) civil society and (8) law enforcement agencies.

These institutions – or 'pillars' –comprise the executive, legislature, judiciary, the public sector, the main public watchdog institutions (e.g. supreme audit institution, law enforcement agencies), as well as political parties, the media, civil society and business as the primary social forces which are active in the governance arena. Thus, the NIS is generally considered to comprise the pillars depicted below, which are based on a number of foundations in terms of political, social, economic and cultural conditions.

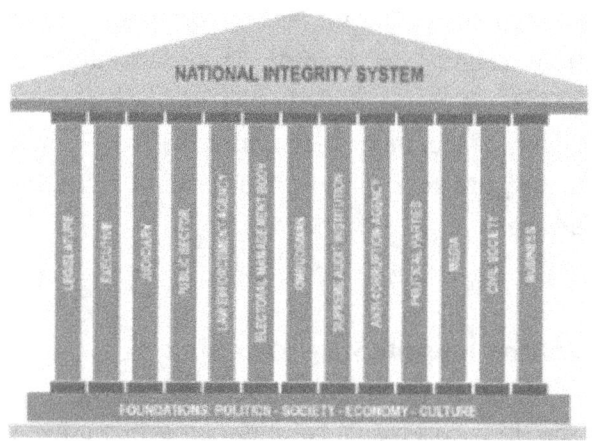

The Temple Diagram of National Integrity System

The pillars are interdependent, a weakening of one pillar results in an increased load being shifted on the others. Where several pillars weaken, the systems can no longer support sustainable development and effectively collapse. Examining a National Integrity System requires identifying gaps and opportunities for corruption within each of the pillars and then coordinating the work of the governments, civil society, and private sector into a coherent framework of institutional strengthening. The reasons for building an integrity system may differ from country to country. There are three broad, almost generic, objectives are identified: rule of law, sustainable development, and quality of life. In most countries that have embraced the reform effort, inadequate rule of law could turn out to be the *critical* bottleneck for progress.

National Integrity System Assessment

The NIS is based on a holistic approach to preventing corruption, since it looks at the entire range of relevant institutions and also focuses on the relationships among them. Thus, the NIS presupposes that a lack of integrity in a single institution would lead to serious flaws in the entire integrity system. As a consequence, the NIS assessment does not seek to offer an in-depth evaluation of each pillar, but rather puts an emphasis on covering all relevant pillars and at assessing their inter-linkages. Such a holistic "system analysis" is necessary to be able to appropriately diagnose corruption risks and develop effective strategies to counter those risks. The analysis is embedded in a participatory approach, involving the key anti-corruption agents in governments, civil society, the business community and other relevant sectors with a view to building momentum, political will and civic pressure for relevant reform initiatives.

On a cross-country level, the NIS assessment creates a sound empirical basis that adds to our understanding of strong or weak performers. Results can create a sense of peer pressure for reform as well as an opportunity for learning from those countries that are in similar stages of development.

The assessment examines both the formal framework of each institution, as well as the actual institutional practice, highlighting discrepancies between the formal provisions and reality on the ground. This in-depth investigation of the relevant governance institutions is embedded in a concise context analysis of the overall political, socio-economic and socio-cultural conditions in which these governance institutions operate. A thorough review of laws, policies and existing research studies constitutes the main data source for the assessment for the formal framework and the context analysis. To collect information on the practice of the relevant institutions, a number of key informant interviews are conducted with knowledgeable persons from the public sector, civil society, academia and other sectors.

The draft NIS report and scores form the basis for a consultative National Integrity Workshop convened by the national chapter to discuss and validate the NIS findings, and, most importantly, to identify recommendations and priority actions for policy and advocacy activities. Participants include anti-corruption and governance experts drawn from governments (including donors, where relevant), the private sector, the professions (e.g. lawyers, accountants), media and civil society. The outcomes of the consultative workshop are added to the draft NIS report, which is then published by the national chapter as well as TI-S as a NIS country report. Most importantly, the outcomes of the consultative workshop are used to inform advocacy activities by the TI national chapter as well as other anti-corruption stakeholders in the country.

A key purpose of the NIS assessment is to inform and guide the work of the national chapter. Experience shows that one of the principal weaknesses of political economy analyses is the failure to translate findings into concrete strategies and actions for change. Therefore, a last and critical step of the process is to transform the recommendations resulting from the NIS assessment and workshop into a strategic and concrete action plan for the national chapter (as well as its partners and allies).

The aim of the action plan is simple: to improve the integrity of the governance system in the country. Because each NIS action plan must take into account the specific objectives emerging from the NIS assessment, the distinct political and social contexts, and the variation in resources available to each NC, the specific objectives and content of each plan will be different. For this reason, this section takes the reader through the process of strategizing action planning, rather than prescribing what needs to be in the plan.

The National Action plan

A key stage in this process is the convening of an internal action planning meeting, during which a political will analysis is conducted. Translating dialogue into action is a critical step in the process of building a National Integrity System. A simple model of a framework that might be employed by an integrity workshop to develop an action plan. The same principles apply to all action plans, whether they are National Integrity Action Plans, municipal or other sub-national action plans: First, to be successful, the effort must be wholly owned and driven by the subject country. Public opinion surveys, which proved successful in other countries, can be used. Implementing the national action plan, for example, will typically involve the auditor-general's office, the ombudsman's office, prosecution agencies, the civil service, public procurement agencies, governments departments, and professional associations among other groups. The process of devising a National or Local Integrity Action Plan is event-driven. Stakeholders should be held accountable for achieving results.

Examples of such initiative by the open government partnership (OGP) forum are formulation of a National Action Plan (NAP) that participating countries co – create with civil society. The action plan covers a 2 year period (usually reviewed and renewed after every 18 month) and consists of a set of commitments that advance transparency, accountability, citizen participation and technological innovation. All major countries like US, UK, Australia, Germany, Israel, Mexico, Nigeria, New Zealand, Norway, Sweden, Finland, Denmark, Canada ,Ireland , Philippines, Brazil , South Africa ,Indonesia etc. have been actively following the plans and some are already on their 3-4rth national action plan like US , UK etc. .

The NAPs are put together with the help of unprecedented consultations and contributions within and outside government, including with a broad range of departments and agencies as well as public, civil society groups and organizations, foundations, academia, intelligentsia, and the private sector.

The countries are exploring various methods, processes to improve accountability and transparency along with national integrity, and are willing to put a framework with time-bound, well-monitored outcomes to work out successful comprehensive, integrated national action plans.

Like Australia has integrated its national action plan with national integrity system, South Korea that has been topping UN e governments surveys and is acknowledged as the world's best online provision of public services has launched its citizen centric Gov3.0 initiative that aims to apply and spread the governments operation paradigm with key values of "openness, sharing, communication and collaboration" throughout the entire government based on e government and other achievements. Its national action plan -3 (NAP3) incorporates various plans and programs to enhance transparency, citizen participation, integrity and good governance through effective implementation and achieving international standards.

CHALLENGES TO REFORM

There are many challenges. First, the question of the sequencing of reforms. This will differ from country to country, but actually working out precisely where to start in the process is an important one, as it will dictate much of the path ahead. It is in this context that the "national integrity system workshop" can be most effective, providing as it does an opportunity for all stakeholders to participate in a process that otherwise tends to be dominated, for no good or compelling reason, by lawyers.

A particular challenge is to identify the appropriate (and clean) partners in a given country. There may be many who offer themselves, but the outsider must be able to determine what hidden agendas there may be and what individual motivations are as well as gain a reading on where the people concerned stand in their community. This dictates a special role for civil society in a country from the very outset to ensure that the reform process is fostered with the right "champions". The road blocks, too, need to be identified from the outset and the base line of acceptable (or perhaps better described as tolerable) conduct which the people are prepared to live with, defined.

The credibility of enforcement and watchdog agencies is crucial to the building of public trust and confidence. Credible agencies will attract public co-operation, both as complainants and as witnesses. An institution lacking in trust will not. And at the heart of credible institutions lies their manifest and popularly accepted integrity. Their leaders must role model conduct of the highest kind.

The donor community and civil society also must play their roles both as part of the problem and as part of the solution. They are part of the problem because in many quarters they are viewed as having turned a blind eye to corruption in the projects they have been funding, and to tolerate the misappropriation of public funds to suit their own ends. However unfair some may think this to be, it is a perception that is very real. And in many instances, there is substance to the complaint. Therefore, donor organizations must re-examine their own practices, something that many have been doing. And as part of the solution, there are activities, which donors can, should and do fund, but it is essential that these be locally owned and driven.

Whatever may have been the position in the past, most countries now have the human resources to tackle their own problems, but they may need access to information, the tools they need to undertake the job and, at times, a word of encouragement. Thus, the donor's role is to be low key, supportive and facilitative. The more conspicuous the roles of the donor and civil society, the more likely the efforts are to bear fruit. The donor community can; in particular, back up the data collection processes needed to empower civil society to hold the civil service accountable—to turn public servants into servants for the public. And they can help stress a focus on the bribe giver, and not just the bribe receiver.

This is particularly the case in so-called "grand corruption", where for a generation or more exporters from the industrialized countries have been accustomed to bribing officials in developing countries to win business or to create what in many cases became "white elephant" projects. Frank acknowledgement of the role of the rich countries in contributing to the present decline, and with it an equally frank admission that no country can claim any sort of moral supremacy when it comes to corrupt practices goes a long way towards cementing a meaningful partnership. The "hand that gives" must also be addressed at the national level, but concerted action against the "grand corrupters" from abroad creates a climate of
Change and the moral ground necessary to address forms of corruption at lower levels.

In the conclusion, the process of building national integrity systems is as important as the content. Successful reform requires a country to integrate and harmonize all reforms in to a National Reform Program, including sector reforms, financial reforms, economic reforms, constitutional reforms, civil-service reform, decentralisation, army demobilization, privatisation, and legal reforms. Essential to curbing corruption is undertaking and maintaining the public's confidence in the State as an institution. It is dependent upon the people's loyalty to its philosophy and policies regarding the development of the society's social, economic, and political welfare.[119] (NIS -Prepared by Petter Langseth, Ph. D, Programme Manager, Global Programme against Corruption, Centre for International Crime Prevention, Office of Drug Control and Crime Prevention, United Nations Office at Vienna UN& TI source book 2000, NIS transparency.org)

Let us see how can we use these tools and mechanisms to reform and transform India:

Reforming and transforming India

The structure has been erected by architects of consummate skill and fidelity; its foundations are solid; its compartments are beautiful as well as useful; its arrangements are full of wisdom and order; and its defences are impregnable from without. It has been reared for immortality if the work of man may justly aspire to such a title. It may, nevertheless, perish in an hour by the folly, or corruption or negligence of its only keepers - the people. Republics are created - by the virtue, public spirit, and intelligence of the citizens. They fall, when the wise are banished from public councils, because they dare to be honest and the profligate are rewarded, because they flatter the people, in order to betray them.

- Dr. Sachidanand Siha (while presiding at the inaugural session of India's Constituent Assembly, 9 December 1946).

As per the international guidelines and framework suggested by TI (transparency International), the National Integrity System in India broadly could be considered as the sum total of democratic institutions, laws, procedures and practices that would present a holistic picture of India's integrity landscape as regards to basic constitutional, democratic principles i.e. integrity, accountability and transparency. The NIS of India can be depicted as a temple with a golden dome supported by a series of pillars that form individual elements of the integrity system like Legislature, Executive, Judiciary, and Public sector, Law Enforcement Agencies, Electoral Management Body, Ombudsman, Supreme Audit Institution, Anti-corruption Agencies, Political Parties, Media, Civil Society and Business.[120]

The golden roof (dome) of this temple is balanced on the beams of peace (the rule of law); progress (inclusive and sustainable growth and development) and prosperity (quality of life) for all that are the very objectives of democracy in the country. All the pillars are interdependent, have to be strong, and together must work to keep the roof of the temple intact and balanced. If any one of these "integrity pillars" fails, all other pillars get overloaded and if several weaken, the roof will collapse. Therefore, the success of India does not depend on any particular pillar but on the quality and integrity of all the pillars collectively. Integrity system ensures that power is exercised in a manner that is true to the democratic values, purposes and duties entrusted to, or held by, the institutions, office bearers and governments as directed in the Indian constitution.

The foundation of this temple is built and sustained by democratic core values, rules, rights and practices of the society that upholds this temple and supports the pillars. These core democratic values are ethics, integrity, freedom of speech, the right to information, strong and effective law and legal processes, transparency and accountability, fair and just elections, independent monitoring and regular evaluation, effective public management and services etc. If these values, rules and practices are weak then the whole foundation will be fragile and all the pillars together would not be able to hold and support the system. These are the fundamental conditions that build trust, confidence and credibility in governance and administration across all the organs of the state i.e., executive, judiciary, and all other public institutions. Without these fundamental values, the whole system will fail to gain any credibility or legitimacy from the citizens whom they represent or intend to serve.

As directed by TI, a strong National Integrity System ensures better governance across all aspects of society by maintaining transparency, accountability, integrity and service in all the pillars and fulfilling their constitutional and legal mandate in daily business. Ensuring integrity and accountability means that the public sector and governments are serving the public with utmost sincerity, effectively and efficiently, through reliable service operations, impartial justice, transparent policies and processes, effective public resources, public finance management and a strong public feedback and grievances redressal mechanism in place.

These democratic systems, values and practices are the primary factors that make a nation poor or prosper. How well all the pillars are developed and how strong the foundation is that would make all the difference as we have seen across the world; the nations with strong integrity systems, effective public service deliveries, strong ethical and accountable administrations and robust law and order environments; enjoy high progress, high living standards and integrated, peaceful cohesive societies- a perfect outcome that every country dreams and thrives for!

For example, the Scandinavian or Nordic model in the countries like Sweden, Norway, Denmark etc. that is considered the epitome of utopian social democracy with its dynamic approach to social development that relies on social and economical equality, universal welfare, unity, social security, pro-labor policies and environment individual freedom, effective, efficient, professionalized public services, fair and just rule of law, open and free trade, and active state etc. What is important to learn that these countries, after a long period of trial and error, have succeeded in maintaining a perfect balance between capitalism and socialism. No wonder they top every global social index like happiness index, social progress index, sustainable development goals (SDG) index and are considered the least corrupt countries in the world. Though there are still some challenges they face like immigration issues and cost considerations but to a greater extent, they represent a perfect social democratic -welfare state model for the world to follow.

Many other countries have also reformed their old models and shifted towards inclusive and sustainable social market economy (known as the third way) with a well-developed, effective integrity system and are constantly striving to achieve a healthy balance between socialism and capitalism; are considered best countries to live and work like Germany, Australia, New Zealand, Switzerland Austria, Netherlands etc. Closer home, the Asian miracle economies Japan, South Korea, Singapore, and Malaysia etc. too followed some of these practices and has successfully advanced to higher income and higher social progress group countries. On the other end of the spectrum, we have those nations like North Korea, South Sudan etc who are still under authoritarian rule, with highly dysfunctional integrity systems and weak institutions, law and practices devoid of any social integrity, freedom or human dignity in the society.

Between these two extreme social models, there are many countries, including India who were able to break free of authoritarian or colonial regimes and embraced democracy yet, the dream of a balanced and robust social democracy still seems distant; as they have failed to reform their policies and systems to achieve the perfect balance between socialism and capitalism. These countries (including India) despite being social democracies and welfare states as directed by their constitutions are largely driven by the capitalist economy with most policies and processes favoring the globalization at the cost of social deprivation. Politics and bureaucracy both are performing below the expectation level of the people in general; the ethical values and integrity of public administration are deteriorating. Poor public service delivery, chaotic law and order and skewed policies resulting in uneven development, extreme socio-economic inequalities, contrasting living conditions and a dysfunctional society have created a crumbling integrity infrastructure that has eroded democracy of its hefty social ideals and people of their constitutional rights!

Ironically, before independence, the people of India had been long subjugated under feudal and colonial regimes where the entire system in the country i.e. the institutions, rules, policies and practices were designed and maintained to serve the rulers. If a ruler was fair and just, the public was in luck, otherwise, exploitation and slavery were the common social orders in those times. The majority of rural masses were forced to work under rich landholders, Zamindars and upper caste Thakurs and feudal families as bonded labors and were denied the basic facilities like quality education, health and employment opportunities. During British Raj, the entire state and central administrative and legal machinery were employed to collect and deposit the loot in the British treasury at the expense of the general public so much that the country went bankrupt while England flourished.

The British very cleverly divided Indian society by introducing their language and education system in India that was designed to colonize and dominate the masses while a small section of rich and powerful elite class was made partners in crime to facilitate the dominance and continued loot. The central service officials, administrative staff and local allies were trained to serve the masters and ignore the public plight and demands. Unfortunately, post-independence, as they say old habits die hard; things have not changed much as far as the systematic loot of country's revenue and resources, the dominance of the selective few and public disregard of the plight and pleas of the masses are concerned. It is highly ironical as it completely defies the democratic framework of our constitution and the aspirations of our leaders who fought and sacrificed their lives for freedom from these very tyrannical rules and practices!

The dream and promise of the long tedious struggle of people of India was freedom and the prize was the democracy - "Poorna Swaraj" (complete self-rule) based on the lofty principles of dignity, equality, liberty, social and economical justice and prosperity for all. The term democracy is derived from the Greek words, demos meaning people and Kratos, meaning power. Democracy thus means the power of the people- a system of self-rule where people rule themselves by choosing their representatives or leaders directly or indirectly.

In the words of Abraham Lincoln, it is a government of the people, by the people and for the people.

Though, in some forms, democracy can be exercised directly by the people; being a huge country with diverse cultures and ethnicities, India opted for indirect democracy where the people of India choose their representatives through voting and delegate them the powers to represent their decisions and concerns.

This core idea of democracy that people choose and delegate executive and legislative power to politicians to serve their interests; in turn politicians must form policies and practices to decide how the public resources and services should be used to serve the people and fulfill the promises and mandates entrusted to them; is what makes the dream of poorna swaraj come true. For instance, when a particular constituency chooses and elects its representative, the elected member of parliament's duty, in turn, must be- choosing policies, budgets and services that will improve the lives of people in his constituency, getting work done as promised, checking public money is spent for and on people wisely. The MP is ultimately accountable to the people who elected him and serve the constituency in the best capacity as the ultimate power to re-elect or reject lies nowhere but in the hands of people of his constituency. The same goes for the entire political landscape across the country.

This is the power and promise of the democracy where the ultimate power to elect or reject remains in the hands of people of the country that gives them control over their destiny and authority over those who they choose to govern and serve.

As quoted by **Lord Acton** who famously wrote- "power corrupts, and absolute power corrupts absolutely," - **The true democratic principle, that none shall have power over the people, means that none shall be able to restrain or to elude its power.**[121]

"Democracy implies that the man must take responsibility for choosing his rulers and representatives, and for the maintenance of his own 'rights' against the possible and probable encroachments of the government which he has sanctioned to act for him in public matters." (Ezra Pound, "ABC of Economics," 1933).[122]

This participatory social power makes the people living in a democratic society, the ultimate guardians of their own freedom and basic human rights as directed by the constitution of the country that recognizes that inherent dignity and the equal and undeniable rights of all members of the society. It is the foundation of freedom, justice, and peace in the nation. In that sense, democracy is not just about setting democratic institutions or set ideas and principles but it also includes democratic practices, policies and procedures that evolve with time as societies evolve and become more aware of their own power and rights.

In short, democracy is the institutionalization of freedom but it is not static; it is a dynamic evolutionary process- a way of living and working together that needs participation, periodic revisions and reforms to achieve the purpose and ideals it strives for. Freedom, after all, means responsibility not freedom from responsibility and it comes with a price. The price is the active participation and social responsibility of citizens to maintain and preserve democratic infrastructure- ideals, institutions, policies and processes in the country and ensure that these are working effectively and with integrity and the vision and outcome of democracy is accomplished.

In other words, for democracy to flourish and succeed in achieving its ultimate objective i.e. peace, progress and prosperity for all, citizen must be active participators in the process not passive spectators; for the success of the governments and the entire system is only their responsibility no one else, as ultimately it is the people who will do or undo it. A passive, apathetic and indifferent citizenry would give away its potent democratic power to few to misuse, exploit and abuse their individual and collective rights, ultimately collapsing the foundation of social freedom and peace in the country. This means that democracy does not only put ultimate power in the citizen's hands but also puts the ultimate responsibility to safeguard their rights and interests by playing their role individually and collectively in the entire democratic system i.e. institutions, rules, processes and practices etc. as government is only a single pillar in the democratic system that consists of various public and private institutions, legal bodies, organizations and associations and a democratic society does not depend upon governments for their existence, legal rights or authority!

Unlike societies ruled by monarchs, dictators or authoritarian governments; where all the institutions, rules or processes are controlled by the ruling governments and the entire system is accountable only to them; in a democracy, governments along with all the institutions, processes and practices, are ultimately accountable to the people of the country. Thus in a democracy, the powers of governments are limited and as per the constitutional law, governments/ states exist only to serve the people and are obligated to protect the constitutional rights of the citizens who gave their loyalty (votes) to the governments/ states. This makes citizens and private organizations free of control from governments and in this free space they can exercise their rights and responsibilities to fulfill and protect the core fundamental values of true democracy i.e. the rights of freedom of speech and expression, freedom of religion and conscience, freedom of assembly and protest against any exploitation or social or political issue, equality of law and right to constitutional remedies. What is more important to understand that these fundamental rights are the constitutional rights of the citizens that exist independently and cannot be influenced or legislated by the whims of any government!

This mutual, two-way relationship between the citizens and governments in a country had been aptly described by Thomas Jefferson in the U.S. declaration of Independence – **"We hold these truths to be self-evident, that all men are created equal, that they are endowed by their Creator with certain inalienable rights, that among these are life, liberty and the pursuit of happiness. That to secure these rights, governments are instituted among men, deriving their just powers from the consent of the governed."**[123]

That is why it is said that democracy is "government by discussion" and any social ill or misery that exists in a country is not due to mal-governance but due to the inaction and passiveness of the citizens who instead of exercising the power and the rights bestowed upon them by the constitution; choose to suffer quietly and helplessly. The failure to stand up for their own rights or hold oppressive and irresponsible governments or officials accountable for their misplaced concerns, ill-designed policies or mismanaged funds, resources and services; is the real failure of democracy.

That is what the chief architect of Indian constitution Babasaheb Ambedkar famously cautioned – **"By independence, we have lost the excuse of blaming the British for anything going wrong. If hereafter things go wrong, we will have nobody to blame except ourselves!"**[124]

That is why our constitution directs that - **"It shall be the duty of every citizen of India to develop the scientific temper, humanism and the spirit of inquiry and reform"**.[125] At the least, they should educate themselves and create awareness regarding the critical issues challenging their country so that they can use their power to vote intelligently and responsibly. Ultimately, a successful democracy would depend upon an active, aware, literate and knowledgeable citizenry whose active participation and criticism of reckless or regressive policies and officials would lead to a more open, evolved and progressive society. A free country must provide this fundamental freedom to its people; in order to govern themselves; freedom to express themselves openly, publicly - in speech and in writing!

That is why the future of democracy depends not on governments, institutions, or practices but on the participatory role of its citizenry as not just the beneficiaries or voters but as the active participators in the collective choices and policies that affect their lives. And not only participating in policy making or budget designing but also monitoring, evaluating and controlling the outcomes. In other words, the future of democracy would depend on public control and political equality exercised by the citizens of the country and creating a system where the governed choose those who should govern and for how long and the policies and practices to be followed; formulating public manifesto and mandates, establishing fair and effective processes of governance, developing accountable, transparent political, public administrative and judicial mechanisms to ensure integrity and legality of the governance.

That is what the vision of freedom and promise of democracy 'Of the people, for the people and by the people' entrusted by our constitution to us. This is the ultimate power vested in the hands of people of India by our constitution, the longest one in the world that opens with the sentence- "WE, THE PEOPLE OF INDIA, having solemnly resolved to constitute India into a SOVEREIGN, SOCIALIST, SECULAR, DEMOCRATIC REPUBLIC and to secure to all its citizens:JUSTICE, social, economic and political; LIBERTY of thought , expression, belief, faith and worship;EQUALITY of status and of opportunity; and to promote among them all FRATERNITY assuring the dignity of the individual and the unity and integrity of the Nation.........do HEREBY ADOPT, ENACT AND GIVE TO OURSELVES THIS CONSTITUTION.[126]

The constitution of India has provided us with a comprehensive democratic framework to guide and govern the country and has made sure that the objectives specified in the preamble that constitutes the basic structure of the Indian Constitution; cannot be amended. It has laid the foundation of Indian democratic system consisting of democratic institutions, process and practices on the premise that the system is established for the sole purpose of protecting the fundamental rights of all the Indians that are: Right to Equality, Right to Freedom, Right against Exploitation, Right to Freedom of Religion, Cultural and Educational Rights and Right to Constitutional Remedies. [127]These rights are fundamentals, protected by the judiciary, and are non-amendable. As we discussed earlier, aside from these fundamental rights, the constitution has also provided instructions for equal social opportunities for all through the "directive principles of state policy," which directs the state to secure a social order for the promotion of welfare of the people and entitlements like "the right to an adequate means of livelihood, free legal aid, "free compulsory education for all children" and "the right to work."[128]

It is said the absolute power corrupts, so to make sure that there is no abuse, misuse or ill concentration of the power in the system, the constitution of India established the main organs of the basic structure of the democratic system accordingly—executive (the elected governments and cabinet of ministers), legislature (elected members of parliaments MPs and Members of legislature assembly MLAs) and judiciary (High court and Supreme Court); defining their powers, demarcating their responsibilities and regulating their relationship. These organs are independent and are supposed to keep a check on each other's activities and processes to ensure that the basic guidelines and objectives of the constitution are followed and maintained perfectly. This power sharing is horizontal and an impartial judiciary that is independent of any influence of the legislature and the executive is one of the main strengths of the Constitution. The Supreme Court is given the highest authority and guardianship of the constitution and every Indian including government and politicians is equal before its law.[129]

The vertical power sharing system established India as a union of states with a cooperative federal structure with a clear division of powers between the Centre and the states, each enabled and empowered by the Constitution to enact and legislate within their field of activity.[130]The constitution has also provided a strong democratic institutional infrastructure where a number of autonomous institutions were set up to play key roles like Election Commission which is responsible for holding free and fair elections, Public Service Commission which is responsible for providing effective public services to all and an Auditor General (CAG) which is responsible for conducting independent audits of accounts of the governments and its agencies. There are another state, non-state organizations and advisory agencies like CBI, ATS, and NITI Ayog etc. who play important roles in their respective capacities.

The most dynamic feature of the constitution of India perhaps is the fact that it is not static but evolving with time through fresh interpretations or amendments. The fact that it is one of the most frequently amended constitutions in the world reemphasizes its objective and purpose that is constant growth and progress for the nation and its people. The right to constitutional remedies is the most powerful fundamental right of the people of India that gives them the power to rule, revise, reform and revolutionize the system if it fails to deliver.

What's more important to understand is that the entire democratic infrastructure with its institutions; processes, rules and practices, is set up for one purpose only and that is to serve the people of India. It is easy to forget that people are the starting point and focus of the entire democratic process and get lost in the haze and maze of political and institutional hierarchies and intricacies. In other words, institutions, processes and practices are the means, people are the ends! All the organs of the state including legislature, executive, judiciary and all other public institutions are ultimately accountable to the people of India as it is the constitutional duty and responsibility of the institutions and official, elected or service bound; to gain legitimacy from the people whom they represent and are mandated/ sworn to serve. Thus, to ensure that elected officials and others holding public posts should act in the best interests of the citizens they represent; governments and public sector need to be accountable and responsive to people, not only for the policies, processes and practices but for the use of public revenues and resources too.

Although frequent elections ensure that the power of democracy remains secured in the hands of people and keep the popular control of governments yet, they cannot ensure the continuous accountability and responsibility of governments to the public. Therefore, this is the responsibility and duty of the parliament to not only choose appropriate policies and practices as per the public mandates but also to provide complete transparency and accountability of their decisions and actions to the public as well. The bottom line is that no effective accountability of governments is possible without public scrutiny or inspection that is the fundamental right of people as per the constitution.

Apart from electoral authorization, continuous accountability; public participation and consultation in policy making, implementation and monitoring the outcomes through independent agencies or ombudsman (lokpal) are also necessary for democracy to succeed in the country. Public consent, public accountability and responsiveness are the hallmarks of democratic institutions, failing which, the power balance and distribution of opportunities and resources tend to get skewed in favor of few powerful and corrupt sections. Additionally, many biases in policies and priorities also result in power imbalance like media focus on middle class or rich and famous, parliament policies debates favoring business class, the legal system or tax system favoring rich and powerful, banking sector bailing out big industrialists or influential corporates etc. Then there is huge power imbalance and resources wastage through the various forces of corruption that find their way through the leaks and creeks of the faulty system and processes.

We all know that corruption and weak governance are the biggest obstacles in achieving prosperity and equity for all, that's why eliminating these weaknesses is not only a moral but economic necessity for India to become a superpower. Improved governance and bureaucratic processes along with deep anti-corruption reforms can raise the GDP growth rate significantly. To define governance- it actually is the process of taking the decisions to manage country's resources and affairs by using the authority – political, economical, administrative or other and implementing them effectively. From this perspective good governance means :–

Choosing appropriate policies and priorities to ensure basic amenities and social security to citizens to live a life with dignity- Utilizing natural resources and national income effectively to provide them equal social and economic opportunities to improve their standard of living -promoting inclusive and sustainable development to provide hope to all for a promising future- creating space and means for participatory democratic activities in public affairs- dispensing free and just legal and judiciary services to all maintaining transparency and accountability in every function of governance , ensuring high ethics and integrity in all activities and services to citizens and most importantly fulfilling the commitments and mandates made to its electorate to repay the trust and faith invested by people in their representatives.[131]

Former Indian President Mr. R. Venkataraman defined good Government as the one that "is stable and truly representative of the majority of the people; maintains its territorial integrity and national sovereignty; accelerates economic growth and development; ensures the welfare of all sections of people, and renders justice without delay". [132]

That is the role the constitution of India has assigned to the government through establishing the democratic institution and processes i.e. independent legislature and judiciary and a system of checks and balances through vertical and horizontal power distribution and supporting agencies and commissions. The world bank has described key attributes of good governance as political stability; Government's effectiveness, which includes the quality of policy making and public service delivery; accountability; civil liberties; rule of law, which includes protection of property rights; Independence of the judiciary; and control of corruption. According to UN, good governance has some major characteristics - It is participatory, consensus oriented, accountable, transparent, responsive, effective and efficient, equitable and inclusive and follows the rule of law. It assures that corruption is minimized, the view of minorities is taken into account and that the voices of the most vulnerable in society are heard in decision-making. It is also responsive to the present and future needs of society."[133]

A participatory democracy and the rule of law require freedom of expression and a sound legal framework that ensures full protection of basic human rights.

Accountable and transparent governance requires accountable and ethical administration and processes. Responsive, effective and efficient governance requires high integrity in all the organs of the system. Unfortunately, the present situation in our country presents a contrasting picture of good governance as the politicization of bureaucracy and criminalization of politics have led to a dysfunctional integrity system with various conditions that are weakening the pillars of integrity in the country. Absence of democratic and moral political infrastructure…delayed and inadequate justice processes….lack of solidarity, trust and cooperation between political parties and citizens….weak and ineffective institutions…..corruption…..communalization of democracy… weak or negligible social responsibility or corporate responsibility displayed by civil and private organizations …..negative media ….. a passive, apathetic society and lack of tolerance and harmony in the country have made the dream of a robust democratic system supported by good governance an implausible possibility today.

In the light of emerging integrity tools and initiatives being adapted in various countries and the subsequent encouraging results and positive outcomes, it is important to assess the crumbling public institutional system and old, outdated processes in India as we have seen such assessments provide benchmark for analyzing the strength and effectiveness of a country's institutions of accountability in addressing corruption and mismanagement. Also, it is clear that when institutions and sectors within the National Integrity System work together and are in sync; they help create an environment that promotes effective and sound democratic governance and discourages corruption and mismanagement.

The word 'integrity' is derived from the Latin integritas that means upright or reliable, or intact and as the antonym of corruption, which means disintegration, or deterioration of the original state. If a person is unable to perform his duties in a reliable and upright manner the then he would be called corrupt and the same goes for all officials and institutions. If they are not able to hold the original values, purposes and duties for which power is entrusted to them, then the integrity system will deteriorate and eventually collapse.

As assessment of our National Integrity System based on several pillars like - Parliament, Executive, Judiciary, Public Administration (bureaucracy), Local Governments, Police (law enforcement agency), Comptroller and Auditor General (supreme audit institution), Election Commission, National Human Rights Commission, CBI, Anti-Corruption Commission, Planning Commission (NITI-Ayog), Political Parties, Civil Society, Media, and Business etc- would show the weak levels of integrity and lack of synergy amongst the NIS pillars that is critical for the system's overall effectiveness. As we know, any weak pillar, particularly in the government, public sector or judiciary directly or indirectly would affect all the other pillars creating an imbalance in the overall system.

The further assessment of our national pillars would show that while India is the largest democracy in the world with a strong inclusive constitutional and sound legal framework; inadequate practice and implementation of those and a weak political will to reform its crumbling " white elephants" institutions fail to provide accountable and effective democratic governance in the country. A prevalent culture of noncompliance, a dysfunctional parliament, an authoritative closed executive, an overburdened insufficient judiciary, an unaccountable and highly inefficient politicized bureaucracy infected with nepotism and corruption and a self-serving criminalized police force have been unable to provide a strong foundation that is essential for nation building. Inadequate law enforcement against corruption, low awareness of citizens of their rights and inadequate access to information, lack of accountability and transparency in governance , so-called independent commissions lacking credibility and public trust, a dynamic yet disconnected private sector, a hugely diverse and powerful yet somewhat irresponsible and sensationalized media and a socially diverse , aware yet inactive, dormant civil society together mark a weak integrity system that is unable to achieve its ultimate potential due to such internal weaknesses and challenges.

As a result, despite being the largest democracy in the world and an emerging super economy, India has failed to ensure effective law and order, sustainable growth and development, providing protection to its citizens and smooth functioning of state institutions that are the fundamental rights of its citizens. Petty party politics and ever-growing hostility between parties have eroded parliament's dignity and scope for constructive discussions and consensus. A lack of political will to bring out badly needed substantive reforms and lack of accountability and integrity in all key pillars in the system have resulted in ever-increasing social inequalities and conflicts, deterioration of law and order, abuse of power and resources and violation of citizen's fundamental rights in the country.

The politicization of bureaucracy has eroded the integrity and credibility of Indian public sector. Instead of serving the public that is the constitutional duty of the public servant, they serve the political masters and it is not unusual to see the entire bureaucratic landscape changing when governments change. Their unholy loyalty earns them many rewards and awards along with high strategic positions pre and post retirement. Even positions that were constitutionally reserved for non-political, neutral, or detached posts like governors or some eminent board positions are routinely given to the loyalists. An ethical governance could be measured by the yardsticks of the rule of law and absence of corruption apart from various other measures. For instance, the rule of law means that the guilty are properly punished yet as we see hardly any corrupt official or politician is ever punished or lost money/assets ever recovered and as far as corruption is considered, well…. the multitude and spread of it in our country is so wide that it has eroded the entire system of its credibility and integrity.

The lack of integrity and accountability and huge discrepancies between law and practice across the sectors show a need of deep, strategic intervention and urgent reforms in every sector for effective implementation of a strong National Integrity System. Many countries who have undertaken such initiatives for reforming their integrity pillars, adapted a comprehensive strategy based on some key principles which stress on the importance of realistic, ever-evolving reforms that are specifically designed to solve issues and achieve clear goals. They have come to understand that there is an interdependence of policy, politics and administration as political reforms determine policy priorities that in turn drive the administrative reform priorities and together these reforms determine the development of the country and its natural and other resources.

Some such popular key guiding principles for reforms are -a realistic, result oriented framework , clear goals ,enabling administrative structures, building capacities and developing skills for better administration and service including increased professionalism to complement staff's technical knowledge and enhance their performance and productivity, better policies, priorities and strategies , introducing initiatives like a code of conduct to improve ethics and morale, efficient and pragmatic system and leakage proof processes, effective public service and financial management through creative use of information and technology etc.

The management and operation of public finances should be the top priority for administrative and reform challenges in the public sector. Some effective tools such as Financial Management Information Systems (FMIS), procurement and asset/wealth declaration laws have helped minimize loopholes for corrupt practices and misuse of public financial resources in many countries. A Sound public management system is also an essential part of the reform process as it supports collective control, prioritization, accountability and efficiency in the management of public resources and service delivery, which are critical to the achievement of national policy objectives and goals, including Sustainable Development Goals. The adoption of Information and communication technologies (ICT) in many countries has been effective in reducing public sector corruption by transforming both the governments' internal work processes and external relationships with its citizens. The impact of ICT as a useful and practical policy tool for reducing corruption in addition to traditional methods i.e. administrative reform and law enforcement is seen in many countries like South Korea, Japan, and the US etc.

There are enough examples that support the principle that ICT plays an important role in public management reform by delivering better quality public services with less waiting time and cost, helping citizens find jobs and better public services, facilitating public engagement , helping community development, enhancing public productivity in turn, supporting good governance and improving governments accountability. This portal is also linked to all the institutions (central and local governments, educational institutions, and overseas diplomatic missions, judiciary, and other major public institutions to provide one-stop services.

Traditionally, in India, periodic administrative reforms introducing new policies and law enforcement have been used to address a range of issue yet, the lack of an effective public management system and accountability infrastructure has hampered the effect. Later, various strategies like enhancing the efficiency of bureaucracy, merit-based promotion and competitive exam based recruitment, improved regulations and other transparency-accountability mechanisms were also introduced to de-politicize the system albeit unsuccessfully.

Effective, Innovative and creative use of Information and communication Technology (ICT) can reduce unnecessary interventions by public employees that endanger the abuse of power, and help to monitor public employees' behaviors at a low cost. ICT also contributes by transparently providing information to the public, and can build a full proof system with watertight processes that can block all the loopholes and scope of leakages and pilferage of revenue and resources. With time bound flow charts, well monitoring and evaluation processes that are needed to prevent public employees' corrupt practices by transparently providing information about government's policy-making and service delivery processes to the public. In this approach, the public is defined as customers, and the government is considered the service provider making public service delivery become more accessible to the public. [134]

Though India has made remarkable strides in ICT yet, it leaves a lot to be desired as even after making a huge expenditure in digital infrastructure; it has not translated into better service delivery performance or towards increased transparency and accountability of the public sector.

For that matter, despite regularly introducing a large number of policies, processes and commitments, the efforts have failed to bring much-needed reform in the integrity infrastructure in India. Rampant corruption, mismanagement of resources and revenue, misplace policies and priorities, inadequate law enforcement, delayed and insufficient justice, poor public service delivery, apathetic, unaccountable public employees, power drunk unapologetic elected members, crumbling institutions, toothless commissions and agencies and deteriorating politics indicate a weak integrity infrastructure that needs urgent and radical reforms.

As we observed earlier, a brief analysis of the pillars of integrity ranging from Parliament, Executive, Judiciary, Public Administration (bureaucracy), Local Governments, Police, Comptroller and Auditor General (CAG), Election Commission, Anti-Corruption Commission, National Human Rights Commission, CBI, Planning Commission, Political Parties, Civil Society, Media, and Businesses etc. shows a system that has so much potential to turn the country into an advanced and prosperous economy yet, is unable to reach its ultimate potential due to various forms of corruption, mal-administration and mis-management of resources, that have hollowed out the very foundations of this integrity temple.

So, the question arises why even after several decades of government reforms and a dozen five-year national plans; much-needed change in the system has eluded the country?

Why does systemic corruption and mismanagement of country's resources and revenue still prevail despite a large number of efforts to fight it?

Why have the reform frameworks, monitoring processes and deterring mechanisms failed to establish improved law and order, better public services and enhanced development in the country?

The real issue however, in India is not the weak institutional infrastructure; as the Indian constitution gave us a strong democratic institutional framework with an effective power sharing structure; rather it is the poor, inadequate democratic processes and practices that are proving India's Achilles' heel and are the main causes of deterioration of democracy and integrity infrastructure in the country. When it comes to the performance of our democratic institutions, it is way below average and deeply compromised by various social, economic or political limitations that have been continuing from the past. For instance, our electoral system, revenue department or education system though are massive and resilient yet there have been no significant reforms considering that advancements in science and technology have grown by leaps and bounds. In fact, after independence, if any reform has really worked, it was the economic reforms in the 90s that changed the economic landscape in India. The other organs are still largely following British era rules and processes. There is a continuing decline of trust in governments offices and public sector and a crying need for deep reform as they have failed to live up to the expectations of the constitution to promote policies and services for the social well-being of its citizens. The fact is evident that majority of citizens are denied the most basic essential services and their modest expectations still remain unfulfilled.

The public officials and elected members still treat the authority as being bestowed upon them and behave as masters instead of serving the public. Criminalization of politics and politicization of bureaucracy has eroded the system of checks and balances and any scope of an effective reform for transparency and accountability resulting in nepotism, unresponsive conduct, apathy and degeneration at all levels and declining public trust in the whole system.

The declining public trust and faith in governments and public sector is due to many factors like lack of integrity or good leadership qualities in governments, inefficient and poor delivery of services, misuse and mismanagement of public resources, corruption, excessive red tape, ineffective reorganization and structural changes or poorly implemented initiatives, too much political or capitalistic interference, among other things. At the core, it is the failure of translating theory (rules, guidelines, schemes, speeches) into practice (processes, implementation, deliveries, outcomes) in public administration and governance.

They need to walk the talk! Public trust is a fundamental principle of office and requires full integrity and accountability of public officials and employees as directed in the constitution, and in the oath they take before taking office. It says that office of public power cannot be the workshop of personal gains and public employees and officials must be accountable to the people and serve them with the highest responsibility, justice, integrity efficiency and loyalty. The same goes for both elected and non-elected officials. Any misuse and the abuse of power is a breach of trust of the citizens.

An unresponsive government and public sector are responsible for declining public trust in the system. Restoring public trust, accountability and integrity thus should be the primary objectives of good governance. That would require massive reforms in institutions, systems, organizational structures, processes and practices. It would also require leadership and capacity building reforms, civil participatory reforms and behavioral and mindset reforms like introducing new public management mechanisms that consider people as customers or clients and as personal stakeholders in the government. Therefore, meeting the needs of customers (citizens) should be given high priority rather than giving attention to the bureaucracy.[135]

This is the clear dictate of our Constitution- the goal of good governance is to serve people of India effectively and efficiently and fulfill their basic needs and constitutional rights. The government and states must make them the first priority and we, the people of India need to make sure that they do it – by demands or commands (reforms).

Ironically, while drafting the directive principles in constitution that instructed states and central governments to secure a social order for providing equal social opportunities and entitlements like the right to live with dignity, adequate livelihood opportunities, free compulsory education to all , free legal aid, and right to work ; it was argued that making them justiciable or enforceable by the court would not be practical for a poor country like India that was bankrupted and looted by various invaders for ages. However, our leaders were hopeful and had faith in the democratic power that our constitution placed in the hands of people - to elect or reject the governments if they fail to perform their constitutional duties or fulfill their promises and mandates. They ensured that the citizens are provided enough rights, tools and means to maintain a robust democratic infrastructure in the country.

Frequent elections, an independent judiciary and a system of public appeals -PILs and RTI (right to information) made sure that the citizens could exercise their power and challenge the states and central governments to fulfill their needs and secure their rights. The constitution also made sure that all elected officials and public servants by constitutional oath are bound to serve the public with utmost dignity, sincerity and accountability in daily government's and public affairs. Moreover, being a welfare state, all the government organs and machinery are also bound to provide basic needs of the citizens as per the directive principles in the constitution.

There is also a provision of citizen activism along with judicial activism to check the misuse of power by states/governments. Any socially active citizen can challenge the states/governments for his rightful provision of information, service or resources through filing a PIL or RTI and ask for immediate actions and remedies. There are many examples of such activism from the judiciary or citizen like recently where the apex court directed the government to immediately release overdue funds for MGNREGA for rural people and also allocate sufficient funds to meet the demand of rural people in response to a PIL filed by a local NGO "Swaraj Abhiyan".

The apex court said - "it was extremely unfortunate that the government had no provision for providing compensation to the workers, and it was regrettable that it cleared the pending wage bill for 2015-16 only during the pendency of the case. It ordered the Centre to release all outstanding funds for MGNREGA to the states and directed it to pay compensation for delayed wages to farmers in drought-hit areas." The court further directed the Centre to ensure that the Central Employment Guarantee Council is immediately constituted under provisions of the MNREG Act within a maximum period of 60 days and asked it to proactively request state governments to establish the State Employment Guarantee Council within 45 days.[136]

Though it is another issue that the verdict was used for political mileage by both ruling and opposition parties yet the fact remains that the power to bring change is still in the hands of people and they must use it properly to secure their individual and collective rights and constitutional provisions. Regrettably, this potent power of choosing our own governments and holding them responsible and accountable for providing decent jobs, health, education, housing and other basic amenities to live a life with dignity; is exercised only during elections every five years in our country. As seen often, in most states there is an anti-incumbency verdict by the citizens; rest of the time this power lay dormant and left unutilized instead of confronting corruption, mismanagement, poor service delivery of public services, misuse of national revenue and resources or demanding complete accountability and transparency in policies and processes in daily lives on a continual basis.

India has come a long way since independence. It is no longer an impoverished or bankrupt country surviving on aids or begging for help. India is a rich country with a GDP crossing $2 trillion mark this year. It is the fastest growing economy on the path of becoming a super power. Yet, even after having enough resources and fiscal capacity, the state and central governments have repeatedly been failed to deliver the basic services or fulfill the needs of citizens. Inadequate employment opportunities, corruption, mismanagement of resources, socio-economic inequalities, poor quality of public education institutes and health services, deteriorating public services, widespread poverty and destitution are still plaguing our country as we discussed in previous chapters. The rapid economic progress has failed to deliver the promise of democracy to people as large section of society is still struggling for basic facilities. The goal of universal health, literacy and social security for all remains a distant dream. Vast rural areas continue to be denied opportunities for gainful employment, public health services, or basic amenities like roads, electricity, potable water, transportation etc.

As we discussed, the higher GDP growth rate or consumption figures have not translated into better services or living opportunities for all. A small section is reaping the fruits of growth yet the masses are still hoping for better days. With over 70% of India's wealth in the hands of top 10% of people, bottom 40% still struggling to keep both ends meet, over 90 % of the nation's workforce working in unorganized sector without any social security or fixed income, more than 70% of rural poor and 60% of urban population (urban poor living in slums , pavement or footpaths) still waiting for better education, health, employment opportunities, for better public services, facilities and infrastructure ; the promise of freedom and democracy still seems a distant dream for majority of Indians. What is more worrying that the limited income and resources of the country, instead of trickling down to those living at the bottom, are mostly lost through corruption in the various layers and loopholes in the system or are being wasted due to mismanagement or lack of transparency and accountability mechanisms.

The population has been increasing steadily and so are the requirements and expectations of the people. The desire for growth and better living standard is making people more aware of their rights and need for social and economic justice especially for equal opportunities for employment and proper distribution of national income and resources. The intolerance and impatience of the new generation with the old system and ways is like a volcano waiting to erupt. Yet, our political parties and leaders, instead of taking up these issues head on and providing substantial reforms or solutions; have managed to divert the nation's attention in petty and trivial issues. Worse, instead of discussing the pros and cons of the policies and their effects and implications, the whole nation is divided on social or communal lines. Our society has become too polarized where large sections of people and Media get influenced by personal charisma or hyped image of the leaders or act out of loyalty to the parties or family dynasties. This is called identity politics. Most governments have been led by clean leaders who have goodwill among the people yet cases of massive corruption and mismanagement happen under their very nose. Most of the voters are fooled by the larger than life image of the leaders and their political rhetoric without any regard to real facts and outcomes of policies or how they are affecting their lives or national environment.

The loyalty of political parties, public sector or a large section of business community towards particular leaders is understandable, as they have formed a mutually beneficial society. What is surprising that pressure groups like a large section of educated and socially aware citizens, Academia, middle class, Media, social and private organizations etc. who have the access, expertise, information and resources to confront the policies and assess the outcomes with definite facts and figures and who can demand for social accountability and transparency; choose to ignore the hard facts and get distracted with the hype, political drama or party rhetoric! The question arises who is going to pull up the states and government for their failure to fulfill their constitutional duties towards constitutional rights and provisions of the citizens if these pressure groups are unable to confront these crucial issues? We all know how the poor and ignorant masses have still been used as pawns as they are easily influenced and manipulated by skewed policies or hyped promises - packaged and presented as pro-poor handouts!

After independence, every government, with every 5-year plan, claimed to be pro-poor and pro-villagers yet their pathetic condition shows the royal rides they have been taken through for decades by all successive governments. Even today, the policies that are harmful and affect the poor most are packaged as pro-poor or pro-villagers and they still are being taken for a ride though. they are totally oblivious to this fact. For instance, demonetization hurt the poor, farmers and informal sector – daily wager and laborers yet, the entire step was packaged and sold as pro-poor, pro-farmer policy and sadly they believed it too. Instead of debating the loss and gains of demonetization, and asking for facts and figures, the issue was encashed by all the parties and ignored by the experts and policymakers so much that no one is willing to put a number or calculate the multitude of damage or gain! We might even never come to know the loss in the informal sector born by daily wagers and poor sections perhaps, as the GDP growth rate is mostly calculated based on formal economy and consumption of middle and rich classes. Moreover, the question to be debated is, did demonetization achieve its objective? Did it really solve the issues of corruption, fake currency, digitalization, or tax evasion?

Black money amounting to billions was supposed to come back in the banks, did it come? What about the black wealth in the foreign banks or assets...were they recovered? On the other hand, when India's job sector and agriculture sector were already suffering from low growth; are the accumulated losses of demonetisation - job loss, crop loss, wage loss and loss of livelihood or agriculture resources justified? Arresting poverty and unemployment should be the first and foremost priorities of government given the explosive situation in our country, everything else should be secondary. All the policies and plans must focus on job creation and poverty eradication along with agriculture sector's growth yet, the focus is on everything else but on these issues! Moreover, the money that was supposed to be recovered should have been used for social sector but with agriculture sector allocation still remaining under 1 % of GDP, with slight increase in education and health sector (which even after multiple recommendations and warning still remains below world average); the point is what was the need for this step and who is going to take responsibility for the losses and chaos?

As for our increased GDP growth rate, India is like a growing teenager today so its consumption would be greater than the adult economies who have reached a certain saturation and stability after a period of high growth. Moreover, the point to consider here is that while many other developing countries like Asian Miracle economies- South Korea, Japan or even China in the similar stage had a much higher growth rate (about 8 to 10%) and were able to lift majority of their people into higher income category, higher living standards and provide social security; India is still punching too below its weight! Given the resources and population, we should be maintaining at least 10% of GDP growth rate to catch up with others.

We must remind ourselves here, that that while our leaders love to tom-tom about India's growing GDP at PPP (dollar exchange rate) taking over other developed countries like the European Union and others; by the same measures, over 90% Indians are living below poverty line of these countries that is 14 to 16 dollars a day! Yet, no one is willing to acknowledge that, to top it, our policy makers have the audacity to keep the poverty line of India at a pathetic figure (Rangarajan line ie 47 Rs a day- urban, 32 Rs for rural poor) that should be called the starvation line and even at that pathetic figure, around 1/3 population is still living below that!

At a time, when the Indian economy was poised to grow at a higher ever rate; that is the greatest priority of India if it is to fulfill the demand of its citizen; any move that puts a break or pulls it down should be questioned and debated by the entire nation but as it so happens in India; the issue was hijacked by the political parties and made into a circus and the whole nation along with media got distracted by the blame game drama. As usual, the suffering poor were taken for a ride again by packaging demonetization as pro-poor or pro-farmer even as it was they who had to bear the brunt! Regrettably, they felt victorious and happily welcomed the step as the general assumption was that the rich and powerful are being penalized and the wealth recovered would be redistributed for their welfare. Unfortunately, nothing substantial happened, apart from mere lip servicing as every policy or action belied the promise.

Moreover, the hyped budget allocation that cannot even fulfill the full demand of temporary jobs for 100 days (MNREGA) for our rural workforce leave aside doubling their incomes; was packaged as the highest ever pro-farmer budget by our policy makers! Similarly, even renowned economists, national advisors confirmed that India has the fiscal capacity to provide social security or universal income to the poorest section of India, no such action was taken while the subsidies to the rich and privileged, amounting a huge percentage of GDP still continue as government has to keep all the voters happy. Ironically, the bad loans and tax exemptions to the rich and powerful costing such a high percentage of GDP could fill the gap for social security to the vulnerable class. With allocation for education and health too still remaining below the world average; even after many recommendations from the experts all over the world; one must ask how our policies are still being sold as pro-poor or pro-farmer? Unfortunately, the naïve, ignorant poor and farmers still buy such empty promises and are taken for a ride again as they always have been by all successive governments!

As we discussed earlier, that while the intention of the government might have been good and a demonetization is a good tool for reform, it appears to have been rushed, poorly planned and resulted in undue pain and inconvenience caused to millions of honest Indians. Moreover, such a drastic move needs to be backed by robust social security, infrastructure, and proper implementation mechanisms. We need to ask ourselves if it really served the purpose it was intended for i.e. eradicating black money and corruption as the main causes of corruption and black money are due to the systemic loopholes and lack of accountability in public sector and governments handlings that still go unaddressed and unchecked. Or is it is another classic case of the ignorant electorate being misled and manipulated by political parties?

Again, as we discussed earlier, this issue has nothing to do with the political loyalties or preferences. It is not about the political drama or criticizing or condemning the government. It is about the promise of democracy to its most vulnerable sections and the roles and responsibilities of its primary stakeholders (people of India) to protect their fundamental rights and provisions.

When educated and socially empowered citizens lose the power to question the policy makers and instead get carried away by the misplaced loyalties, inclinations, party ideologies, identity or individualistic politics; the power of democracy is wasted and becomes a useless tool instead of the mighty weapon it was meant to be- to protect the dignity and security of society especially of those who need to be saved. Any such policy or misplaced priority that pulls India's growth down or affects a million lives needs to be debated and confronted. In a democracy, a good policy means ensuring what is good for all, not for the selective few. The primary requirement for a successful democracy is that people of the country must be committed and loyal to the cause of greater good, not to any individual leader or party ideology and that goes for all, including elected and non-elected public officials, media or other sections of the society.

We are a country where it is said that an innocent must never be hanged even if it means letting hundreds of criminals go scot free. In Gita, when Arjun asked Krishna what Dharma is, he replied that whatever is good for the common good over individual good is the real Dharma. Even Mahatma Gandhi warned policy makers that any action or decision that harms the most vulnerable section of society could never be justified or rectified. Yet, every time the most vulnerable and weak sections of our society are sacrificed at the altar to please and appease the rich and powerful. This is the stark reality of our politics that every successive government, every successive economic policy and 5-year plans have been packaged and presented as pro-poor, pro-farmer yet, pathetic conditions of the bottom strata show the ugly truth hidden and sadly the façade' still continues....

As the primary stakeholder and ultimate guardian of democracy, the people of India not only have the rights but also the ultimate responsibility to question the policy makers and power holders on any policy or plan that affects the livelihood of citizens especially, of the most vulnerable sections of society. Questioning and asking for complete transparency and accountability for every policy, action, service or process that is not suitable for the common good is the debt we must pay as the inheritors of the legacy of freedom and democracy, handed over to us by our previous generation with great hope and faith. As an enlightened society and successors to their dream, our loyalty, our Dharma should be the welfare of common people of India; everything else i e party loyalty, preference or ideal worship should be secondary if wish to keep the spirit of freedom and fire of democracy alive in our nation!

But it so happens in our country that instead of fulfilling their constitutional duties and responsibilities, states- governments indulge in politics of confrontation , communalism, empty promises etc and as a result, instead of assessing the work done or demanding their constitutional rights and promises fulfilled, the electorate in the country gets distracted over this politics of polarity and election rhetoric.

This is the tragedy of democracy in our country that every serious issue is lost in this confrontational and communal politics. The political parties use these critical issues to pull each other down or score brownie points and the entire parliament and legislature, along with media and people of India with their skewed priorities and loyalties are drawn into this senseless battle and get polarized while the burning problems are sidetracked without any conclusion, consensus, substantive actions or solutions.

Instead of measuring and evaluating policies, processes, gaps between budget allocations and their outcomes through regular report cards or asking for transparency and accountability in all their affairs, politicians are judged on their oratory skills or creating hypes of virtually nonexistent social achievements most of the time. Instead of judging the schemes and policies by the hard facts and figures like how many jobs were created….how many primary or secondary enrollments were done…. how many were provided skills and vocational training…how many of them got absorbed successfully or evaluating other health and educational parameters; unfortunately, people in our country remain divided over party or identity politics.

Politicians must prove their credibility and should be judged on their past performances, target achieved and promises fulfilled before making any new ones yet, in spite of poor or nil achievements, we repeatedly see governments and politicians making big promises, indulging in chunavi Jumalas (political rhetoric) and sell big dreams and worse, people still buying that! As citizens, it is our duty and responsibility to call their bluff and ask for report cards of their promises and past performances before believing empty lip services or new rosy promises. We must ask for monthly, quarterly and yearly report cards. For instance, how much money was allocated to which department? How much was used on salaries? What was the target? How much of it was achieved -facts and figures? We must have real-time information on every single rupee that was allocated and spent.

It is worth repeating that as the primary stakeholders in the world's largest democracy we, the people of India, have every right to participate, monitor and question all the decisions, functions and actions of our chosen representatives and Governments   i.e. policy making , planning, implementation, review and monitoring, financial affairs ,working transparency, accountability measures and reforms etc. There are hundreds of schemes governments keep floating, millions are spent on salaries, development, purchase….there are hundreds of Government institutions, agencies and employees working on issues like eradicating poverty, unemployment, illiteracy, infrastructure and development etc. but where is the accountability? Who is checking the money allocated, spent, duration, effectiveness, time-bound outcomes or performances? We have selected our representatives but are they really doing their jobs? What about their promises and mandates, which they used to come in power. Have they fulfilled those and proved their proficiency? Who is questioning them? Who is monitoring them? Are the national audit agencies doing their jobs honestly? Who is following up on discrepancies and mismanagement?

"Perhaps nothing in our society is more needed for those in positions of authority than accountability." – Larry Burkett.

The time has come for us, as citizens, to stand up, take collective social responsibility and demand our rights and accountability in all government and public affairs as unless we have a clear accountability system, nothing is going to really change. Unless we set up an Independent Accountability and public information system and create an interface – a democratic space, where the Governments (local, state and central), all the ministries, MPs, MLAs and public officials are answerable and accountable for their decisions, policies, processes and actions to the people of India, we cannot expect any true reform in the current scenario. Every elected politician or public official must give his report card of what he has done for his constituency and for people who voted for him and to whom he swore to serve. They must prove their sincerity and credibility before asking for vote or trust of people again. We must have citizen's charters/ portals where the total budget, revenue and expenditure of every department, every head and outcome must be explained, justified and scrutinized.

We must demand total transparency…. all departments…all sectors from top to bottom under public scrutiny. Every citizen of India has a right to know where our national revenue or resources are going. How much national wealth and resources are being wasted on corruption, leakages, bad loans to influential people, revenue forgone or tax exemptions and subsidies? All the governments – states' and central must be accountable for every single policy decision, action and rupee spent during their tenure.

Now that India is no longer a bankrupt country and states' and central governments have enough funds and fiscal capacity, what are their excuses for not being able to ensure the welfare and social security for all the citizens of India? They must make provision for and implement the directive Principles in the Constitution i.e. the right to life with dignity, right to quality education, right to quality health services, right to food and right to employment for all. Today, India has more than enough wealth and resources to provide quality education, health, employment, food, housing to every Indian yet the mismanagement of resources and funds push millions of Indians struggling for these basic facilities and provisions.

As we discussed the data in previous chapters, with 1/3 of our population is living the below poverty line in dire condition in slums or on footpaths without basic food, health or education facilities, almost half of India living in multi-dimensional poverty without any decent shelter and job opportunities; around 1/3 of our children undernourished and stunted, millions of youth waiting for jobs, over 90% of our workforce working in informal sector without any social security or fixed income, 69 % of India living in villages that lack proper infrastructure or quality health or education facilities, over 90% of our workforce unskilled, thousands of farmers committing suicides every year, what plus 7% GDP growth or 2 trillion economy are we talking about? Where is the growth happening in India? Where are the fruits of growth and national resources & revenue going when we are unable to provide better living standards or quality basic services to the majority of Indians?

It is not about the promises and schemes that are launched every day to divert attention or sell new dreams. We must ask for the previous year's performance report cards of every state …from every government. How many Indians were skilled, out of them how many got jobs? How many rural and urban poor were given employment guarantee, shelter, or basic facilities? What were the education and health targets and what are the achievement, improvements? What about the budget allocations- how much of it was actually spent on what head and what was the outcome in fact and figures? What about the unspent amount- where did it go? What happens to the consolidated fund at the end of the year? What about the revenue generation of the states or funds and aid received?

Why the allocation for agriculture is under 1% of GDP that cannot even guarantee temporary employment requirements leave aside doubling their income when thousands and lacs of crores are being wasted on NPAs, tax exemptions of the rich and powerful? Why subsidies amounting to almost 3 % of GDP to the privileged section are being allowed when the allocations for education, health and social security are still way below average and recommended percentage? What about foreign aid and borrowings- where do it all go, what was the outcome- results- facts figures?

For instance, in the recent election, our leaders promised to create a new young India by providing skill training and creating 250 million jobs in 10 years as almost 10 to 12 million youth enters the job market every year in India. Various schemes were launched with lots of hype and fanfare yet only 1. 53 lacs formal jobs were created in 2015 that was the lowest in 7 years! In last 3 years as per the target i.e.

75 million jobs, not even 1/3rd of it is achieved. Out of which many are lost due to demonetization and other misplaced policies and priorities.

Similarly, we need to skill at least minimum 80 million of them every year to reach the figure of 400 million by 2022 as promised and if we have to provide employment opportunity to all of them, yet, not even 25% of it is achieved. Even the "Skill India" mission that was launched with so much fanfare and promises to make 400 million Indians employable in seven years, in the first year, could manage to skill about 1.76 million but less than half of them completed the course; and of those, only a fraction of them could actually be matched to jobs. According to data from the National Skill Development Corporation, till date close to 19.92 lakh individuals have been trained under PMKVY while only $1/3^{rd}$ of them have been placed.

According to a recent report by **India spend**; net enrollment in vocational courses in India is only about 5.5 million per year, compared with 90 million in China and 11.3 million in the United States. Though, there is an increase in net enrollments recently, yet, compared to other countries, we are way behind. We know that India already has the lowest number of skilled workers- a pathetic 2 to 4 % of the total workforce is skilled as compared to 68% in the UK, 80% in Japan, and 96% in South Korea. 60% of our engineers remain unemployed every year.[137] Just imagine the frustration, after years of hard work, studies and competitive exams they put through just to find themselves without any job prospects!

Jobs and skills in India are the most serious issue ...a waiting volcano to erupt if we don't engage our youth constructively, their restlessness and frustration will result in social unrest and upheaval and our GDP numbers would mean nothing. It should be every government's first priority to provide jobs and better employment opportunities to the youth of the country.

Similarly, forget about fulfilling their constitutional duties and obligation and providing regular jobs, shelter, land, quality health and education and social security to all the citizens, even the measly, temporary 100 days employment guarantee (MNREGA) and loan waivers that are far too inadequate for the rural population is being hyped as highest ever or blessings or favors from our political parties.

Sadly, even after 70 years of independence and being a socialist and welfare state, the budget for social sector spending remains merely 7% compared to other countries that is over 30% or 18% in developing countries not to forget the allocation for health and education that is still far below the world average even after our leaders promised to double it in their election manifesto; while the national revenue in the form of lost tax revenue, tax holidays and bad loans to big businesses amounting lacs of crores could have filled this gap significantly. Allocation for the most marginalized population like Dalits and Adivasis too remain too low as against the recommended minimum 4% by the experts. Worse, out of this low allocated amount, a large portion never reaches the beneficiaries and is often remain unspent while million suffers due to mismanagement, corruption and lethargy of public officials.

Yes, the state and central governments and public officials are accountable and answerable to every Indian for every rupee coming and spent. They are accountable for every job, house, health or educational shortfall in the country. Again, it is not about current and previous governments, states' or central governments or how they are better or worse than the others. It is about the democratic right of equity of every Indian in national resources and national income that must be provided on a consistent basis. Not in future or after the elections or with new promises, dreams or new schemes. More importantly, why has it not been done till now? Why not last year or before that? Why the current budget still has no provision for that? We must ask the questions from every party and elected member across the country. They must be held accountable and answerable to people of India with facts and figures and their performance reports ...no more chunavi jumlas or rhetoric please.

Before asking for nation's trust or cooperation, or selling any new dream or hope, they must answer these queries, prove their sincerity and credibility, and fulfill the oath they have taken to fulfill every constitutional directive and guidelines.

Otherwise, people of India must make sure that their fundamental constitutional and democratic rights are fulfilled, by demand or command! Instead of governments making misplaced policies, investments or having misplaced priorities or skewed party mandates, it is the responsibility of people of India to create their own mandates/national plans and make sure that every government from top down, up to local municipalities follow people's manifesto and implement it effectively and efficiently with time bound monthly and yearly action plans and outcomes. Failing which, the power to recall and revoke must be used by combining citizen activism with judicial activism which is the potent weapon of democracy bestowed upon the people of the country by our constitution.

As per the constitution of India, state and central governments are responsible for revenue generation and equitable redistribution of national revenue and resources yet millions of landless or houseless rural and urban poor are living in pathetic conditions while a small section of middle and upper class (10 %) of the total population enjoys the benefits of growth and development thanks to the flourishing private sector. As we discussed earlier , India has enough fiscal capacity and resources to provide social security to all its citizens, especially the marginalized sections yet gross mismanagement and misplaced priorities of our national revenue and resources continues to keep millions in deprivation and suffering while our politicians indulge in mere lip service instead of initiating substantial reforms, actions or ensured outcomes.

What is the use of hyped schemes or budget allocations if they do not translate into ground realities or produce results? Moreover, where does it all go? More than a dozen ministries and thousands of crores of national revenue failed to achieve even a quarter of targeted jobs or ensure a decent salary growth in the informal sector. Imagine the same scenario in any private sector organization. Such gross mismanagement and efficiency in achieving targets would have resulted in the entire management being shown the door! Yet sadly, in our system, such accountability and professionalism remain a distant possibility. There are hundreds of government, semi governments bodies, and agencies for environment control or related issues in our capital and metros, a huge portion of our national revenue goes in maintaining and running them yet every monsoon the condition of our roads and civic infrastructure is in shambles. Our municipalities are some of the worst service providers and fountainheads of

corruption and misused resources. The pathetic conditions of our public schools and health facilities make one wonder where do all the budget allocations go? Sadly, with all the development rhetoric our politicians brag about, except for some selective urban areas, the real development remains a paper horse or chunavi jumla in our country! The point remains that our public sector and its machinery that is supposed to serve the people is serving themselves and except for some changes here and there, mere lip service is being doled out to the people.

It is time to ask for report cards from our politicians and hold them responsible for every promise, every failure, and every target that was not achieved before we trust any future promise or dream they might sell to get votes! Not every five years but monthly, quarterly and yearly report cards with every rupee allocated, spent and results in hard facts and figures not the hyped schemes or allocations. They are accountable to every voter and only their performance and past work is what should earn them our trust not empty future promises, rosy picture or skewed vote card tactics.

It is time to rise above party loyalties, idol worship or dynastical sycophancy and ask for complete transparency and accountability from our politicians and public employees no matter which party or ideology they may represent. People of India's loyalty should be towards the people and the country only. No more party manifestos during elections, but time-bound action plans with definite outcomes and progress monitored by people on quarterly, yearly basis instead of every five years, to make sure that the national resources and revenue are being utilized properly and distributed equitably among the citizens, especially among the ones who need it most. Every government, every ministry, every public office must be judged on their monthly and yearly performance and be held responsible and accountable for missed targets and poor services.

We must realize that governments are just the representative of the people of India, to serve India not to rule or dictate. It is high time we stopped depending and begging for our rights and took charge to play our role as the primary stakeholder in the country to demand and command what is rightfully ours. It is time to remember, that SWARAJ (self-governance) means the governance of the people, by the people, for the people. The preamble of constitution that starts with "We the people of India" and ends with "we do hereby adopt, enact and give to ourselves this constitution" is not just empty words, it means that the people of India have the ultimate constitutional authority and governments and public servants must serve them and ensure their well-being. In a democracy, the highest authority is given to the people of the country, to hold the governments and state machinery accountable for their policies, actions, services and for the management of national revenue and resources. In that sense, the people of India are given the ultimate guardianship over the nation's resources, revenue and governance.

A government that fails to generate enough revenue due to its incompetent machinery i.e. ministries, slack administration, skewed policies, misplaced priorities, mismanagement and allows huge losses of limited national resources on account of tax exemption, revenue forgone or subsidies to powerful and privileged group at the cost of its most vulnerable section, cannot be called a welfare state. As we discussed earlier, NPAs, loan waivers, readjustment or restructuring of corporate loans amounting lacs of crores that our national banks regularly indulge in, while denying better livelihood opportunities to the most vulnerable sections, belies the promise of a pro-poor economy. This gross misuse and mismanagement of national income and resources is the biggest corruption in our country! As APJ kalam wrote – "It is not difficult to fathom that political corruption is easily the most dangerous of all forms. In any mature or emerging democracy, the quality of the political leadership can mean the *difference between* a welfare *state* and a *bankrupt* one," [138] It is time to demand complete transparency and accountability from our politicians and public officials for lost or misused national revenue and resources!

In every budget, there are lots of promises, investment pledges, new schemes yet most of the allocations are on paper and never actually get translated on ground. Every year there is a vision shown to people for 2020, 2030, for better days ahead but we must ask - what about the past year? How many promises and pledges have been translated into action and most importantly, what was the outcome in figures and facts? 5 years is a long time and anti-incumbency voting is not the solution as in these five years, without regular monitoring and accountability mechanisms, the governments and the state's machinery get a free field and most of the national revenue, wealth and resources are wasted or siphoned off and never recovered. As we see, every political party during election uses corruption cards and pledges to change and reform the system yet except some nominal changes here or there, things remain the same and voters have no choice but to vote for change again.

For last several decades, this vicious cycle is going on and it would go on unless people of India wake up and take charge. It must be stopped and we must put the pressure on the governments from day one, on performance, transparency and accountability; for every policy, every action and every rupee; instead of waiting for 5 years when too much water has flown under the bridge! The revenue, resources and opportunities lost in these 5 years never come back, we all have seen that. No corrupt minister has been jailed or assets recovered, on the contrary; new alliances and mutually beneficial relationships are formed every day once the elections are over!

We all know that corruption is not an outside job but an inside mechanism in our system. Every misuse or mismanagement of public office, resources or funds is corruption- every misplaced policy or priority is a scam- every rupee wasted through leakages and cracks in the system instead of reaching the end beneficiary is corruption yet, instead of creating water-tight processes and structures that should ensure not even a single rupee slipping through leakages or loopholes, or tracking the money flow right from the top through the various layers of the system; that is supposed to be the fountainhead of real corruption; the politicians are using the corruption card for manipulating vote cards by exploiting our hopes and expectations.

Instead of making strict laws, punishing the guilty and recovering lost national revenue or assets, they form a mutually beneficial society with criminals or scamsters to utilize their money muscle or power that safeguards their interests rather than securing the national interest. The facts are evident as hardly any political party or politician has ever been booked for corruption charges or the lost wealth or resources recovered from various frauds and scandals that rocked the nation. Moreover, those who were charged with corruption or scams still roam scot-free and our electoral commission has been helpless in stopping them to contest again! Even the lists of corrupt and black money holders provided by global corruption watch agencies and Wikileaks etc. are ignored or brushed under the carpet.

This shows a mockery of law& order and politics that is the source of all the issues prevailing in the country today. When the system itself is ineffective and corruption or mismanagement of resources and revenue is the rule rather than an exception and supposed caretakers are busy perusing their own interest instead of acting in the larger interest of society; any reform or change will invariably fail. In short, when corruption in any form i.e. moral, financial, political or institutional is an internal mechanism then, any reform or change no matter how well designed and implemented, would not be able to get results unless external pressure is applied to identify and rectify the problems.

A further analysis of some of our crucial national integrity pillars and political landscape shows a worrying picture -

A poor parliamentary control, confrontational politics, a weak opposition and legislature, a dominant executive and the culture of boycotts, blame games or passing the buck instead of discussing crucial issues and finding solutions, have eroded the dignity and credibility of our political infrastructure. MPs and MLAs are not held accountable and often are engaged in various scams or scandals, our electoral system is unable to filter out criminals or secure opportunities for honest candidates as money and muscle power dominate the election scenario in the country. Instead of high risk and low gains, politics has become a high-gains, low-risk game and a safe haven for criminals or power mongers. Over 30% of those elected are charged with various criminal offenses and occupy important seats and instead of setting up fast track courts or put them in the limelight for speedy trials, lack of any serious punishment or penalty, our system provides political impunity to them. There are cases of controversial appointments, promotions, eliminations of judges that affect the independence of Judiciary. There is also an ongoing tension between the executive, legislature and judiciary has resulted in overburdened and inadequate judicial infrastructure in the country.

Other independent agencies and commissions like the office of the Comptroller Auditor General (CAG) or Anti-Corruption Agencies are supposed to keep a tight check on corruption but they are not totally free from political influence and are unable to play their constitutional roles. There is no real-time checking. They are like the doctors who conduct a post-mortem after the patient is dead! Too little, too late! Even Media, barring some exceptions, is not free, has become politicized and biased reflecting political or corporate interests rather than questioning the integrity or accountability of our power holders. No wonder, the big scams are brushed under the carpet after the initial TRP gathering headlines. There is no proper investigation or follow up except for few cases. For instance, the water irrigation scam in Maharashtra some years back raised a big hue and cry, election were fought and won on cashing the issue and big promises were made to the suffering farmers and families of those who were driven out of their land, many committed suicides due to losses, distress and climatic conditions but as usual, after the election, the issue was conveniently forgotten. The farmers who lost their livelihood, land or rather were manipulated or forced to part with their land are still waiting for justice but the political parties, media who encashed on these scams, are quite. No one is booked, no money is recovered and everything is hunky dory between the parties for now…. new alliances are made…. new equations are formed as we see quite often in most cases, opposing parties join hands for mutual benefits and the voters are taken for a ride…..as usual!

Even the recent elections were fought on the issue of billions of dollars stacked in foreign banks and the promise of recovering it within 100 days and bringing the criminals to justice yet, till date no foreign money or black assets have been recovered, forget about jailing the scamsters, no substantial action has been taken on the lists provided by global agencies, banks or Wikileaks. The real black money holders and their black wealth stayed tucked away safely in new foreign tax heavens (there are 100 tax heavens in the world so even if we take action against some of them, would not really stop the outflow) while real areas that are breeding grounds of corruption i.e. public sector and high-level politicians-businessmen-bureaucrats nexus are never addressed.

As we discussed earlier, corruption is a systemic problem and our public institution, processes and loopholes in the system are the real reasons for leakages and scams so blocking them and making water-tight process must be the first step to tackle this issue as once the water has flown over the dam, trying to get the black money back would be just a wild goose chase!

As advised by international organization like TI (Transparency International and member country profiles) corruption is a systemic problem that needs to be tackled through strong reforms and revolutionary strategies. There are many such tools and international assistance available to counter corruption and mismanagement as we explored in the previous chapter, like Open government data forum, Transparency International's national integrity system initiatives and anti-corruption toolkits. These initiatives are based on prevention, enforcement and suppression and are considered some of the greatest tools and methods in the world for helping countries fight corruption and are extensively used by many governments who are really serious about eradicating the menace of corruption from their countries.

Unfortunately in India, all successive governments have failed to utilise these global tools and initiatives to develop a comprehensive framework for arresting corruption, mismanagement or reforming public sector that brings us back to the root of such failures - the lack of the outer or third force as it is called by many all over the world i.e. an active social capital – citizen's movement to hold the entire system accountable and corruption free. As OGP describes – "In a democracy, public participation as strategic partners in government's decision-making and policy-making processes is not only possible, but also necessary as it is through active participation and civic engagement, citizens help societies and economies grow and hold their governments to standards of integrity, accountability, transparency, and responsiveness. Public participation, therefore, enables an effective democratic decision-making process that is required for a healthy, inclusive, and a more sustainable economic, social, and political development. Active citizen participation promotes and demands openness, effective and sincere service delivery and can pressurize governments to meet the needs of citizens, address their concerns and provide required information that goes beyond transparency and accountability principles and their traditional role as mere beneficiaries."[139]

For democracy to flourish, citizens must take an active part in public life, sharing their ideas and opening their minds to the opinions of others, and taking ownership of the well-being of the country." (Meskell, 2009)[140]

A robust integrity system has many components like the high integrity of public officials, public trust in governance, policies, practices, institutions and integrity guardians that form the foundation of the system. An integrity guardian as it is called by global experts is an agency with oversight and control powers concerning integrity violations like corruption, misuse of resources, bribery, conflict of interest, misuse and manipulation of information, sponsorship, just, of aids and cronyism.

Many countries all over the world have put in place integrity systems or ethical frameworks to support and enhance the integrity of public officials. These ethical frameworks include regulatory measures such as codes of conduct, anti-corruption agencies or risk assessment strategies apart from existing audit and regulatory bodies that are a part of the integrity system yet their effectiveness in achieving high integrity and improving public trust in governments is still questionable. Thus, there is a growing need for a neutral and effective integrity guardian that can make an impartial assessment and provide constructive, trustworthy solutions. That is where the role of social capital (active citizenry, media, the private sector, CSOs etc.) of the country comes in. An active and socially responsible civil society, independent, free and alert media along with a supportive private sector can provide that external pressure or force that can revolutionize the entire integrity framework of a country.

Yet, this tremendous democratic power lies dormant and is wasted when citizens' efforts are scattered and they are unable to unite and demand their rights. There are many factors like social acceptance of corruption, lack of accountability, transparency and integrity, tolerance of poorly implemented justice and law enforcement practices, lack of severe penalties or punishments, systemic loopholes; lack of collective action and coordination in establishing a high integrity - accountability system and reforms; that result in overall failure of social capital or civil society's role in revolutionizing the national integrity system in a country.

The failure to initiate and implement such reforms hence, turn into a social inertia or collective inaction where even if general public disapproves such practices and is aware of the negative impact and consequences on the social environment in the country; very few are interested in establishing or promoting clean and effective institutions and the status quo continues. The point remains that when the system itself is inefficient and corrupt and there is not enough motivation and very little political will to bring out deep radical reform and establish the highest order of integrity for the fear of losing control on public resources, power and capital; who is going to bell the cat? When so-called toothless external authorities, commissions or agencies impose rules but are unable to tame the monsters of corruption, mismanagement, abuse of power and resources due to weak monitoring and lame penalties or justice processes, what other options we are left with? Who is going to apply the external pressure to dismantle old outdated, deteriorating system, processes to establish a new, vibrant, transparent, accountable leakage proof system with 0 corruption, 100% accountability approach that serves and delivers as required?

We need to realize that the usual, old remedies and traditional approaches of reforms would not work anymore as if they really did, we would have had a new vibrant, robust system and effective services by now! The fact that it is still missing even after 70 years of independence, calls for radical approaches and solutions. Cynicism, criticism, feeling helpless or trapped in the game also would not serve anymore as we have done that enough! What is needed to successfully reform the whole system is not an internal fix or a cosmetic political makeover but a revolutionary collective action that would break down the old systems, processes, practices and would establish a new open and impartial system with strong pillars of integrity, transparency, accountability, trust and service.

Such initiatives have been observed in the countries that made successful transitions from thoroughly corrupt to significantly less corrupt systems of rule and were able to establish institutions that benefit the larger society, like Sweden, Denmark, New Zealand, Australia, UK, Hong Kong, Malaysia etc. It clearly demonstrates that a collective will and action involving, i e political, economic, and social sectors, is necessary to bring out radical changes in the country.

The global researches and studies show that an effective model for successful reforms and integrity system depends on some key internal and external factors like – public intolerance for corruption and mismanagement, external pressure, societal or international independent integrity guardian agencies that have the power and resources to investigate and scrutinize all types of integrity violations; a free, independent media and civil society groups that can access and publicize the Information and internal factors like ethical policy framework and practices in government sector, strong political will and ethical leadership, openness and accountability infrastructure etc.

But most importantly, the critical factors that make a nation successful in implementing these initiatives are the quality of its institution and public participation in reforming and maintaining the high standards of quality, ethics and integrity in these institutions. These institutions like Judiciary, Police, electoral body, and parliament, planning commissions, CBI and other agencies form the backbone of the country and their balance and perfect functioning is crucial for the progress and development of the country. However, internal factors like ethical framework and government's monitoring and enforcing certain reforms have seen to be ineffective and insufficient unless the external factors like public and media pressure

(third force) and other external guardians (investigating and regulating agencies) join the efforts forming a synthesis that would enforce each other.

Thus, when there is not enough will or adequate measures from the top to change the system, pressure to reform through collective social action and coordination is the push that initiates the institutional reform movements and through this bottom-up approach, citizens can reject political exploitation and stand as watch guards against corruption and mismanagement of national wealth and resources. A well developed and strong social capital hence, becomes the most important pillar in any integrity system and can compel all other actors' - the legislature, judiciary and other law enforcement bodies, the private sector as well as the governments to act through a holistic and integrated mechanism to reform and transform the nation.

A weak integrity system has a cascading effect on overall development of people and the country as it becomes the source of all illegal, immoral, and unproductive activities, destroys people's trust in its leadership and authority in the system and challenges the very foundations of social and economic environment hence, this is the collective responsibility of all the stakeholders to strengthen it and make it corruption free.

As we saw a recent survey by the global corruption watch agency Transparency International (TI)- 2017 stated that India has the highest bribery rate among the 16 Asia Pacific countries surveyed that included people paying bribes for getting basic work done. Even back home, the recent annual report of Central Vigilance Commission (CVC) tabled in parliament says in 2016 there has been an increase by 67 % in corruption complaints received against various government departments with the Railways topping the list. As we discussed earlier, India ranks lowest in Doing Business among the BRICS nations in the recently released World Bank's ease of doing business index for the year 2017 - (Russia (40), South Africa (74), China (78), Brazil (123) and India (130).[141]

What is clear from these reports that given the scope and complexities of this phenomenon, traditional approaches and processes would not work anymore. Even if a strong ethical policy framework and strict processes, rules and regulations are introduced and implemented, people can always find loopholes or means and ways to sidestep and manipulate their ways through it. That is the reason that despite various reforms and regulations, the quality of our institutions and public service delivery remains pathetic. This shows that only through a multi-pronged approach and synchronizing energies between different integrity pillars in a synergetic framework, can the effective reforms and resolutions be achieved.

It is time to come together for reforming and rebuilding the entire foundation of our system, starting from our parliament to executive, judiciary, public system, police, various agencies and commissions along with business, media and social sector. A complete overhauling of our crumbling, old, outdated integrity system is critically overdue. Considering the multitude of corruption spread in our country that is described by some experts as a multi-headed monster and the subtle ways it works through the entire system, it is the social responsibility of citizens to unite and counter it with greater force and all their might!

Unless we dismantle the existing faulty systems and block all the loopholes and cracks, reform and revolutionize our institutions; processes and practices and create a new vibrant system based on trust, integrity, transparency and accountability, time-bound, performance-based policies and action plans, strong review and monitoring techniques, innovative and adaptive strategies and measures , more inclusive and integrated engagement with all the stakeholders in the country i.e. community, media , civil, public, private and various service and sectors; no real or sustainable reform or transformation can happen. There would be some cosmetic changes here and there but no substantial results would be achieved. The faces will keep changing but India will remain the same!

Unless we monitor every single rupee coming in the system and track the flow of money through every layer from top up to top down, till the end user or target; unless we take inventory of national assets and resources and make sure that they are distributed and utilized properly ; unless we set up transparent processes and practices and ask for accountability for every policy, scheme and action from every office-holder, power-holder elected or non-elected; no matter which party or wing he belongs to or loyal to, things would not change. Unless we take radical measures and set up strong methods and processes to increase state or institutional credibility and responsiveness, introducing zero tolerance mechanisms for corruption and mismanagement, build new democratic spaces for citizen activism and empower them, design better budget utilization plans and ensure better delivery of services; things would not change. Unless we harness the individual strengths of all the national integrity pillars i.e. civil and private sectors, media, independent agencies and law enforcement agencies etc. converge and synergize them into an integrated framework to reform and transform the system, things would not change!

It is time to create a new order, a new synergy by combining and converging social activism (civil, media and private sector activism) with political and judicial activism and create new transparent structures, processes and reforms across all the national pillars and create a new system that has no place for leakages, loopholes for corruption, mismanagement, misplaced policies and priorities, manipulation or lapses between targets and outcomes.

The time has come to demand good governance, accountability and transparency in all public affairs. Given the magnitude of corruption and accountability-transparency issues existing in our country and constant failure of national 5-

years plans to achieve sustainable growth and development for all; it is clear that the governments] cannot handle it alone but needs to act in concert with other sectors like civil society and business sector to protect the public interest. Therefore, we all need to tackle these issues in a holistic way with all the players involved i.e. citizens, governments, private sector, Media, global agencies, local players etc. coming together to form strategic partnerships; create a new robust national Integrity system, set up an independent national integrity unit and develop a national vision with concrete action plans, processes and time-bound targets.

The initiatives we explored by global agencies, like World Bank, UN, Transparency International , UNDP, SDSN, OXFAM and Open Government's Forum etc. have provided a holistic framework , strategies and tools to develop integrated and comprehensive social accountability and national integrity systems with all the national pillars coming together for achieving common purpose and goals. As suggested by these agencies and experts, we must break the old democratic model and paradigm that made citizens give away their rights to few in power and promoted complete reliance on governments and public sector to deliver the public goods. In this old model, the private sector and civil society are kept on the fringe and are not considered as important pillars or agents for change, the focus is on the development of executive activities of governments and the legislative and judicial sector are also left neglected. Similarly, the entire attention of policy makers is focused on budget allocations and developing various schemes while little thoughts are given to monitoring, revising or evaluating the outcomes and impacts. Moreover, the governments and public sector have a free field to play as there is no outer agency to hold them accountable or demand transparency.

We must break this old pattern that no longer serves us and embrace the new emerging paradigm where there is a convergence of different sectors like governments, private sector and civil society to improve integrity and accountability in every area in the country. We must learn from various global initiatives and country experiences and adopt the new approach that is based on a multi-stakeholder, multi-dimensional, multi-faceted collaboration between civil society, private sector and governments that would determine policies and priorities that guide laws and regulations and distribution of resources through market forces.

The time has come now to create a new paradigm with a new approach with the belief, that elected leaders and public sector employees are responsible for fulfilling the needs of public by providing sustainable development through proper distribution of national wealth and other resources and citizens must hold governments and public employees accountable individually and collectively for delivering the promises and fulfilling commitments as per their respective job portfolios.

We must realize that lack of integrity, transparency and accountability in governments and public sector is the most crucial reason that has delayed the sustainable development in our country and use all the tools available like national integrity system, independent national integrity unit, public delivery surveys, integrity workshops, integrity pledges and islands of integrity to help governments ministers, municipalities and public employees increase transparency, trust, accountability and performance. We must unite- the civil sector, private sector, Media; and collectively and constructively challenge and push governments and public sector to institute integrity, accountability and transparency in all matters. As we know, left to their own, the governments and public sector would not use accountability and integrity as effective tools to reform or perform. We have been observing it for decades now and must realize that for that to happen, both internal and external pressure is needed- a combination of political will with public pressure. This new approach, as suggested by TI (Transparency International), acknowledges the power of public pressure and encourages the policies and processes that focus on the public that constitutes the 98% of the stakeholders in a country against the governments and public sector that is less than 2% of the total population.

We must play our role as a vibrant and socially aware civil society in building integrity and preventing corruption by adopting and introducing new innovative approaches, systems and processes for developing holistic integrated strategies for educating the citizens and raising general awareness through media campaigns (print, TV, news, papers etc.), conducting regular integrity workshops for all stakeholders to come together for discussion and finding solutions, introducing Citizen's charter and other public empowering monitoring tools like periodic service delivery surveys, online feedbacks, public grievances centers and portals, developing a national integrity Unit/ Plan and regular surveys and assessments on corruption at national, municipal and local level, involving media to investigate and inform public on corruption etc.

As a paper by Petter Langseth in an anticorruption conference for UN many years ago (Prevention: An Effective Tool to Reduce Corruption) suggested Media must play its role as a free, impartial and independent sector with investigating capacities that can be the game changer and prove to be the most important pillar in the nation building process. By drawing attention to corruption, journalists can turn corruption from a seemingly low risk- high gains activity for those involved, to one that is high risk –no gains![142] It can be a key player in nurturing democratic elections by educating people and making them more aware of their candidates' motives and goals. Independent media reporting – free from owners/editors' influence, investigating journalism workshops for training and awareness-raising among the journalists, developing high integrity, result –oriented, public service mindsets are some initiatives that are reported to have had a positive effect on curbing corruption and mismanagement in the countries. Overcoming business – TRP-political limitations can enable media fulfill its role as "nation builders" by focusing on public education-awareness activities and investigative journalism as suggested by TI and global experts. [143]

It is time for all national stakeholders i.e. Media, private sector and citizens to come together as a team to play their respective roles and responsibilities in nation building process and create a revolution to create a new India that is built on the foundation of integrity, participatory democracy, mutual trust and coordination. It is time for a social revolution and conscious evolution, it is time for people of India to come together to form a Team India and play their roles and responsibilities in building a new India. Let us all come forward to join this evolutionary revolution movement and transform our country into a heaven on earth. Let's see how we can do it...

Team India

Team India - An Idea whose time has come......

A small body of determined spirits fired by an unquenchable faith in their mission can alter the course of history. - Mahatma Gandhi

Never doubt that a small group of thoughtful, committed citizens can change the world. Indeed, it is the only thing that ever has. - Margaret Mead

The quantum physics' theory of critical mass and phase transition is a well-known phenomenon. It shows that a small stimulus can trigger a number of atoms lining up in phase with each other and when it reaches a certain critical mass, there's a phase transition and suddenly all of the light becomes coherent. This is the principle for laser light where all the atoms form a coherent pattern that is influenced by a sudden phase transition caused by some atoms reaching a certain critical mass. Similarly "collective transformation" would occur when a "critical mass" of "individuals align to create a change in society.

As individuals change, eventually a critical mass of people will be reached and the whole society will have a new, effective way of doing things or in other words when enough individual people share common objectives and beliefs, a critical mass will be reached which will create a force field of such intensity that everyone in society will share this belief. "Team India" is such a belief which can change our country if applied effectively.

It is time for people of India to come together for a revolution that would lead us to our conscious evolution and transform it into a heaven on earth.

Yes, it is time to break all those old paradigms, systems and processes that have blocked India from achieving her highest and greatest democratic potential and create a new India where the new, vibrant systems with well-synchronized pillars, transparent, accountable processes and practices, work towards achieving the shared goals of peace, progress and prosperity for all. Like a body, where all the organs and systems are well synchronized and are working in harmony to keep all the cells happy and healthy; we too must come together- all the organs in the country - to keep this collective body of our mother India with all her 1.3 billion cells; happy, healthy and prosperous. It calls for a revolution and massive reforms.....not a destructive revolution but an intellectual one that would lead us to our conscious evolution- by rejecting what does not serve us anymore - by choosing best strategies and processes that would serve our highest collective good and help us achieve our collective ultimate potential.

"Yes we can – team India" is such a belief which can change our country if applied effectively. We, the people of India, share the same vision, the same idea, and the same dream of a free and prosperous India; free of corruption, poverty, violence, communalism, terrorism, unemployment, illiteracy etc. We all dream of a developed India with a booming economy, sound infrastructure, food, job, health, social and national security for all.

It is time to achieve the dream handed over to us by our forefathers; carry their legacy forward and repay the debt of those who sacrificed their lives so their children can live in a free India - happy, healthy and prosperous. Now it is our turn as inheritors of their hard-earned freedom and democracy, to make their dream come true! We need to come together again to free India from the monsters of corruption, poverty, illiteracy, unhygienic conditions, poor infrastructure, communalism, unemployment etc. that are keeping the people of India chained and unable to achieve their highest potential and prosperity.

We need to unite as one mind, one soul, one body as team India with a multi-dimensional, multi-stake holder and multi-lateral approach to reform and transform the entire system and design effective strategies, action and implementation plans to create a new India that works for all. Yes, it calls for a revolution! Indeed, every revolution is good as it asks for a change – a fundamental change to rule out what is not working and start all over again with a new foundation for a better outcome. It is a call to let go the past and choose a new future.....better, brighter with the experiences, inventions, discoveries, technology advancements our country has acquired. We have the best of means and tools to choose and create the best. All we need is a spiritual and intellectual revolution for our collective conscious evolution. Today we are a step away from making the changes for the betterment of our entire country.

As we explored earlier, we already have all the resources – Manpower, brainpower, technology, wisdom - we have everything in abundance. We have the brightest brains on earth with us -economists, scientists, entrepreneurs; the largest pool of workforce, best financial and technical institutions, science and technology at our fingertips, abundance of bio, mineral and chemical resources, service and strategic sectors, massive youth power, largest agriculture resources, brightest economists, intellectuals, analysts, academia, highly enterprising and successful corporates and industries, professionals and global support - we have it all! We just lack the collective will and vision to turn India into a developed country and the happiest place on earth to live in. We must take the responsibility to create a new India to make the dream of our previous generations come true and forward the legacy to our children.

What can we do?

Ask not what your country can do for you; ask what you can do for your country- JFK

History has witnessed whenever a courageous mind stood up and took cudgel for all that is right and just, all the universal forces have come to pave the path for him; be it Mahatma Gandhi, Mandela, Lincon, Martin Luther King or anyone with a genuine cause to make the whole world a better place.

Frankly, there is nothing that we, the people of India or shall we call it the "team India" cannot do.

How do we do it?

The constitution of India has a clause that says, "It shall be the duty of every citizen of India to develop the scientific temper, humanism and the spirit of inquiry and reform."[144]

All we need today is some progressive thinking heads with the scientific temper to inquire and find solutions, some caring hearts to enlighten the society and some working hands to reform and transform the country. Together, we can create a vibrant "Team India" to design our dream future where every issue in the country is collectively analyzed and solved. Team India, in turn, should create a wisdom pool and a neural network (India – think tank) where people with revolutionary ideas and specialist and experts from all the sectors can come together for brainstorming, discussing and formulating comprehensive solutions, strategies and action plans to combat all prevailing issues like lack of integrity, transparency & accountability , sustainable development, growth & prosperity for all, poor Infrastructure & development, poor public services, unemployment, corruption, communalism/ terrorism, unhygienic conditions, health issues, illiteracy , poverty, socio-economic inequalities etc.

In other words creating a democratic -social, interactive platform where socially active and aware citizens and experienced professionals from various sectors like Media, private, public, civil sectors i.e. experienced economists, technical experts, specialists, authors, corporate honchos, entrepreneurs, intellectuals, philosophers, academia, journalists , youth organizations, philanthropists, NGOs, retired judges or defense personals and people from all walks with bright ideas can come together as a team to discuss various national issues and create an integrated, holistic national vision with multi-pronged democratic systems, processes, practices, comprehensive strategies, integrated structures , reforms and time-bound action plans , implementation-monitoring- review -public awareness teams and task forces for transforming India into a developed country. We must work towards creating a new India where all the citizens are living in peace, harmony and prosperity and are offered enough opportunities to achieve their individual and collective ultimate potential. In other words, the goal of Team India should be to make every Indian's dream of peace, progress and prosperity come true!

This is the dream of every citizen of India – peace, progress and prosperity for all. That needs strong rule of law, communal harmony, sustainable and inclusive and growth, quality education, health and job opportunities for all. It would need the equitable and proper distribution of national income and resources to all through improved, well designed and prioritized policies, processes and time-bound action plans. It would need good governance serving with integrity, transparency, accountability. It would need efficient public service delivery, improved public management- financial system and monitoring processes to stop huge financial and human resource wastages in public sector that result in a shortage of resources for development activities. It would need linking schemes with outcomes and social goals and a complete overhauling of the crumbling integrity structure of our governments, state machinery and apathy, lethargy of our office and power holders. Moreover, it would need active citizens' involvement that is the most critical factor for successful democratic governments to operate in an efficient and responsive manner and live up to their public obligations.

As we discussed earlier, given the magnitude of corruption, mismanagement of power and resources, repeated failures of national 5-years plans and political mandates to achieve substantial results; poor public services and integrity-accountability- transparency issues existing in our country, it is clear that the government cannot handle it alone. Therefore, we all need to tackle these issues in a holistic way with all the players involved i.e. Team India, government, private sector, global agencies, media, local players etc. coming together to design holistic strategic approach and Procedures to tackle corruption and mismanagement of national revenue and resources. As suggested by global experts, we need to design specific methods like prevention, enforcement and suppression measures, integrated in ethical, legal, social and institutional governance framework with concrete steps and time-bound actions; that will get all the pillars across the country on a single coherent framework, working towards the shared goals of good governance, effective public service delivery and financial management, political and public accountability and transparency, sustainable development and the rule of law. Put simply, developing a comprehensive strategy and action plan to achieve the common goals of peace, progress and prosperity for all.

As seen quite often, so many well-intended schemes and development programs have been launched regularly by successive governments but very few see the light of the day due to inefficiency, misplaced priorities or outright lethargy and apathy of office holders and of those in power. It is crucial to enhance the effectiveness of the public funds on social goals. The role of Team India along with media, social organizations and private sector would be thereby, catalytic and critical to maintain pressure i.e. play a watchdog and ferociously guard the budgets and policies to prevent any misuse, misappropriation or manipulation.

It would need creating a new power structure and accountability mechanism in addition to existing ones and establishing the third force – Team India (citizens, Media and private sector) to play the role of ultimate guardians of democracy and integrity in the country. As we discussed in earlier chapters, as per the constitution, all the democratic institutions, processes and practices are ultimately accountable to the people of India only. Team India should create a national democratic space and interactive platform where by using various democratic tools, processes and global initiatives like social responsibility, social accountability, participatory democracy, transparency, national integrity system assessment and reforms, Open Government Data, ICT etc., citizens can exercise their democratic rights.

For instance, by using setting up systems like independent integrity assessment unit, public information infrastructure, social accountability interface etc and using democratic tools like right to information and right to participation, citizens can reverse their traditional roles and common passive practices like Dharma (protest) , playing the victim or powerless mute spectators into active participatory democratic roles and practices like "citizens with rights" , " integrity guardians" or " champions of reforms". They can harness the power of democracy by adopting new approaches and paradigms that recognize the power of public pressure (power of 98% stakeholders (public) vs. 2% stakeholders (governments and state machinery) on policies and processes in the country [145]as we explored earlier - suggested by global social accountability experts and organizations like TI, UN, UNDP etc.

We know left to their own, governments and public sector would not use accountability and integrity as effective tools to reform or perform. We have been seeing it for decades now and must realize that to make it happen; both internal and external pressure is needed, a combination of political will with public pressure.

So, the point is not that whether the governments would do it or not for, had it been the political will, we would have had our dream India by now! We have already waited far too long. The failure to achieve the "vision 2020" launched in 2000 to reform and transform India (that is perhaps, one of the most intelligent, comprehensive and effective blueprint with well-researched, meticulously designed strategies and time-bound action plans by one of the greatest scientific minds and visionaries of this century - late Dr APJ Kalam) by successive governments, is a testimony of that. Had it been implemented sincerely, India would have been an advanced nation by now with a thriving rural economy and sustainable urban development. Instead, those crucial nation-building years had been lost in corruption, mismanagement, and communal politics. We cannot afford to lose any more years given the explosive poverty, social and economic inequalities, unemployment and communal issues in the country!

For that matter, as we have already explored, our political parties have failed to achieve any of the lofty ideals and dreams of democracy of our leaders and visionaries who constituted India as a welfare state and directed states to provide every citizen with basic rights i e life with dignity, social security, jobs, quality health and education facilities, proper infrastructure, equality of opportunities, proper distribution of national revenue and resources etc. As even after seven decades of independence, governments after governments, plans after plans (India is on its 12th five-year plan now), budgets after budgets; for the majority of Indians, the dream of the fulfillment of these basic rights still remains a pie in the sky.

It is time for people of India to come together as team India to acknowledge and accept the failures of successive governments, reform the system and transform India. We need not wait for political will anymore or any other future vision of 2020 or 2030 for this dream to happen, as we have seen in Indian politics, tomorrow never comes! We have already lost precious time…no more dream selling, promises for future or empty visions without solid ground actions. Before buying any dream or hope, we must ask for past report cards with facts and figures and account for every year gone by- every failure- every promise that was not fulfilled- every single penny that was allocated but not spent or failed to get the desired outcome.

We must ask questions, about the promises that were not fulfilled, mandates that were not followed as we see our leaders regularly making huge commitments and show a rosy picture of future to woo voters. Instead of citing various, random new schemes or proposed plans and hyped budget allocations; they must provide the detailed account of targets and outcomes of every previous scheme and initiative launched and that only should be taken as a proof of their commitments and sincerity not mere lip servicing or election rhetoric!!

We have seen how other countries raced ahead of us and today, not only they have per capita income almost 5 to 10 times of us, but have achieved all round development in all other areas as well i e infrastructure, living standards, health, education but we are nowhere near our dream vision. Thus, the onus is on us to make this dream come true for our future generations. It is time to reject those skewed policies that failed to achieve results, reject those party mandates and promises that have not been fulfilled. It is time for people of India to exercise their democratic right and by using the tools and practices like social responsibility, social accountability etc, claim their place as "citizens with rights" instead of "beneficiary with needs" [146]or "mute spectators" and take charge of national policies, budgets, processes, action plans and outcomes. It is time for people of India to create their own vision and mandate – "India manifesto" and time-bound national action plan and make it happen through collective will and actions. It is time for us to make a new, perfect system with 0 corruption and 100 % transparency and accountability with water-tight processes with no scope for any leakages or mismanagement and take stock of every penny, every policy, every scheme, and every outcome.

Once we have a perfect accountable system, transparent processes and people's manifesto (a national action plan for sustainable development with perfect monitoring and evaluation mechanisms) in place; governments may come or go; no one would be able to take people in the country for a ride with empty promises or misleading mandates, as to win people's trust, they will have to comply and perform. We must realize that India's destiny is not in the hands of few people in power. India's future will depend upon the collective will, choices and actions of her citizens. Therefore, the point is not what this or that government did or how they are doing better or worse than the others. The point is -what India can and must do with all her resources- huge workforce, large knowledge pool, ever-growing youth power, science and technology resources, massive land area and bio-mineral resources!

It is time for us to unite and take charge of our future and claim our roles and rights, as unless we take collective social responsibility for fulfilling the basic goals of peace, progress and prosperity for all us and demand social accountability to change the entire system, things would not really change. Experts all over the world emphasize the collective nature of social accountability as a defining feature that is an on-going and collective effort to hold public officials and service providers to account for the provision of public goods that are the constitutional obligations of the states such as primary healthcare, education, better job opportunities, safety, sanitation and social security etc. They suggest that social accountability is a tool through which citizens can demand and enforce accountability from those in power. The aims and claims of these initiatives impact overall well-being and empowerment of citizens, vibrant democratic governance and better and efficient management of aids.

The global researchers like Marie Chene (TI) who tried to find out why some countries like NEW ZEALAND, DENMARK, FINLAND, SWEDEN etc are cleaner than most countries suggest that well-performing countries characteristically, have a long tradition of government's openness, civic activism and social trust, with strong transparency and accountability mechanism in place; allowing citizens to monitor their governments and hold them accountable for their actions and decisions.[147] These 'demand-side' initiatives are led by citizens and social actors with support from many state or non-state actors like private sector service providers, CSOs etc. and provide social interfaces that go beyond the formal democratic institutions of elections, recall of representatives or internal government's audits to hold the states and its agents accountable to common citizens. These four key principles or concepts of transparency, participation, accountability and integrity are deeply intertwined, as they form a strong democratic infrastructure that provides an interactive social platform and tools which enable informed, active citizens to stand up for their rights and hold their leaders accountable for their actions, policies, decisions and management of public resources as well as for failures to perform their constitutional democratic duties and achieve promised outcomes.[148]

"democratic governance goes beyond the building of institutions and includes developing the very relationship between institutions and people, to ensure that institutions are responsive to individual and community aspirations, to support participation and, in so doing, address imbalanced power dynamics" (UNDP and OHCHR)[149]

Team India must aim to create such a synergistic power structure based on mutual discussions, negotiations, compromises, coordination and co-operations that would create a more inclusive and coherent society and get all the stakeholders working towards realizing the common goals of creating peace, progress and prosperity for all the citizens in the country. This would require building specialist teams and harness the collective expertise and potential to optimize policies and resources and reduce wastage and misuse of national revenue and resources. It would require dismantling the old leaky systems, poorly designed and implemented processes and create a new robust national integrity system to get all the stakeholders on the same page for achieving shared goals of good governance, better public services, better management, 0 corruptions and 100% transparency and accountability across all the pillars.

As we discussed earlier, a systemic integrity system is the most important factor for sustainable growth and development in a country as it is based on the strong pillars of transparency, accountability, trust and service. It is a multi-pronged approach that creates a sustainable framework and combines various areas like building integrity system in a society, establishing the rule of law, strengthening institutions, building civil society and governments capacities, improving administration and public service delivery and last but not the least, pushing government sector for result oriented performances.

It would also require building social accountability and ITC enabled public information infrastructure for bridging the gap between citizens and governments to collect, analyze and repackage information in easily accessible and understandable formats to empower citizens and media so they can use the data to exercise their rights and demand complete integrity, transparency and hold governments and public officials to account. It would also require developing a comprehensive national action plan for inclusive, sustainable growth and development by converging all the national resources under single umbrella initiatives and creating specific action teams and task forces to translate strategies into definite actions and results.

Team India should create a think tank (expert team) by inviting technical experts, specialists, well informed professional from all the sectors involved i.e. Media, IT, Civil and Private sector, retired professionals like judges, economists, technocrats, corporate honchos, social experts, eminent personalities and enlightened citizens , academicians , Intellectuals and technical geniuses from our esteemed institutions like IIM and IITs etc. for brainstorming and creating innovative, creative solutions and action plans for all the issues facing the country today .The idea is to create specialists' team (team India) vs. generalist teams (governments and public sector) to harness the vast pool of knowledge and technology that has made India a powerhouse abroad and realize its full potential by optimizing its resources.

Unfortunately, while the whole world acknowledges and is benefited by India's intellectual and technical exports, India has been unable to harness and utilize this power to create inclusive and sustainable higher growth and development for the country. While our private sector is going from places to places using this vast pool to maximize their profits and assets, our government sector though, having their own think tanks and task forces like NITI AYOG etc. is unable to do so. Considering India's performance on crucial areas recently, it would need a radical transformation to change the things happening in the country. As we see often, most demand-side national policies and projects are based on generalist centric approach in our government system and that leaves the huge knowledge powerhouse, technical resources that are India's greatest strength; un-harnessed and un-utilized in the process of nation building. Even if specialists are hired through lateral arrangements, their scope, freedom and capacity remain limited due to the power structure in the government system.

Team India can create a knowledge bridge by creating expert teams (India -think tank) that can actively work with the policy makers from inception to designing, monitoring and achieving desired outcomes and come up with creative and innovative alternate solutions with comprehensive strategies, reforms and action plans in every key strategic area and challenges in the country - from economic to social, environmental or technological. It would require our experts to scrutinize every key decision and policy that affects the lives of the people directly or indirectly and present better alternates that could avoid wastage of national resources and revenue on account of poor policy designs or lack of expertise and specialization, not to mention misplaced priorities and skewed motives; and expedite the rate of growth and sustainable development.

Let's face it. India, today, has abundant manpower and brainpower along with ample resources and technology to achieve at least 9 to 10 % GDP growth per year, that is crucial for inclusive growth and development and that China and other miracle countries had managed to achieve for almost a decade. By not utilizing these resources and technological expertise, India is losing its miracle time. Team India and think tank should develop an expert panel and policy framework and work across sectors using policy audits and presenting policy alternatives by integrating macroeconomic policies with microeconomic factors and human rights to ensure inclusive, sustainable growth and development. Team India should also aim to bring the policy matters out for public debate and to encourage collaborative efforts and engagements. Every issue in the country can be analyzed and solved by our think tank and implemented as per mutual agreements. Team India with its think tank can converge all the existing and proposed plans, schemes and processes; formulating comprehensive strategies to set up single umbrella initiatives for various objectives and societal challenges. It should set up **action & implementation plans, review, monitoring and public awareness teams and specific task forces** for executing the strategies and plans into action.

In other words, our think tank can maximize the policy effectiveness and optimum utilization of national resources and revenue while minimizing the wastage or mismanagement of the same with their expertise and specialized solutions, creative, holistic, innovative strategies and action plans. It can push India to achieve her highest, collective potential and transform it into a new advanced country.

A comprehensive, holistic and integrated strategy to achieve these objectives thus, should include:

- A- Creating an India - Think Tank (Expert team)

- B- Creating a National Integrity Infrastructure

- C- Creating a National Public Information Infrastructure (social accountability infrastructure)

- D- Creating a National resources pool

- E- Creating a National Action Plan (sustainable development goals and prosperity for all)

- F- Creating review, monitoring, public awareness teams and task forces

Let us explore the steps in details:

A) **Creating a " Think Tank"-**

Team India should create a think tank (expert team) by inviting technical experts, specialists, well informed professional from all the sectors involved i.e. Media, IT, Civil and Private sector, Retired professionals like judges, economists, technocrats, corporate honchos, social experts, eminent personalities and enlightened citizens , academicians , Intellectuals and technical geniuses from our esteemed institutions like IIM and IITs etc. for brain storming and creating innovative, creative solutions and action plans for all the issues facing the country today like poverty, socio-economic inequalities, illiteracy, unemployment, environmental issues, communalism, social , health and hygiene issues etc.

As discussed earlier, Team India with its think tank can create a knowledge bridge between the government and citizens by using ICT and social accountability tools to ensure 100% transparency and accountability across the government and public sectors - in all the policies, processes and practices across all departments. It can then converge all the existing and proposed plans, schemes and processes formulating comprehensive strategies to set up single umbrella initiatives for various objectives and societal challenges.

Through applying these accountability and transparency Initiatives and converging all the resources, policies, schemes and expertise under single umbrella initiatives, Team India would ensure effective, optimum utilization of national resources and revenue and minimize the losses through corruption or mismanagement. With their creative and out-of-the–box ideas and solutions and innovative strategies, action plans and task forces, Team India –think tank can revolutionize the entire system and processes and help India achieve its highest collective potential and destiny. The collective power and potential of our Team India- think tank can push India into the highest spheres of social and economic progress in no time and transform it into a miracle economy - a feat that has eluded our country for so long!

For instance, India has made remarkable strides in ICT and e-governance yet, the current state of these initiatives leave a lot to be desired as providing a vast amount of information and making huge digital infrastructure expenditure have not translated into better service delivery performance or improved transparency and accountability of the public sector. To ensure good governance and better service delivery, it is crucial to have a robust information structure and effective public interface that could help people to hold the governments and public sector accountable. The failure to provide effective tools and mechanisms for social accountability and public scrutiny in policy matters and public affairs, unfortunately, results in wastage of national revenue and resources due to integrity and accountability violations like corruption, misuse of resources, bribery, conflict of interest, misuse and manipulation of information, sponsorship, misuse of aids and cronyism.

The indication is that even after launching good initiatives like Digital India and other hyped schemes, in the latest edition of 2016 UN's e-governance survey, **("E-Government in Support of Sustainable Development")** performance of our e-government is quite humiliating considering the level of IT professionals- experts, technological advancements and abundance of resources in the country. Among 193 countries, India ranks too low at 107 on the Index that is derived from 13 different parameters. The recent global IT report (WEFORUM) shows –" Despite many improvements in its political and regulatory environment (78th, up four) and in its business and innovation environment (110th, up five), India has slipped down two positions to an overall rank of 91 for using good governance to achieve sustainable development goals." [150] While there have been some marginal changes scored in recent years, India has failed to match the rapid pace that other Asian countries are moving with like South Korea and Singapore who made it in top 10 along with the top countries like Australia, NZ, Sweden and

Denmark etc. India's poor performance puts a big question mark on our technical and e-governance capabilities.

Similarly, as we discussed earlier, the recent 2017 Global Corruption barometer report by the Transparency International (TI) declared India the country with the highest bribery rate in Asia Pacific region with 69% Indians reporting to pay bribes for most basic public services like governments healthcare, public schools, police, court and other utilities or for getting identification documents compared to other countries like Japan and Hong Kong where only 2 to 4% have reported having paid bribes.[151]

In the World Bank's 2017 report on "ease of doing business" too, India ranked 130 out of 190 countries against countries like South Korea (5th), the UK (7th), Sweden (9th) etc. Even among BRICS group, India ranked lowest (130) compared to China (78), Russia (40) and South Africa (74). The index is based on indicators like getting permits, credits, electricity, property and payment of taxes etc. for starting business.[141]

To achieve the goals of shared prosperity, high growth rate, sustainable development and maintaining peace and harmony in the country, we need to address these issues urgently and tackle them collectively. We cannot deny anymore that the real issue in our country's progress and performance in e-governance and other important areas is not a technical one. At the core of it, everything boils down to poor policies, poor administration of schemes and processes and gross mismanagement of revenue and resources. The whole system is very laid back and there is very little motivation in bureaucracy to change old systems and flawed processes. Unless we change policies, processes, structures, and people's mindsets in the system and get rid of the administrative inertia and social apathy, no amount of technologies or innovative plans would work!

We know that today when e-governance has become a development indicator and benchmark for civil participation worldwide, it can play a critical role in bringing more inclusiveness, efficiency, credibility, trust, accountability and transparency in the government and public sectors and can prove to be the most powerful tool for sustainable development and delivery of basic services. But for e-government to realize its impact on development, it needs to be accompanied by measures to ensure access and availability of ICT and make public institutions more accountable and responsive to people's needs.[152]

Utilizing the knowledge pool and their expertise, team India should create an information infrastructure using ICT enabled initiatives like social accountability and open government data to play the role of an "information intermediary" or "knowledge bridge" between governments and citizens, collecting, analyzing and repackaging information in easily accessible and understandable formats with the help of graphics and flow charts etc. to empower citizens and media so they can use the information and data to exercise their social rights ; demand complete integrity, transparency and hold governments and public officials to account. They can design specific programs that can supplement and complement existing horizontal and vertical accountability mechanisms and that are based on demand-side accountability (what people must know and demand) as against the supply side accountability mechanisms (what governments and it machinery provide).

Team India should implement these social accountability initiatives in diverse governance contexts, from front-line service delivery to national policy processes that would in turn lead to strengthening civic engagement in policy and planning and building responsive and capable institutions. All over the world, these 'demand-side' initiatives are led by citizens and social actors with support from many state or non-state actors like private sector service providers and provide social interfaces that move beyond the formal democratic institutions of elections, recall of representatives or internal governments audits to hold the time-bound and its agents accountable to common citizens not every five year but on a continual basis.

It would require creating a national information infrastructure as a two-way " government to citizens and citizens to government (G2C – C2G) "single window interface" between the citizens and government across its machinery i.e. all ministries, municipalities, public offices etc, where Team India working with global agencies like Transparency International (TI), Transparency &Accountability Initiatives , Open Governments Partnership (OGP), OECD, UNDP etc. can promote more open and accountable governments, with the ultimate goals of eliminating corruption, empowering citizens, encouraging economic competences, harnessing innovation, and improving the delivery of services. Though, as we discussed, we already have some existing government to citizen platforms but the information and data provided remain inadequate and ineffective and there are not enough social accountability, integrity tools and processes to achieve the purpose.

Team India- think tank can harness the new data revolution and develop innovative applications and structures like citizen database e-clouds (C-clouds) connecting with governments e- clouds (G – clouds) exploring possibilities of various satellite and mobile based applications. It should establish a network of shared access and information between governments and public and can provide tools for citizens to monitor performance in the delivery of public goods and services, give feedback, submit grievances, and contribute towards developing constructive solutions. Such a network can become a powerful interactive platform for people to come forward to offer mutually beneficial solutions that advance the common good and social interests instead of feeling alienated, clueless or powerless and promote productive relationships and alliances between governments and citizens. This can build networks and reservoirs of trust among people and with governments, enhancing both community trust and trust in governments.

Similarly, the Open Government Partnership can offer an opportunity for governments to share best practices in transparency reforms and the inclusion of both government and non-government participants can facilitate collaboration between key stakeholders. Team India should continue to nudge governments and other organs toward increased transparency, continued reforms by as well as complement and reinforce ongoing reforms by spreading social awareness, providing easy, quality information to the public and monitoring implementation. Team India must work with the Governments in total partnership from conceptual planning, action & implementation planning to review, monitoring and reforming. Their participation through all stages of the policy process— planning, advocacy, implementation and monitoring will create an open and transparent system of information that will serve as a link publicizing and disseminating to stakeholders their needs and concerns regarding the effects of policy. The concept of national decision-making processes based on the accountability of the state to its citizens is increasingly accepted by influential actors in both governments and civil society all over the world.[153]

By creating this public information infrastructure based on social accountability tools with a new robust integrity infrastructure that would ensure high integrity of public officials, public trust in governance, policies, practices, institutions and converging all the sustainable development goals into national action plan, establishing implementation, monitoring teams and task forces operating at local, state and national level ; Team India can profoundly amplify all efforts to ensure transparency, accountability, and participation in governance and make the entire system with all the national pillars and public institutions, zero corruption and 100% transparent and accountable. Participating and following all policies and their outcomes, budget allocations and outputs; tracking every rupee going in the system to its end use would ensure our national resources and revenue being utilized properly and effectively for achieving the goals of shared prosperity and inclusive growth. It would also enable the citizens along with team India, to play their role as ultimate integrity guardians and caretakers of the national wealth and resources.

Once the integrity and social accountability infrastructure are in place, Team India can harness the individual strengths of all the national integrity pillars i.e. Legislature, Judiciary, civil, private sectors, Media, independent agencies and law enforcement agencies etc. converge and synergize them into an integrated framework to reform and transform the entire system. This would lay the foundation of a new India with new democratic systems, structures, processes and practices that would make the dream of freedom and promise of democracy – SWARAJ- self-governance; that is by the people, for the people and of the people; come true.

B) Establishing A National Integrity Infrastructure

However, we all know that a new India cannot be built without dismantling the old faulty, leaking systems, crumbling institutions, poorly designed, and maintained processes and practices. It would require building a new vibrant system with multi-dimensional, multi-stakeholder strategies, approaches and revolutionary reforms in public administration and governance; mindsets and behaviors and in civil sector's inclusion and participation, to achieve the results. In short, team India should aim to revolutionalise and reform the entire integrity system, create new power-sharing structures and build a new temple of integrity on the foundation of trust, accountability and transparency to achieve the shared goals of peace, progress and prosperity for all as without changing the weak foundation; no plans, no efforts will bear fruit. We have seen that despite regularly introducing a large number of policies, processes and commitments, the efforts have failed to bring much-needed reform in the integrity infrastructure in India. Rampant corruption, inadequate law enforcement, delayed and insufficient justice, poor public service delivery, apathetic, unaccountable public employees, power drunk unapologetic elected members, crumbling institutions, toothless commissions and agencies and deteriorating politics show a weak integrity infrastructure that needs urgent and radical reforms.

As we discussed in the previous chapter, to make sure that there is no abuse, misuse or ill concentration of the power in the system; the constitution of India distributed the democratic power by establishing the system of checks and balances i.e. horizontal (equal) power structure between executive (the elected governments and cabinet of ministers), legislature (elected members of parliaments MPs and Members of legislature assembly MLAs) and judiciary (High court and Supreme Court). The Constitution made vertical power sharing structure between the Centre and the states, that enabled each to enforce and legislate within their field of activity and other autonomous democratic institutions like Election Commission which is responsible for holding free and fair elections, Public Service Commission responsible for providing effective public services to all and an Auditor General (CAG) responsible for conducting independent audits of accounts of the governments and its agencies. There are other state and non-state organizations and agencies like CBI, (NITIAyog) etc. The idea was to have a power balance by making the democratic institutions checking and balancing each other to ensure maintaining the rule of law and providing service to people through the smooth functioning of the entire government system and its machinery.

Yet , a brief assessment of our National Integrity System that is based on several pillars like (as per Transparency international's (TI) national integrity system model) : Parliament, Executive, Judiciary, public Administration (bureaucracy), Local Governments, Police (law enforcement agency), Comptroller and Auditor General (supreme audit institution), Election Commission, Anti-Corruption Agencies, CBI, Planning Commission (NITI Ayog), Political Parties, Civil Society, Media, and Business etc. shows the weak levels of integrity and lack of synergy amongst the NIS pillars that is crucial for the system's overall effectiveness. And we know that any weak pillar, particularly in the government, public sector or judiciary; directly or indirectly; would affect all the other pillars and weaken the foundation of the integrity temple.

While India is the largest democracy in the world with a strong inclusive constitutional and sound legal framework, inadequate practice and implementation of those and a weak political will to reform its crumbling " white elephants" institutions fail to provide accountable and effective democratic governance in the country. A highly confrontational politics, a highly dysfunctional parliament , a predominant culture of defiance, an authoritative closed executive; an overloaded judiciary, a criminalized police force and politicized bureaucracy with unaccountable , inefficient staff ; have been unable to provide a strong foundation that is essential for nation building. Inadequate law enforcement against corruption, low awareness of citizens about their rights and inadequate access to information, lack of accountability and transparency in governance , so-called independent commissions lacking credibility and public trust, a dynamic yet disconnected private sector, a hugely diverse and powerful yet somewhat irresponsible and sensationalized media and a socially diverse , aware yet inactive, dormant civil society; demonstrate a weak integrity system that is unable to achieve its ultimate potential due to such internal weaknesses and challenges.

As a result, despite being the largest democracy in the world and an emerging super economy, India has failed to ensure effective law and order; smooth functioning of state institutions; promote sustainable growth and development or provide social and economic justice and security to its citizens that are the fundamental rights of its citizens. Petty party politics, blame-games and ever-growing hostility between parties have eroded the parliament's dignity and scope for constructive discussions or national consensus. A lack of political will to bring out badly needed substantive reforms and lack of accountability and integrity in all key pillars in the system have resulted in ever-increasing corruption, deterioration of law and order, abuse of power and resources and violation of citizen's fundamental rights in the country.

Setting up an Independent National Integrity Unit – Guarding the guards[154] -

We know that achieving the objectives of peace, progress and prosperity for all, would require creating a new national integrity temple built on mutually supportive pillars, including all the stakeholders in the country i.e. executive, parliament, judiciary, watchdog agencies, media, private sector, civil society and law enforcement agencies and applying a holistic approach, using all the tools of integrity like establishing an independent national integrity unit in collaboration with reputed technical and management institutes in our country like IITs and IIMs . The integrity unit can conduct regular national integrity assessments, integrity workshops, public surveys and based on the findings, can design national integrity strategy, cross-sectorial reforms and action plans. It can also create the implementation, monitoring, review and reform teams for all sectors like government, parliament, judiciary, police and other law enforcement agencies etc. The national integrity assessment team, using the formats suggested by TI for assessing all the integrity pillars - their strength, weaknesses, and recommendation; should identify gaps and loopholes for corruption and mismanagement within each of the pillars and coordinate the work of the governments, civil society, and private sector into a coherent framework of institutional strengthening.

The lackluster approach and delay in implementing the Lokpal by our most important national pillars i.e. executive, parliament and law enforcement institutions show that setting up an independent integrity unit cannot be left on them. Despite all hyped anti-corrupt and pro-reform election rhetoric, there is no political will or efforts to implement it successfully by our politicians. This demonstrates the level of political hypocrisy and mockery of public sentiments existing in our country. Therefore, the onus lies on the citizens of India (as Team India) to apply the external pressure and work with other stakeholders ie media, private sector, Academia, technical experts (IIM, IITs etc) CSOs, NGOs and global agencies like Transparency international, OECD, UNDP and Open Government Data etc. to establish the "third force" by creating an independent integrity unit to revolutionalise and reform the national integrity infrastructure.

We must come together with the mission to promote a corruption-free society where high levels of effective rule of law, mutual trust, integrity and accountability are upheld and corruption as a systemic issue, in all forms i.e. moral, ethical and financial is addressed and arrested. It would require all stakeholders to work on several fronts and collaborate with all branches of governments and many parts of society to curb corruption, promote good governance, build integrity, improve public services and create an enabling environment for the private sector. The three principal activity areas as suggested by many global agencies are- improving public sector service delivery by focusing on public sector accountability and legal reform in order to re-establish rule of law; building integrity by promoting governmental accountability and transparency and building prevention and suppression anti-corruption capacities across the sectors ie public sector including parliament, watchdog, enforcement agencies, business sector, judiciary and civil society, particularly by strengthening civil organizations, active citizen groups and the media.

The real impact of this initiative would not only be anti-corruption or pro-integrity benefits but also, improved public service delivery, the established rule of law and an enabling environment for the private sector. The national integrity unit along with Team India can focus on the goals of promoting good governance, ensuring sustainable development –prosperity for all, establishing the rule of law and ensuring effective public services. By conducting integrity assessment surveys of all the pillars for assessing their systemic weaknesses like poor strategies or implementation plans; untimely or inadequate budget allocations; lack of monitoring and evaluation processes and gaps between targets and outcomes; it can recommend and design a national reform strategy. By implementing and monitoring these reforms in collaboration with government and public sectors, Team India and integrity unit can establish a robust integrity infrastructure in the country that would ensure 0 corruption and 100% transparency and accountability across sectors. Through mutual support, all integrity pillars can combine their strengths by applying core values and practices for better synergy and synchronization. In short, the national integrity unit along with Team India can play the role of the ultimate guardians of integrity – "guarding the guards" in the country.[154]

Note - An integrity guardian as it is called by global experts, is an agency with oversight and control powers concerning integrity violations like corruption, misuse of resources, bribery, conflict of interest, misuse and manipulation of information, sponsorship, misuse of aids and cronyism.[155]

Following are the guidelines from Transparency International (TI) and Anti corruption country strategy Sierra Leone) for designing a strategy for building integrity as we discussed in details in the previous chapter (global tools and guidelines):

STRATEGY AND TOOL KIT FOR BUILDING INTEGRITY[103]

One of the strategies is to initiate a process that will lead all the stakeholders to identify their
Roles and recognize that "they are either part of the problem or part of the solution."
The process of strengthening a National Integrity System begins with a national dialogue,
followed by a national action plan. To promote national reform, the following prevention and
Integrity tools have been developed:

- National integrity system assessment
- Surveys focusing on service delivery
- Integrity or corruption Surveys
- Municipal and Sub-national Integrity Workshops
- External oversight in tender process
- Enforce code of conduct including declaration and monitoring of assets
- National Integrity Workshops (NIWs) (broad based action planning)
- The Integrity Pledge
- Islands of Integrity
- National Integrity Steering Committee (NISC)
- National Integrity Unit (NIU)

Some more tools [156]-

Whistle-blower provisions and protection: a key mechanism to overcome the culture of tolerance of corrupt practices, people must be provided with the means to report responsibly any abuses of power or acts of corruption

Vigilance units: groups appointed throughout the public sector with responsibility for verifying compliance with integrity pacts, codes of conduct and anti-corruption rules and procedures.

Integrity testing: random checks on those in vulnerable positions.

Citizens Charters: set out the public services a government agency will offer and how it will respond to members of the public.

Service delivery surveys and report cards: publicized reports of tests of anti-corruption standards and targets, based on verified surveys, which departments will welcome as recognition of due performance and justification of appropriate

Review and reform teams for every pillar review, integrate, and harmonize all reforms in to a National Reform Program, including sector reforms, financial reforms, economic reforms, constitutional reforms, civil-service reform, decentralization, privatization, and legal reforms.

Formulating a time bound National Action Plan to implement processes and reforms with key pillars collaboration.

Key Principles

- Local Ownership
- Increase accountability through increased transparency
- Enforce access to information to all
- Balancing of powers across executive, legislative and judiciary
- Broad-based capacity building
- Public empowered to monitor the state
- Administration based on rules
- Rule of law
- Overall objective is improved service delivery and high-quality growth
- demonstrations by a range of key leaders of commitment to change
- Transparency: openness in dealing with the public and public opinion
- Accountability: responsibility for the performance of public duties and being answerable for all
- acts and omissions

- Meritocracy: promotion of the most talented and able to perform
- Deregulation: systematic removal of unnecessary regulations, processes and procedures
- Standardization and automation: simplification and widespread use of technology
- Efficiency of service delivery: progressive performance improvement
- Professionalism and competence: investment in recruitment and training
- Public participation: active engagement of civil society and the media
- Change management: measures which facilitate change, for example, capacity building and awareness raising
-(Guidelines form TI)[157]

We should draw lessons from the past planning failures, reform failures and from other countries' successful anti-corruption and reform strategies to develop a comprehensive new national strategy that would make all the integrity pillars zero corruption and 100% transparency and accountability based. A multi-dimensional , multi-stakeholder partnership based, holistic and integrated, multi-pronged strategy using technology-based designs, realistic planning, prioritizing reforms; combining technical expertise of various sectors; involving local actors like NGOs and independent agencies, watchdogs and other implementing partners; setting strategic priorities and sequencing, effective coordination, monitoring and evaluation mechanisms to link all the national integrity pillars with a shared goals platform.

It would require designing and implementing massive reforms such as -Public Sector Reforms that focus on prevention through civil-service reform and public-expenditure planning and management- Legislative reforms to strengthen parliament role not only in overseeing the executive but also the passing of new legislations and bills - Legal reforms , that strengthen the rule of law. It would also require building "integrity infrastructure", that is a positive, proactive preventive approach to counter corruption and to promote effective public service delivery as well as ensuring that public power and resources are used for the public good. As seen all over the world, creating a national integrity system to support preventive measures is more effective than any other specific measures to fight corruption.

It would require all the stakeholders with team India with its national integrity unit to integrate and harmonize all reforms into a National Reform Program as a time-bound national action plan, including sector reforms, financial reforms, economic reforms, constitutional reforms, civil-service reform, and legal reforms etc. as suggested by World Bank.[158] The national integrity unit can follow TI's guidelines and other effective reform strategies and practices used by some of its member countries.

Team India should also create an anti-corruption task force to address a range of issues and processes including: public information-sharing, policy-making and planning; the analysis and tracking of public budgets, expenditures and procurement processes; monitoring and evaluation of public service delivery, supervising anti-corruption measures and complaints handling mechanisms .[159] The task force can serve as a single umbrella initiative for convergence and co-ordination of all sectoral strategies and activities in the country against corruption.

In India, Traditionally, periodic administrative reforms introducing new policies and law enforcement have been used to address a range of issues yet, the lack of an effective public management system and accountability infrastructure has hampered the effect. Later, various strategies like enhancing the quality of bureaucracies, merit-based promotion and exam based recruitment, improved regulations and other transparency and accountability mechanisms were also introduced to de-polities the system albeit unsuccessfully. In some countries, new reforms based on business management strategies like running the public institutions professionally like big corporate companies with CEO-style leadership, expert teams and scientific analytic tools, performance management based on time-bound targets and result oriented strategic management with innovative ICT programs and interfaces are being sought to improve public sector delivery and accountability.

As we explored earlier, effective, Innovative and creative use of Information and communication Technology (ICT) can reduce excessive intrusions by public employees that result in power abuse and can prevent misconduct and mismanagement by public employees. ICT also contributes by transparently providing information to the public, and can build a full proof system with watertight processes that can block all the loopholes and scope of leakages and pilferage of revenue and resources. With time-bound flow charts, well monitoring and evaluation processes, it can prevent public employees' corrupt behavior by transparently providing information about governmental policy-making and service delivery processes to the public. In this approach, the public is defined as customers, and the government is considered the service provider making public service delivery become more accessible to the public.[160]

For instance, by harnessing civil participation and private sector's professionalism, public (customer) management system, financial management, and incentive-based performance systems; Team India along with other players can reform our public sector and governance.

Team India together with private sector and media, should converge technical expertise and technological infrastructure for designing and developing innovative tools like citizen's cloud and governance clouds (on public information interface) where all the ministries, departments and municipalities are connected through common software and platforms and are able to provide mobile-based public services. All public official elected or non-elected must earn their salary by performing with integrity and accountability or the right to recall their tenure must be introduced and exercised. All the MPs , MLAs and public sector employees must submit monthly and yearly reports of their performances, targets, achievements and publish on public information interface for public appraisals and scrutiny. Innovative, interactive mobile-based information interfaces like "know your leaders" where their personal and professional credentials, work done for the voters/constituencies, monthly and annual report cards are analyzed and are available on fingertips, will increase the credibility and performance of our government and public sector by multifold.

Similarly, by combining the individual strengths of various pillars like civil activism with judicial activism and technological expertise of private sector and technical institutions (India think tank), Team India can reform and revolutionize our electoral system. Using transparent processes and accountable mechanisms like citizen database clouds and government e-cloud, it can create a firewall that filters the corrupt and criminal candidates at the source itself. Team India can select and implement various tools and tips provided by global organizations like open government data (OGP), UNDP, and TI etc.

-By establishing a legal framework that ensures its impartiality, effectiveness and transparency; setting clear criteria for selecting electoral officials and candidates based on their past records, personal integrity and capacities; making all nominations/ candidates public on the citizen information interface and introducing innovative web and mobile applications like "know your candidates" with the vision, mission statements of the candidates with their detailed portfolios and personal details - assets disclosure, criminal records etc. , it can invite public scrutiny, debates and comments period before selecting the candidates.

- By establishing budgetary procedures that guarantee the ability of election administration to act impartially (free and independently from political pressures), effectively (with timely and adequate funding), transparently (budget proposals and the budget documents made publicly available in a timely and easily accessible manner) and accountably (through legislative oversight and public scrutiny). (OGP) [161]

- By setting up special fast-track legal cells with public monitoring agencies (Team India along with other players like media, CSOs , global agencies etc) to scrutinize all the candidates before and after elections; conducting speedy trials and high priority cases under public and media limelight, making politics a high risk, low gains zone instead of low risk, high gains zone. That would keep candidates with criminal records or charges out of the system and would encourage honest people to enter politics. By ensuring zero corruption and 100% transparency system and processes in campaign financing and other budgetary processes or introducing revolutionary structures like state financing for election and keeping a cutoff /maximum- minimum expenditure sealing; a revolutionary reform in Indian politics can be brought. It would eliminate the use of money and muscle power in the election process that has blocked honest, compassionate and socially motivated people from entering politics for so long.

It is high time that we dismantled the old democratic model and processes that are no longer working for the higher collective good and opt for better systems and practices that work for all. It is high time to review and reform our election system and processes and come up with better processes and practices like introducing direct democracy and participatory practices that are the truest forms of democracy and can provide a solution for all the social, economic and political issues in the country.

Another pertinent question we need to ask ourselves is whether we, as a highly diversified society, are matured enough for parliamentary democracy based on the British model? Has it served the purpose it was meant for? Is it truly representative of our people ….is it not a scourge of our current ills? With the majority of our population living in abject poverty and illiteracy and no minimum threshold or qualification required for entering politics, we have a large number of politicians from criminal backgrounds whose only reason to do politics is to enjoy the perks of power, accumulate illegitimate wealth and seek political impunity. In a country like ours where vote bank politics have polarized society, votes are bought by bribing or misleading naïve voters, money and muscle power rule the election process; horse trading (buying MPs and MLAs for proving majority), dynastical sycophancy, ideal worship, party coercions, policy or ideology limitations are the political norms; direct democracy seems to be the only way to ensure reliable and accountable governance and democratic panacea. More so, it will encourage renowned, honest, sincere, and above all educated and enlightened people to come forward as potential leaders.

If only people of India could opt for direct democracy and select honest candidates directly bypassing party politics and money power; a new era of democracy in the country can begin. In the current form of our representative democracy, people give away their potent democratic power and destinies to a few people that is a dangerous practice as we know that absolute power corrupts and makes people egotistical that, in turn, leads to abuse and misuse of power and politics in the country. True democracy is a participatory democracy where people have a control over policies and decisions as we explored earlier, and direct democracy will ensure that the power is properly balanced in the system. By combining civil activism and judicial activism with technology, Team India should strive to set a model for direct democracy where by using the information interface and social accountability tools, citizens can participate in electing honest candidates with proven credentials and clean backgrounds instead of choosing parties with limited options and undeserving candidates. Voters would also be free to approve or reject particular issues rather than be compelled to agree with limited visions and ideologies of political parties. Using the web and mobile technologies, a transparent and direct participatory interface on national issues and election process can be created that can revolutionize the democratic and political landscape in the country.

A similar review and revolutionary reform programs for other pillars like Parliament, Judiciary, Police, Anti-corruption agencies etc. will establish a new system of integrity based on water-tight processes, 0 corruption & 100% transparency- accountability model. It would create such a solid foundation of the new temple of Integrity that governments may come and go, the core structure of India's integrity and democracy will be held intact by its people forever!

This new integrity infrastructure, combined with citizens' information interface (social accountability infrastructure) and sustainable development goals framework; recommended by the United Nation based on achieving environmental sustainability, economic development and social inclusion; can make India realize its full potential and push it into the category of developed nations with high social and economic progress- on its way to becoming the next Asian miracle economy that it so deserves!

C) **Creating a National Information Infrastructure – (social accountability infrastructure)**

Demand-side accountability, also known as social accountability, refers to a broad range of actions and mechanisms beyond voting that citizens can use to hold the state and providers of public services accountable. Demand-side measures for financial accountability include publicly accessible local governments financial information(including budgets, end-of-year financial statements and periodic implementation progress reports during fiscal year); public involvement in budgetary process through participatory budgeting practices; gender-sensitive planning, budgeting, and resource allocation, reinforced by gender audits; independent budget analysis and participatory public expenditure tracking programs that monitor budget execution and leakage of funds. **(Schaeffer ,Yilmaz)**[162]

Elements of social accountability - (As defined by UNDP)[111]

Preparing community and civil society groups to engage—includes raising the awareness of citizens, building confidence and capacity for engagement, building networks and coalitions.

Collecting, analyzing and using information—includes finding, securing and analyzing information on government's activities, translating it into different formats, styles and languages, and sharing it through the media and social and political networks.

Undertaking accountability engagements with governments—includes using instruments such as scorecards, audits and budget analysis to engage with a government, either by using existing formalized spaces for participation in planning or policy cycles or by developing new ones, or by mobilizing social protests.

Using information from accountability engagements with governments—includes advocacy, lobbying and campaigning work to follow up on the delivery of commitments.

Broadly defined, accountability is the obligation of power-holders to take responsibility for their actions. It describes the dynamics of rights and responsibilities that exist between people and the institutions that have an impact on their lives, in particular,

the relationship between the duties of the state and the entitlements of citizens (UNDP)[163]

At its core principle, social accountability can be described as a vibrant, dynamic and accountable relationship between states and citizens supporting each other's efforts to ensure sustainable and equitable development. There are two popular forms of accountability i.e. 'horizontal' or 'vertical' as we discussed before. Horizontal accountability operates within the parallel pillars of the state (executive, legislature, judicial bodies,), providing formal, institutional checks and balances to guard against abuse of power; vertical accountability operates outside the state. Social accountability is known as bottom-up or demand-side accountability as unlike other forms of vertical accountability, such as periodic elections, social accountability can be exercised on a continuous basis or can be demanded as against the supply side accountability that is supplied by various pillars. It is a form of participatory democracy that allows the proactive and informed citizenry to engage directly in governance activities ranging from local service delivery and budget planning to national development policies, demand complete transparency and accountability, and play their role in constructing states that are more democratic.(UNDP)[164]

Building an information infrastructure that would work as a two-way interface (G2C-C2G, using citizens' clouds and e-governance clouds) as discussed before, is crucial for social accountability to work and achieve improved e-governance, transparency and accountability in the country. It would create an interactive platform that would allow citizens to seek information from governments in such areas as policies, budgets, expenditures or compliance with national and international legal frameworks as well as develop new, innovative and creative solutions for easy access to information and improved quality of services. The platform can also educate citizens on their rights and make them more aware about legal and institutional procedures; encouraging active and effective participatory democratic structures, practices and processes. Team India should collect, analyze and present data in more interactive, innovative and easy to understand formats with graphics, flowcharts and tracking mechanisms in real time for empowering citizens to hold their governments and public employees accountable for their policies, decisions and actions.

Data revolution

Team India should adopt innovative global data initiatives and harness new data collection techniques, technologies and methods to move India towards an advanced data culture and statistical literacy and use more sophisticated approaches to produce and analyze data and for data visualization, and communication.

The traditional data collection methods like official data, household survey, administrative, and census data, is found somewhat limited and inadequate to meet the data challenges in the country. The rapid rise of innovative technologies and widespread scope and capacity of data to play a critical role in national policies and programs has raised the bar. This data revolution can change the way governments and public sector use statistics, analyze data, and modernize the entire data process. Team India must use these innovative approaches to build the information infrastructure suggested by SDSN (Sustainable development solutions network):[165]

Satellite imagery: The cost of high-resolution image acquisition is falling while the availability of images and capacity for automated processing are increasing. There are many applications for such data across multiple goals, such as predicting harvests, disaster response, earth observations, and food security situations; monitoring geographic patterns and likely transmission corridors of diseases that have geospatial determinants; measuring population density and the spread of new settlements; and mapping and planning of transportation infrastructure.

Crowd-sourcing: Global connectivity has created the opportunity for wide-scale participation in data collection and data processing, with applications in road mapping, land cover classification, human rights monitoring, price tracking, species inventories, and disaster response planning, and new applications unfolding regularly.

Smart-meters: The increasing use of smart-metered systems for energy and water distribution, which transmit usage information over communications networks, create novel capabilities to measure and manage service provision. Enel's Telegestore system in Italy is one of the largest and most successful examples.

Smartphone and tablet-based data collection: As described in the SDSN indicator report, many surveys are now being conducted on digital mobile platforms. This practice reduces time and cost for data collection, improves accuracy, simplifies collection of GIS and image data, streamlines integration with other information streams, and opens up the possibility of incorporating micro-chip based sensors into survey processes.

Data mining: New uses have been discovered for data sources emerging from processes not explicitly designed for such purposes, such as social media, mobile call data records, commercial transactions, and traffic records. Proven applications have been developed in a range of areas including crisis response, urban planning, and public health management.(UNSDSN)[113]

Though we have a good digital e-governance framework in the country and there are some good initiatives like Digital India, The National e-Governance Plan (NEGP), Digital India program, G2G, G2B, G2C, OPEN DATA, PRAGATI and other data portals , inter-departmental websites etc. but the information and data provided is not sufficient and leaves a lot to be desired. Our ITC system needs to be more users friendly, transparent and concise. There is a need for more effective and user-friendly citizen-centric interface and convergence of various data portals and information. Like in the Open Data platforms, some very critical datasets are unavailable or outdated, duplicated, incomprehensive and incomplete. The formats also need to be updated, which is more compatible and easily downloadable across devices. The icons and interfaces are not interactive or user-friendly, making it difficult to analyze or compare the datasets. The policies are not very clear and interdepartmental coordination and data sharing is inconsistent.

There is a need for better infrastructure and internet availability. Moreover, there is no awareness about these initiatives amongst the common public and concerned groups. Digital India is a good initiative of the Government of India to integrate the government departments. It aims at ensuring that government services are made available to citizens electronically by eliminating paperwork. But as we see time and again, such great initiatives and programs are launched with great hope and vision but their proper implementation and monitoring is another story.

We need more portals like "Transparency portal" for information on government's spending and fund transfers data, Open Budget Index, "Open Data Portal "for information on government's expenditure and parliamentary proceedings data, "Where Do My Tax rupees Go?" or " Follow the Money" portals where citizens could see in real time how their governments spend taxpayer money and which government service providers receive the largest contracts. Citizens should be able to see the relationships between the various city agencies and the companies that benefit from service contracts and be able to compare the percentage of public spending that goes to education, infrastructure, public transportation in real time. Through these portals, people can share relevant information with each other and with governments, such as the state of infrastructure like roads or school buildings, or if the budget was well and truly spent on deliverable public goods and services like health care. This would create awareness for public policies and programs especially in the outcomes, and help us to measure actual results against the expectations and standards set by policy-makers.

There are many ICT-based social accountability tools, approaches, initiatives and guidelines by many global agencies and organizations like Open Governments' Data, UNDP, Transparency International etc. that have been used in many countries across the world to increase e-governance' effectiveness and ensuring better public service delivery. Team India – Think Tank can design the "short route 'via direct accountability relationships between users and service providers by using a range of innovative transparency and accountability approaches and initiatives from better institutionalized forms of co-governance to public expenditure tracking surveys, citizen report cards and score cards , citizens' feedback loops, community monitoring, aids transparency and social audits etc.[166]

Significant moves in democratization and good governance like participatory budgeting and improved public finance management also have been taken in many countries along with citizen juries and other forms of public hearings, participatory monitoring of national development policies and their outcomes, aids transparency that not only can help increasing the efficiency and transparency & accountability but also make the citizens exercise and claim their democratic rights.

Some more Transparency and Accountability Initiatives around the world are technology-based transparency data portals like US' "We the people" portal, that is a direct interface between president's office and citizen, "Brazil's Transparency Portal" that disseminates information on government spending and fund transfers data, U.K.'s 'Where Does My Money Go' that tracks public spending by open knowledge foundation and citizens report card in Chile. In Mexico, transparency organization developed "Where Do My Taxes Go?" to track budget spending in different sectors and in Argentina, follow the Money trail like "Bahia Blanca's Public Spending" is another tool that allows citizens to monitor public contracts to various agencies and compare the percentage of public spending in various sectors like education, infrastructure, health or public transport etc. in real time as all the municipalities use the same accounting software.

In an innovative endeavor to help inform governments, civil society and the private sector in developing their OGP commitments, the Transparency and Accountability Initiative (T/AI) invited leading experts across the world to share their expertise and inputs in open government best practices and practical steps that the governments around the world could follow to achieve openness. They covered the 'state of the art' in transparency, accountability and citizen participation across 16 areas of governance, ranging from broad categories such as access to information, service delivery and budgeting to more specific sectors such as forestry, procurement and climate finance and published their findings in form of a guide on best practice in transparency, accountability and civic engagement across the public sector. [167]

The Initiatives included following topics –

1. **Aid transparency (Publish What You fund)**
2. **Asset disclosure (Global Integrity)**
3. **Budgets (The International Budget project)**
4. **Campaign finance**

5. Climate finance
6. Electoral transparency, participation & accountability
8. Environment transparency, participation and justice
11. Financial sector reform
13. Land transparency
14. Military and intelligence budgets
15. National security transparency and accountability
16. Open government data
17. Police and public security
18. Procurement – Transparency
19. Right to information

This information interface can make a new social accountability structure that would enhance and complement the existing horizontal and vertical accountability mechanisms in the country and would make government systems, legislatures and bureaucracies at every level, from capital cities to isolated rural areas, become transparent and accountable to the citizens for their decisions, policies, institutions, processes and activities. Using the social tools i.e. voice, participation and empowerment, citizens can push the governments to be more responsive to their rights and agendas (people's manifestos - national action plan) ultimately transforming them into responsive, inclusive, welfare states and perform their constitutional role and duties, that is the most important democratic function of the states in order to re-establish their legitimacy on an on-going basis as against the traditional accountability mechanisms, such as periodic elections.

Team India should develop a comprehensive framework to utilize various global approaches and tools with the aims to dismantle the existing faulty systems , plug all the loopholes and cracks and reform and revolutionize old, outdated institutions, processes and practices to create a new system based on integrity, transparency and accountability, time bound performance-based policies and action plans . The new framework must include strong review and monitoring techniques, innovative and adaptive strategies and measures, more inclusive and integrated engagement with all stakeholders in the country i.e. community, media, civil, public, private sectors etc.to ensure a sustainable transformation.

Furthermore, through this interactive information interface, Team India can make people of India along with other stakeholders ie Media, civil organizations, watchdog agencies etc. take stock of the national resources and revenues and ensure their proper and equitable distribution and utilization. By creating transparent structures, processes and accountability mechanisms, better policies and budget analytical tools and services; team India can enable citizens, media and other pressure groups to monitor every policy, track every rupee going in the system to its targeted end to evaluate the outcomes and commitments of governments and hold them accountable for the same. It would address a range of issues prevalent in our system today i.e. uneven social progress and development, wastage of revenue through systemic loopholes, leakages or corruption; mismanagement and unequal distribution of national wealth and resources, misplaced policies and priorities, manipulation and lapses between targets and outcomes to name a few...

D) Creating a National strategy and Action Plan

(Public Manifesto – National mandate)

Building new integrity system and social accountability (information) infrastructure, however, is only half the battle won. These systems would lay the foundation of trust, the rule of law, integrity, accountability, transparency, and participatory democracy. To build a new India that works for all and fulfill the dream of ever Indian of living a quality life in peace and harmony with ample opportunities to progress and prosper, team India should integrate UN sustainable development goals (a blueprint for achieving these dreams) with these systems into a comprehensive, holistic, national strategy framework and develop a time-bound national action plan.

The United Nation (UN) has offered a comprehensive framework for achieving sustainable goals (17 SDG's) [168] that is signed by the most governments all over the world including India, written to people and the planet to eradicate poverty in all its dimensions, strengthening universal peace and freedom and improving the environment. The SDGs contain a universal agenda for addressing the most pressing national and global challenges of the day as part of a shared commitment to end poverty, inequality and injustice regardless of where or how it occurs. [169] They represent once-in-a-lifetime opportunity to achieve peaceful societies and a sustainable future for all citizens, and governments all over the world have pledged to actively engage in SDG implementation through an inclusive approach focusing on People – Peace – Prosperity – Planet – Partnerships.

The **architecture of the UN SDG Agenda** is defined in the outcome Document that is presented in the form of a 'Declaration' preceded by a 'Preamble' in which, the following five fundamental principles are intended to lead the way of the implementation:

People: We are determined to end poverty and hunger, in all their forms and dimensions, and to ensure that all human beings can fulfill their potential in dignity and equality and in a healthy environment;

Planet: We are determined to protect the planet from degradation, including through sustainable consumption and production, sustainably managing its natural resources and taking urgent action on climate change, so that it can support the needs of the present and future generations;

Prosperity: We are determined to ensure that all human beings can enjoy prosperous and fulfilling lives and that economic, social and technological progress occurs in harmony with nature;

Peace: We are determined to foster peaceful, just and inclusive societies, which are free from fear and violence. There can be no sustainable development without peace and no peace without sustainable development;

Partnership: We are determined to mobilize the means required to implement this Agenda through a revitalized Global Partnership for Sustainable Development, based on a spirit of strengthened global solidarity, focused in particular on the needs of the poorest and most vulnerable and with the participation of all countries, all stakeholders and all people.

This Declaration contains **17 SDGs** and **169 targets**.[170]

UN List of proposed Sustainable Development Goals (SDGs) -

Goal 1: End poverty in all its forms everywhere
Goal 2: End hunger, achieve food security and improved nutrition, and promote sustainable agriculture
Goal 3: Ensure healthy lives and promote well-being for all at all ages
Goal 4: Ensure inclusive and equitable quality education and promote life-long learning opportunities for all
Goal 5: Achieve gender equality and empower all women and girls
Goal 6: Ensure availability and sustainable management of water and sanitation for all
Goal 7: Ensure access to affordable, reliable, sustainable, and modern energy for all
Goal 8: Promote sustained, inclusive and sustainable economic growth, full and productive employment and decent work for all
Goal 9: Build resilient infrastructure, promote inclusive and sustainable industrialization and foster innovation
Goal 10: Reduce inequality within and among countries
Goal 11: Make cities and human settlements inclusive, safe, resilient and sustainable
Goal 12: Ensure sustainable consumption and production patterns
Goal 13: Take urgent action to combat climate change and its impacts
Goal 14: Conserve and sustainably use the oceans, seas and marine resources for sustainable development
Goal 15: Protect, restore and promote sustainable use of terrestrial ecosystems, sustainably manage forests, combat desertification, and halt and reverse land degradation and halt biodiversity loss
Goal 16: Promote peaceful and inclusive societies for sustainable development, provide access to justice for all and build effective, accountable and inclusive institutions at all levels

Goal 17: Strengthen the means of implementation and revitalize global partnership for sustainable development.

(UN SDG document) [170]

This new set of SDGs requires setting national priorities and policies and creating a national action plan for achieving structural economic, environmental and political transformation across the country in order to ensure 'no one is left behind". It also requires ensuring good governance, well designed and prioritized policies, transparent and accountable processes, efficient public service delivery, effective national reforms, inclusive and participatory democratic practices, a robust social accountability infrastructure and the effective rule of law.

The holistic nature of the SDGs and systematic approach for financing, implementing and monitoring them, have set them apart from any other previous goals or plans. The approach provides a comprehensive framework for achieving them through the involvement of all stakeholders in the country (governments, citizens, media, private sector, other national and local actors) and for actions at the national and local levels. The SDG also provides an important benchmark for evaluating government's activities. Though, government's think tank and task forces (NITI AYOG and concerned ministries) have taken up the task of implementing the goals yet, the current fragmented approach; based on divided roles and goals between ministries without any comprehensive vision, integrated strategy or adequate citizen participation or consultation; misses the holistic nature of sustainable development. The lack of coordination and integration would increase the risk of working in silos and unable to deliver as warned by the UN.

That is what the recent performance of India in the latest UN Sustainable Development Goals index -2016; that assesses where countries stand with regards to achieving the SDGs and ensuring accountability for that; showed that we have a long way to go as India scored very low at 110th position. India is still way behind its peer groups like Russia (47th), China(76) and a long way from

Sweden (1st), Denmark (2nd), Norway (3rd), UK (10th) etc. to achieve the dream of inclusive, sustainable growth and development for all.

Many global reports and researchers conclude that the success or failure of the countries to achieve these ambitious goals depends on how policies, processes and relations are structured, organized and refined. Some common factors for failure to achieve these goals are- lack of institutional reforms especially public sector reforms, working in silos, unequal distribution and mismanagement of national resources, corruption, lack of transparency and accountability, inadequate data and knowledge gaps, resistance to change and inability to mainstream SDGs into national integrated strategy and plan; lack of social inclusion (stakeholder involvement) and social accountability spaces and most importantly, lack of rights-based approaches such as the right to information or the right to carry out social audits on the use of public funds.

On the other hand, the supporting factors that help countries to successfully implement these goals are –a supportive political system, effective planning agencies and engagement in development of SDGs, using integrated approaches and processes, reliable data and access to information, capacity building for media and civil society, increased public awareness and public participation etc. There have also been various analyses of many positive experiences that show how social accountability principles, practices, and social inclusion have resulted in the successful development outcomes. Involving citizens, media and private sector ensures higher potential utilization and lead to more resources mobilization. Such integrated approach also helps in finding innovative, creative solutions and in harnessing collective potential, expertise and efforts to achieve the shared goals.

That is what the primary requirement set in the UN development agenda and the SDG commitments signed by the governments (goals 16 and 17); that demands continued efforts to broad consultation with and participation of all stakeholders (Governments, citizens, media, private sectors etc.) in designing, implementation and monitoring of development strategies and to strengthening partnerships between stakeholders. The UN agenda states that such a colossal and ambitious task of successful implementation, monitoring and realization of these goals cannot be achieved by the governments alone. It is a national task and a national responsibility that would depend on more inclusive, efficient and comprehensive engagements; commitments and partnerships between all the stakeholders in the country.[171]

In fact, the UN Sustainable Development Goals Agenda has clear-cut themes like: "Goals need to be universal. Ending inequality is paramount. Women, children, youth, indigenous peoples, marginalized communities and differently abled people must be at the center of development. The responsibilities of the rich and powerful need to be spelled out. It is critical to respect and build upon the principle of equitable sharing of atmospheric space, taking into account historical responsibility between and within states as well as inter-generational justice. Commitments by all stakeholders must be time-bound; accountability and transparency are also paramount. Leaving no one behind must mean 'no goal should be met unless it is met for everyone' and ensuring that every citizen receives the opportunities and benefits promised in the SDGs."[109]

"We need your continued pressure to align the investment toward sustainable development. We need your full support for 2015 and beyond (...) we need to keep the doors open for civil society. (...) You are the voice of the people. You can count on the UN. And, please, make your voice loud and clear."

- **UN chief Ban Ki-Moon on civil society's role for SDG[172]**

UN agendas for sustainable development through the years have recognized nine key sectors of society or "major groups" as the main channels through which citizens and people could organize and participate in sustainable development processes. These include women, children and youth, indigenous peoples, non-governmental organizations, local authorities, workers and trade unions, business and industry, the scientific and technological community, and farmers. The outcome document of United Nations Conference on Sustainable

Development in Rio "The Future We Want", reaffirmed that sustainable development requires the meaningful involvement and active participation of regional, national and sub-national legislatures and judiciaries, and all major groups as well as other stakeholders, including local communities, volunteer groups and foundations, media and private sector, older persons and persons with disabilities. In the same document, Member States agreed to work more closely with the major groups and other stakeholders, and encourage their active participation; as appropriate, in processes that contribute to decision-making, planning and implementation of policies and programs for sustainable development at all levels. [172]

The recent Sustainable Development Agenda made several references and mandates for engaging civil society, the major groups and other stakeholders in its implementation and follow-up, according to the Preamble [109], "all countries and all stakeholders acting in collaborative partnership will implement this plan". Other references like - "This Partnership will work in a spirit of global solidarity, in particular solidarity with the poorest and with people in vulnerable situations. It will facilitate an intensive global engagement in support of the implementation of all the Goals and targets, bringing together Governments, the private sector, civil society, the United Nations system and other actors and mobilizing all available resources along with international institutions, academia, philanthropic organizations, volunteer groups and others." In fact, the UN charter has put people at the center of all its agendas with the celebrated words "We the Peoples". The sustainable development goals agenda states - This Agenda is a plan of action for people, planet and prosperity. "We are embarking today on the road to 2030. Our journey will involve Governments as well as Parliaments, the UN system and other international institutions, local authorities, civil society, business and the private sector, the scientific and academic community – and all people. Millions have already engaged with, and will own, this Agenda. It is an Agenda of the people, by the people, and for the people – and this, we believe, will ensure its success." [173]

It further states- "The revitalized Global Partnership will facilitate an intensive global engagement in support of implementation of all the Goals and targets, bringing together Governments, civil society, the private sector, the United Nations system and other actors and mobilizing all available resources", committed to be "robust, voluntary, effective, participatory, transparent and integrated with a principle for follow up and review at all levels to be "open, inclusive, participatory and transparent for all people" and, most importantly that they "will support the reporting by all relevant stakeholders". It also affirms that reviews will be "people-centered, gender-sensitive, respect human rights and have a particular focus on the poorest, most vulnerable and those furthers behind".[173]

The reviews are expected to be regular and inclusive at all levels. "We also encourage Member States to conduct regular and inclusive reviews of progress at the national and sub-national levels which are country-led and country-driven. They shall provide a platform for partnerships, including through the participation of major groups i.e. Civil society, the private sector and other stakeholders, and will engage all relevant stakeholders and, where possible, feed into, and be aligned with, the cycle of the high-level political forum and encourage and promote effective public, public-private and civil society partnerships, building on the experience and resourcing strategies of partnerships." [185]

In that context, it is time for team India - think tank along with all the stakeholders to reflect on lessons from various SDG-related global experiences and social accountability initiatives and figure out how they can further bring positive reforms in service delivery through building integrity and social accountability (ICT based information) infrastructure and support governments to deliver progress towards the SDGs and develop a new framework based on multi-stakeholder partnerships and multi-pronged approaches . At the same time, pushing governments and public sector to make appropriate democratic changes like more open and participatory policy culture and practices, encouraging public participation in order to build dynamic social accountability relationship between governments and citizens instead of continuing with old dominating technocratic policy culture and practices that remain insulated from public scrutiny and alienate public from participating in nation building activities. These initiatives would create a democratic space and framework for citizens along with media and private sector to build capacity, take collective decisions and actions to play their roles as active, empowered citizens with rights instead of being passive spectators or vote banks.

Experts all over the world have identified some key priorities for achieving improved country performance to accelerate progress on the SDGs. Among them are increased data transparency and local accountability in planning and implementation, support to community participation and partnerships, and inclusion, which means specifically targeting public services to address inequality, discrimination and social exclusion.[174]

The task for team India along with other players, therefore, would be empowering citizens to participate actively in various governments activities i.e. creating a national platform for citizen participation and bringing all the stakeholders together, especially social groups with little or no voice and ensuring no one is left behind; raising awareness through various media outlets and channels; filling data and knowledge gaps; taking stock of existing SDG policies, implementation and monitoring framework and prioritizing according to social needs and demands; actively participating in policy cycle (design, implementation, monitoring and evaluation) budget monitoring or deciding development strategies; developing legal framework and transparent and effective accountability mechanisms to protect and exercise citizens' rights. It would open doors for more social inclusion in political space particularly, in those policies and decisions that affect the lives of citizens such as fiscal, monetary and financial policies for development strategies.

Many social accountability initiatives and tools like - social auditing of economic policies and legal analysis of their impact on basic democratic rights that go beyond participatory policy making and budgeting initiatives can bring a healthy integration and balance between macroeconomic policies with microeconomic /

social policies. Through such audit tools, citizens can identify which policies are violating or contradicting their fundamental constitutional rights and take appropriate actions or push alternative policies to counter such negative impacts. For instance, deep cuts in social spending or in crucial sectors like agriculture, education or health may show a violation of government's commitments to welfare state policies and constitutional directive principles. In other words, Team India and citizen's participation, empowerment and affirmative actions, along with other stakeholder's support, would make a sea of difference in India's performance in achieving the sustainable development goals and bring the dream of democracy - peace, progress and prosperity for all, within people's reach. Through active participation and empowered engagement in SDG process, equipped with integrity and social accountability tools; people of India can finally claim their roles and responsibilities in nation building and be the masters of their own destinies!

It would require setting up national integrity system and social accountability (ICT-enabled) infrastructure to ensure a vibrant, dynamic and accountable relationship between states and citizens supporting each other's efforts to promote sustainable and equitable development, improved e-governance, Improved efficiency of public service delivery, increased responsiveness of services to a range of users; Improved budget utilization, better social inclusion - especially of vulnerable, marginalized and traditionally excluded groups in policy formulation and implementation, reduced corruption and improved transparency and accountability in the country.(UNDP) [175]

Collaborating with global organizations like UNDP, TI, OECD, SDSN and Open Governments data (OGP) etc. for various social accountability initiatives and guidelines for SDG implementation and monitoring; will support and advance the ambitious aims of the goals. Moreover, it would build new democratic spaces for participatory democracy and political engagement and ensure that existing spaces are used to the best possible effect to enhance development outcomes by strengthening links between governments and citizens.

This would also require bringing all stakeholders on the same platform, mobilizing all available resources, combing strengths, experiences, potentials and fighting weaknesses. We should draw lessons from the past planning, reform failures and other countries' successful strategies and develop a comprehensive new national strategy to realize the goals. A multi-dimensional, multi-stakeholder partnership based holistic and integrated multi-pronged strategy; combining technical and professional expertise of various sectors; involving state and non-state actors and other implementing partners to link all the stakeholders with a shared goals platform. Moreover, it would create a national framework that can serve as the guiding post for bringing all cross-sectoral policies, collaborative initiatives and activities together – converging to achieve the common goals. Such a comprehensive approach would promote greater synchronization, policy cohesion, integrated approaches and set a benchmark for measuring progress.

Team India- think tank should develop a comprehensive framework (using the key principles and global guidelines) for a national strategy and a national action plan after an extensive dialogue and consultation process involving all the stakeholders.

To set the ball rolling, the SDG implementation process should start with:

- Creating a national democratic space for all the stake-holders to come together and understand the SDG Agenda,

- Start an inclusive dialogue on SDG implementation,

- Prepare an SDG framework and national strategy and align existing plans and strategies with desired outcomes

- Develop a national action plan

Though, local, state and national governments are essential for promoting inclusive sustainable development within their territories and are the main stakeholders in the implementation of the SDGs yet, creating a national plan will require effective and responsive governance that can ensure the inclusion of various stakeholders, creating broad-based ownership, commitment and Accountability. It would require an integrated multi-level and multi-stakeholder approach to promote transformative agendas at the local and national level along with a strong national commitment to provide adequate legal frameworks and institutional and financial capacity to meet the goals.

To be accountable and transparent, a monthly and annual reporting system has to be in place on what is being done to achieve the goals, both domestically and globally, with policy framework ie through social, economic, foreign, environmental, business and industrial policies. These reports must be made publicly available on the public information interface. Team India must join the reporting process, with the aim of ensuring a joint understanding of progress and further priorities. In order to review the progress on the SDGs, especially on the national level, governments must establish such a baseline with clearly defined indicators that make it possible to review progress and make necessary adjustments. Nation-wide ownership should be established through a broad-based partnership that includes citizens along with media, private sector and other groups.

Governments are ultimately responsible for implementation, but team India along with other stakeholders can contribute as implementing partners and as a driving force- through mobilization and by raising awareness to make sure that the Goals are on track. Ultimately, the achievement of goals would rest on the role citizens- team India and other players would play as empowered partners to promote, implement and monitor SDGs and as watchdogs to ferociously guard the policies, budgets and processes by directly engaging with national and local governments. This requires more transparency on national budgets and priorities, and more social inclusion – citizens' participation on every stage of the policymaking, planning, implementation, monitoring and reporting process.

Team India along with other stakeholders can contribute to SDG achievement through:

1. **Engagement and participation:**

   Creating a national democratic space (establishing social accountability based information infrastructure with a two way governments-citizen interface) for facilitating direct and constructive dialogues and actions through various stakeholders' (Team India, citizens, media, private sector, marginalized sections, and other national and local players) participation and engagement in the SDG process. By bringing all the stakeholders on the same platform would build trust as well as form a social bridge between diverse groups and people who are not used to interacting with each other. This in turn would develop a sense of opportunity, responsibility and ownership for SDG challenges, enhance knowledgebase, strengthen local governance and accountability through increased people's participation, and build an enabling environment for various stakeholders especially private sector and civic engagement to mobilize them to share expertise ,creative and innovative solutions and leverage collective action, and engagement across all Goals.

2. Raising Awareness:

Improving stakeholders' understanding and recognition of the value of national and global goals for sustainable development through various media outlets i.e. TV, Internet, print media, social media, local campaigns and other creative approaches; especially in villages, remote areas and with marginalized populations. Raising awareness would get local actors play an active role in the localization of the SDGs and support them to make decisions that contribute towards the achievement of the SDGs.

3. **Advocacy and social empowerment:**

Improving stakeholders' ability to participate and influence the setting of the national policies and action goals during planning, implementation, monitoring and evaluation of the SDG Agenda at local and national level with government and is machinery; would promote human rights, social justice and equity in a way that empowers people, promotes gender equality, recognizes the rights of citizens and protects environment. [176] It would also ensure equal distribution of wealth, resources, opportunities etc. within the country and among present and future generations.

Team India along with citizens can become the voice of the voiceless by including marginalized and deprived sections, youth and women in the national policy making process promoting social accountability, combining social activism with judicial activism to create legal framework to protect democratic constitutional rights and provisions to ensure that no one is left behind. Following the social accountability tools and guidelines from various global organizations and networks like UNDP, OECD, OGP, and SDSN etc., Team India should adopt a human rights approach that will enable identification of groups of people whose rights have been violated, neglected or overlooked in development processes or checking discriminatory laws or social practices that propagate inequality. [177]

Increasing the visibility, inclusivity and impact of advocacy activities and policy responses by using the social accountability (information) infrastructure; Team India should use this space to Identify, engage with, learn from other civil groups and organizations and highlight the actions, pilot projects or remedies that are not effective or unproductive. In this space, using various civil mobilization practices such as research advocacy, lobbying for civil rights, legal aids, collecting public opinion, raising public awareness, sharing technical expertise, filling data and knowledge gaps, monitoring, evaluation and outcome gaps along with other actions, Team India with other players can push the policy agenda and play a critical role as transformers in society which would help building capacities and increase knowledge of citizens towards achieving the SDGs. This will make sure that people become the focus of the SDGs and that the most vulnerable in society are not left behind when these global development goals are being designed and implemented.

4) **Strengthening Governance**:

By ensuring that all stakeholders contribute to policy design, service planning and delivery government not only can improve quality of service, policy effectiveness but also reinforce the legitimacy of the decision-making process and its results and reduce the likelihood and costs of non-compliance. (OGP)[178]

Team India with other stakeholders, using integrity and social accountability infrastructure and tools can support the governance systems and institutions to effectively deliver ambitious and inclusive global goals. Pushing governments to adopt open government data initiative- strategies and practices for instance, would promote the principles of accountability, participation and transparency in the process and engaging citizens, civil society organizations and the private sector as partners to pursue SDG through the policy cycle (namely, during their design, implementation, monitoring and evaluation) would ensure that their needs are identified and responded to leading to higher user satisfaction.

While national and local governments hold primary responsibility for delivering services in their country, the other stakeholders i.e. Team India, Citizens, private sector etc. can also play a key role by collectively shaping requirements, developing policies and demanding better service deliveries particularly in situations where there is a lack of capacity, capability or the will to provide essential services by governments and public sector. They can also identify creative and innovative alternatives to development policies and actions that would better suit the needs of people. The Governments (states and central) must respond to the SDG goals by developing effective institutions and ensuring responsive, inclusive and participatory decision making process by co-coordinating public policy framework. At the same time, address the issues and problems arising from poorly designed and implemented policies that lead to loss of trust, legitimacy and resources. Many countries have moved beyond consultation, towards more advanced forms of participation, and providing citizens and businesses the opportunity to be involved in the co-design and co-delivery of public services.

Going beyond the design and adoption of policies, making citizens an essential component in the implementation of public policies, increasing public understanding and support, designing processes such as co-design and co-production, in which citizens along with service professionals, participate in the design and delivery of the public services; can make participatory democracy a critical factor in achieving the goals. As the UN SDG agenda demands a high degree of policy co-ordination and coherence horizontally (across ministries and agencies), as well as vertically (across levels of governments); it would require significant resources in capacity building, new data and reporting mechanisms and close coordination between governments and citizens to ensure data relevance.[179]

5) Data Collection, Reporting and Monitoring - The progress of SDG in the country would depend on the crucial key processes as suggested by SDSN[180]-

- Collecting reliable data using data revolution, harnessing new technologies and new sources of data

- Building strong national monitoring indicators and

- Increasing statistical capacity

We know data is the most important factor in measuring the effect and impact of SDG process as it is clear that data gaps, the insufficient use of data and differences in indicator values and traditional forms of large-scale data collection delay and hamper the SDG process. To address these issues, the SDSN and UN suggested a "data revolution":

"data collection systems should be low-cost and reliable, and they should ultimately ensure that data is accurate, timely and immediately available to policymakers, the public and CSOs .The data revolution needs to be an inclusive and transparent process that includes statistical experts, CSOs, national human rights institutions, service providers and marginalized populations Furthermore, data should be disaggregated, should focus on the local level and be crowd-based to capture statistics about the most poor, vulnerable and marginalized citizens of society". To realize this ambition, there needs to be adaptable tools for data collection, monitoring and evaluation of processes related to the implementation of the SDGs. Recent improvements in information technology, such as the innovative use of mobile technology in collecting data, create an opportunity to enhance statistics for accountability and decision-making purposes and to create new forms of participatory monitoring .This could be used by citizens to enhance governments and service-provider accountability .(UN, SDSN)[181]

Team India, using information infrastructure (online interactive public interface) must harness new data revolution to shift the way governments and the public sector use data and analytics and move the country towards a well-developed culture of statistical literacy , data sophistication and modernized approach to data production, use, analytics, visualization, and communication as suggested by UN and SDSN . Team India with its technical expert team and task forces as part of the SDG planning and implementation process, should design a set of SDG indicators; conduct a needs assessment for SDG monitoring and utilize various new and innovative approaches to modernize data generation processes such as: geo-referenced data- satellite imagery, crowd-sourcing, smart-meters, smartphone and tablet-based survey for data collection, data mining such as mobile call and social media data records, traffic records and commercial transactions etc.

As explained in the SDG guide for designing SDG strategies these new methods in addition to traditional methods like official data, household survey, administrative, and census data, will play a critical role for tracking the SDGs and shaping governments' policies and programs in the future. It will facilitate real-time monitoring of development results and help in reviewing and revising policies and plans for effective implementation and outcomes.[182]

Beyond supporting data collection and redesigning it to be used for analysis and review, Team India must play the important role of directly monitoring the local implementation of the SDGs by devising a strong monitoring methodology with strong national indictors to measure the progress in a timely fashion. They can produce shadow reports if the government's reports are found inadequate and highlight the loopholes, missing targets, misplaced policies, mismanagement of resources and needs and plights of most poor and marginalized communities etc. They should also set up an evaluation process to assess whether the implementation of these goals was in lines with the constitutional duties of the governments i.e. good governance, participatory democracy, maintaining the rule of law along with protecting democratic and human rights of all the citizens.

By establishing effective data collection, analysis and report mechanisms, focusing on and aligning with the SDGs, Team India will be able to highlight the areas where the implementation processes of the SDGs are effective or lacking and ensure that governments are delivering on these commitments. It would lead to better mobilization and redirection of resources as well as facilitate the implementation of the SDGs and monitoring activities related to the process.

6) **Taking stock and prioritization**:

As suggested by SDSN, Team India along with other stakeholders should take stock and identify priorities with regards to achieving all seventeen goals before implementation. Team India should also identify creative, innovative, alternate solutions that are missed by government departments that mostly work in silos. Identifying data gaps, knowledge gaps and policy gaps and filling them through collective solutions, technical expertise, best practices and inspired actions will streamline the SDG process and its achievement.

Such an initial snapshot can help discern where India is lagging behind in achieving the SDG targets and which areas need priority goal settings. It can also help checking that the goals and policies are not pitted against each other like development at the cost of environmental degradation of macroeconomic policies at the cost of public welfare etc. Setting priorities would also help mobilizing resources, catalyzing actions and awareness to achieve rapid success in the areas that need transformation. It should include all the sectors and bring all stakeholders - everyone on the table to contribute towards achievement of goals and identify priority areas for action.

Following guidelines are suggested by SDSN for stocktaking and prioritization[183]:

- Identify needs by analyzing existing plans and programs
- Set priorities through multi-level and multi-stakeholder mechanisms, placing particular emphasis on inter-regional, inter-municipal and municipal-regional cooperation, in order to involve as many actors as possible
- Identify and build on synergies and links with national SDG strategies Identify synergies and links within local or regional administrations and adapt existing initiatives and strategies to the SDGs and their targets
- Identify the actions and resources needed to implement priority areas of the SDGs - Draft an ad-hoc SDG-based plan for their territory or align existing plans with the SDGs
- Set up local institutional arrangements and governance frameworks to support the implementation of the SDGs
- Mobilize local and international human, technical and financial resources. This includes reallocating own resources, setting up partnerships with universities and other stakeholders, looking for alternative finance channels, pooling and up scaling services and developing capacity building programs
- Involve all local stakeholders in implementation to promote ownership –local, regional governments associations and network.
- Support local and regional governments to improve their human, technical and financial resources
- Promote the exchange of best practices among their members
- Promote decentralized cooperation and effective development cooperation
- Identify policy challenges that impact on the localization of the SDGs and make recommendations for improvement
- Promote the effective and full implementation of commitments to decentralization
- Forge links with key sectoral ministries and the ministry of local governments to collaborate on localization .116

7) Increasing transparency and accountability

Another critical role that Team India should play with the help of other stakeholders (especially with active citizens, media, private sector, judiciary and other law enforcement agencies and local organizations) is, to ensure that governments and public employees are held accountable for SDG process and outcomes. They have to make sure that the social accountability infrastructure includes all the elements of accountability i.e. responsibility, answerability and enforceability as suggested by global experts and agencies.[184]

Responsibility means the authorized staff has well defined duties and performance standards that would make it possible to have a transparent and objective assessment of their behavior. Answerability demands that public officials and institutions present logical and articulate justifications for their actions and decisions to those affected, such as the general public, voters and other institutions. Enforceability requires public institutions to implement mechanisms that measure the degree to which government's officials and institutions abide by established standards, and that enforce sanctions on officials who do not comply and, when needed, ensure that the proper corrective and remedial action is carried out - (SDSN - OHCHR, CESR, 2013). [185]

As SDGs are the commitments from the governments to the people of their countries, governments are responsible for their implementation and answerable to the people for their policies and actions to achieve goals successfully. Failing which, the option of enforceability might be explored by the citizens in the country.

To ensure accountability, Team India and other players should participate and ask to be integrated into development and planning processes at the national and local levels. As we saw earlier, the reasons of SDG failures are closely related to lack of social inclusion and social accountability from the governments. That is why it is critical that Team India, along with citizens and other stakeholders, is included in the SDG process to ensure that policymaking and other SDG related decisions are shaped proactively from an early stage. Getting involved in the full SDG policy cycle (designing, implementing, monitoring, evaluating outcome and impact) would ensure that the SDG initiatives are inclusive and fully reflect public needs. This could be achieved by ensuring that Team India, along with other stakeholders, plays a proactive role as partners in the design of the national SDG strategy and national action plan, as well as in the implementation, monitoring and evaluation of its activities.

Also, using the integrity and social accountability infrastructure, tools and process like citizen charters, participatory budgeting, expenditure tracking, public expenditure tracking surveys and citizen report etc. Team India can highlight the hits and misses and other matters that are not shared by the governments ensuring complete transparency and accountability in the entire process.

Team India with close association with other civil organizations, media and private sector can go form a core group or a task force (sustainable development-prosperity for all) and approach the SDG process in an integrated manner. They can act as a watch dog, guarding budget, aids and other financial issues; analyzing all the existing policies and processes to ensure that government and its agencies align with the SDGs in an integrated and comprehensive manner, ensuring equity of provision and proper distribution of services and benefits for all. Team India should closely monitor government and its machinery (ministries, various departments, associates and agencies etc) to avoid the risk of working in silos and wastage of national resources and revenue due to corruption or mismanagement. They can also explore legal and policy framework to ensure that regular reviews and appropriate corrective measures are taken by governments and its agencies to maintain transparency and accountability in the system. There are many suggestions from various global experts regarding the judicial enforcement route that could identify systematic policy failures and bring structural and institutional changes.

8) Promoting Goal-based partnerships and cross sectoral convergence

As we discussed, the successful implementation and achievement of SDG requires multi stakeholder partnership based on shared goals platform to facilitate multi-lateral association of public, private and other local, national and international actors. Such a partnership would harness strengths of each sector and help overcome the systemic weaknesses by collective solutions and efforts. Team India along with other stakeholders must set up an SDG based goals framework with transparent processes, comprehensive integrated approaches, well designed monitoring and evaluation mechanisms and time bound action plans with clearly defined roles and responsibilities of concerned ministries and authorities. The guidelines to set up goals should be:

- Goals have to be analyzed extensively and pursued with integrated approach taking into consideration all dimensions of sustainable development (social, economic and environmental).
- Goals must aim to promote peace, inclusive societies and the rule of law as the basic conditions to achieve sustainable development.
- Goals have to be comprehensive aligning various themes and avoid conflicting policies and interests.
- Goals have to be universal with a multi-dimensional approach and multi-level association yet easy to communicate.
- Goals have to be measurable with clear targets and indicators with time bound action plans.
- Goals should ensure coherence, coordination and synergetic association with other initiatives and must follow strong implementation mechanisms. [186]

Well-designed and well-crafted goals can provide a shared national narrative of SDG and guide citizens to understand the scope and challenges related to SDG implementation and achievement. The goals would unite communities, mobilize stakeholders from all sectors i.e. citizens, media, private sector, communities, academia, youth, women, trusts, foundations, NGOs and others and motivate them to come together for the shared purpose of achieving the goals. A time bound, well-monitored goals framework with transparent processes and action plan, will drive greater mobilization of resources, and promote innovation, increase collaboration and network of best practices and expertise.

It would bring greater convergence across sectors, promote integrated thinking, and avoid fragmentized policies and approaches that create a chaotic environment and hamper growth and development. Team India must ensure that all the goals are in harmony with each other (not pitted against each another) and all sectors are working with greater synergy and synchronization. Clear time bound goals, targets, indicators; monitoring etc will allow team India, citizens, public and private actors etc. to identify the needs, resources, timelines, priorities, individual and collective capacities and respective responsibilities that would help chart out long-term pathways to achieve sustainable development. This integrated; comprehensive planning and perspective would also help avoid misuse of policies, resources or planning process for short term political or corporate gains.

Moreover, with a strong social accountability tools based monitoring and evaluation mechanism with transparent processes, such a comprehensive goals framework would enable and empower citizens to monitor the progress on each goal and hold governments and its agencies responsible and accountable.

There are seven core processes of goal-based partnerships identified by the SDSN (Sustainable Development Solutions Network) that involve many actors:

1. Shared goals and metrics that provide a coherent narrative for action mobilize all actors involved in a particular area, galvanize the community to develop clear strategies for implementation, and raise the financing and develop the technologies needed to implement them.
2. Advocacy and policy standards to raise awareness of the importance and feasibility of the global goals, mobilize stakeholders, ensure accountability, and translate lessons into standards that other countries can emulate.
3. Back casting and implementation strategies to show how the goals can be achieved through sustained investments and supportive policies.
4. Technology road mapping for RDD&D to identify missing technologies and organize public-private partnerships to address them.
5. Financing and technology transfer to mobilize the right mix of public and private resources to implement goal-based investment strategies.
6. Delivery systems that translate policies, strategies, and financing into outcomes.
7. Monitoring and Evaluation (M&E) to sharpen the understanding of what works, support advocacy, and hold all partners accountable.[187]

Team India should utilize all these global tools and guidelines to design a multi-stakeholder, multidimensional approach by adopting a participatory, consultative and consensus building methodology after in-depth brainstorming and planning meetings with the public sector, civil society, media, private sector along with state and central governments and other development partners to ensure social accountability, inclusion and participation in the development of national strategy.

What's more important to realize is, that we have the collective expertise and resources to achieve a higher degree of success and a much better score on SDG index; that clearly shows that these sustainable goals cannot be achieved by government alone. Any one organ in the country by itself is not capable of achieving the ambitious targets and goals of the SDG framework. It has to be a collective effort from all the pillars / sectors especially, public, private and civil sectors with shared ownership and responsibility for securing our collective future. Team India must work with governments (states' and central) on policy setting mandate and ensuring processes and structures that would create an enabling environment for private sector to collaborate and contribute their technical expertise and other resources for achieving the targets. Creating a national action plan (annual) based on this comprehensive SDG framework and combining it with national integrity strategy for better implementation, monitoring and evaluation should be the combined strategy of all the stakeholders in the country. A multi-dimensional and multi stakeholder partnership where all sectors and state and non-state actors should collaborate on the complete cycle of designing, implementing, monitoring and evaluating the policies and work at national as well as local level.

This new strategy should be based on key features like national ownership, knowledge and technology based design, stakeholders' participation, strategic priority setting and sequencing, effective coordination, monitoring and evaluation as suggested by many global agencies. This strategy should link the SDGs with integrity and accountability strategies, as we know that corruption and mismanagement not only damage a country's economy; political systems, institutions, businesses, civil society but pollute its social, moral, economical and natural environment too. Therefore, it is important that this new national strategy focus on realistic planning, adequate prioritization of reforms, sufficient involvement of non-state actors, and other implementing partners. Other specific priority areas of intervention should include strengthening institutional coherence between the various pillars involved, increasing civil society participation, supervision and converging the resources.[188]

The strategy should follow a holistic, strategic, multi-pronged approach to tackle corruption and mismanagement of policies and resources with a combination of prevention, enforcement and suppression measures, embedded in the ethical, legal, institutional, social and systemic framework of governance in India. It should provide concrete steps and actions to be undertaken in order to progressively eliminate corruption, increase integrity and accountability, ensure better governance and public services, better management of policies, resources, and effective implementation and monitoring of sustainable development goals. The benefits the new national strategy would be a shared understanding of the causes and impacts of Corruption, misplaced policies and mismanagement of resources and to bring together the various measures as a coherent strategy, creating a route to implementation; it will propel the long road to effective public financial management; political accountability, transparency, good governance, effective service delivery and the rule of law that would create the foundation for successful implementation and achievement of sustainable development goals

In short, the new national strategy should be based on an integrated, comprehensive approach that is unlike any previous strategies with focus on building integrity, trust, transparency, accountability, social cohesion and cross-sectoral convergence to achieve the national goals of peace, progress and prosperity for all. [188]

To sum it up, the new national strategy should include the following features:

- Ensuring highest integrity, transparency and accountability
- Ensuring good governance, effective public services, better management of resources and the effective rule of law

- Mainstreaming social inclusion and national information in sustainable development plans and initiatives locally and nationally
- Mobilization of all key stakeholders and other local and national participants and institutions
- Building collective synergies and national support for SDG strategy and its goals
- Participation of all stakeholders at all stages of policy cycle, planning and implementation
- Building capacities and skills required (cross sectoral)
- Convergence of resources across all sectors
- Building implementation teams, review and monitoring teams
- Building public awareness teams to ensure public participation
- Building task forces with specific goals and objectives

To integrate these features in the national strategy, Team India, along with other stakeholders, can set up the following steps:

A) Build an integrity infrastructure

- Set up an national integrity Unit
- Create a national integrity assessment plan for all the national pillars
- Set up review and reform teams
- Create public awareness team
- Create an integrity and anti-corruption task force

B) Build a social accountability based information infrastructure

- Design and set up a two way interface (G2C- C2G) and integrated single window portal

- Create a new data revolution by harnessing new innovative and creative data method and analytical tools
- Create a social accountability based platform for citizens, media and private sector to engage in participatory democracy
- Create a legal framework for protecting social democratic rights
- Create public awareness team to create social awareness
- Create monitoring and evaluation teams
- Create an accountability and transparency task force

C) Create an integrated national action plan

- Create a national platform for all stakeholders to participate and share resources
- Create a national SDG framework to align and integrate with the existing framework
- Convergence of resources and policies - cross sectoral
- Create public awareness, monitoring and evaluation teams
- Create review and action teams
- Create a sustainable development goals task force

Team India can create single umbrella task forces for all the goals like converging all anti-poverty and development policies, plans and initiatives across all sectors (governments, public, private , Trusts, Foundations, NGOs, CSOs, etc.) under single umbrella initiative - Task force- sustainable development and prosperity for all.

Similarly, various task forces can be set up like:

Task Force – National Integrity, Transparency &accountability
Task Force - R & D and Innovative solutions
Task Force – Employment and entrepreneurship
Task Force – Infrastructure Development
Task Force – Education and skill development
Task Force – Health & Hygiene
Task Force – Clean & green India
Task Force - Peace and harmony (anti-communalism and anti-terrorism)
Task Force – Law and order (anti-crime and Social issues) and so on..........

To summarize, the following activities can support and streamline the national sustainable development strategy and framework:

- Lessons drawn from the experience of implementing the previous reform and accountability strategies and processes,
- Achievements and failures of current strategies and policies , Analyzing MDGs with respect to gaps
- Comparative analysis of other countries' strategies' and experiences
- Adopting global initiatives like open data governments (OGP), UN, SDSN, UNDP, TI Transparency international guidelines and tools
- Setting up integrity and social accountability infrastructure
- Setting the national integrity review and reform process to ensure transparency and accountability
- Creating a legal framework for accountability and enforceability using tools like social audits, budget monitoring, participatory policy cycle, monitoring and evaluating the outcomes etc.
- Creating a national dialogue and comprehensive framework to facilitate multistakeholder partnerships
- Stock taking and prioritization, Identification of needs, filling knowledge and data gaps
- Mainstreaming of SDGs, alignment with existing line agencies
- Integrating SDGs into national development plan, including new institutional models

- Interconnection among SDGs and inter-sectoral integration ,Mainstreaming in all sectors with accountability support
- Coordinate SDG planning and implementation strategies, using knowledge tools for integration of SDGs into national plan
- co-coordinating monitoring, evaluation and knowledge management
- co-coordinating the SDG implementation plan
- Setting up a framework for the review process ,conducting public awareness , outreach and communication
- Developing a national monitoring framework and accompanying set of national indicators
- Creating monthly and annual SDG report with actions taken and goals achieved within the targeted action plan and time frame
- Supporting multi-stakeholder data initiatives that connect the data revolution in achieving the SDGs
- contributing to filling knowledge and data gaps, using original data as well as new data in achieving the SDGs
- Contributing technical expertise, creative solutions and resources to SDG challenges
- Organizing workshops and seminars to advance connectivity, collaboration and innovation towards achieving and measuring the SDGs
- Strengthening statistical capacity ,capitalizing on the data revolution, harnessing new technologies and new sources of data
- Integrating all SDG agencies , ministries and authorities under single window platform for citizens' use
- Setting up an easy to communicate goals framework with timelines and follow up tools for public
- Convergence of resources and expertise across the sectors[189]

As we discussed earlier, the real impact of building new integrity and social accountability infrastructure would not be only anti-corruption or pro integrity but also of improved public service delivery, the established rule of law and an enabling environment for the private sector. The national integrity unit should focus on the ultimate goal to promote good governance, sustainable development, and the rule of law and effective public services. It should conduct a national integrity assessment of all the national pillars to evaluate their systemic weaknesses, lack of comprehensive strategies and implementation plans like untimely or inadequate budget allocation or lack of monitoring and evaluation plans and strive to make them 100 % transparent and accountable. By mutual support, all the pillars can combine their strength by applying core values and practices for better synergy and synchronization. Once the new systems and processes are in place, Team India should work towards converging all the needs and resources into single umbrella initiatives under SDG framework to accomplish sustainable goals.

As we have explored, there are many specific area of engagements and collaborations where citizens, private sector and other local players can come together to promote convergence and make a remarkable difference in the way things work. These could be - designing, implementing and monitoring quality initiatives like development and technical programs to strengthen local capacity building, project management and outreach in a cost effective manner; initiating multi-stakeholder policy dialogue, negotiation and quality standards setting; advocacy, campaigning and communication regarding social issues; knowledge management, technology -information sharing and data management; promoting integrity, transparency and accountability in all areas; mobilization and convergence of expertise, resources and funds; R & D, innovation and building capacity etc.

In fact, Team India and private sector together can change the pace of growth and development in the country by contributing their expertise and by converging resources for building capacities across all the pillars i.e. for research, for inquiry, for creativity and innovation, for knowledge transfer, for technology, for enterprising and moral leadership, for higher, equitable growth and inclusive, sustainable development etc.

For instance, by creating a national integrity system and social accountability infrastructure (public interface), Team India can ensure a zero corruption -100 % accountability system for SDG implementation and monitoring framework. It can then invite private sector sector, Trusts, Foundations, Social organizations and activists, visionaries and philanthropists to align their common social objectives, CSR (corporate social responsibility) activities and initiatives with the national

SDG strategy framework to support the shared goals of peace and prosperity for all. By raising awareness, developing resources, facilitating partnerships and developing action initiatives on key issues, they can support the SDG initiatives, focusing on key areas like Investment and resources, knowledge and expertise, innovation and Creative solutions etc.

Convergence is the key!

A nation's progress depends upon how its people think. India has to think as a nation of a billion people. A new socio-economic order based on connectivity force that is binding and invigorating societal transformation including integration of vital growth sectors, connectivity of rural-urban dynamics, networking of human and material resources and convergence of technologies.

– DR APJ Kalam

Convergence is the key for building a new India….

To build a new India, we need to converge our human resources (especially our vast youth power), technological and national resources that we have in abundance and build capacities to work in harmony toward the common goal of achieving peace, progress and prosperity for all. Such a convergence of collective will, ideas, efforts and resources will create a new India that works for all!

Team India needs to create an umbrella under which, all stakeholders, resources, needs, funds, policies schemes and plans can be brought together and converged to optimize results and to achieve India's highest collective potential. By establishing integrity, transparency and accountability infrastructure and creating transparent systems and processes, team India can not only bridge the knowledge, data, expertise, technology or resources gaps but also, can bridge the trust gap that exist between governments, civil and private sectors. Combining the strengths and best practices of all sectors by creating knowledge and expertise pool, manpower pool, resources pool, funds pool etc and synchronizing them towards a common shared purpose; team India can revolutionize India's growth story and put it on the path of becoming the next miracle economy!

For instance, there are various existing / proposed policies, schemes, action plans and processes for various issues like corruption, environmental risks, terrorism, poverty, illiteracy, unemployment etc.; that are plaguing our country and hampering India's optimum growth potential. There are so many institutions, private organizations, Government bodies, NGOs, corporate houses, trusts, foundations, global agencies and individuals who are doing their best to help and eradicate these issues locally and nationally and in their own way are contributing towards India's growth yet the efforts are not focused or coordinated. They all have the same intention and objectives but use different ways and means. Everything is scattered and we all know that unless we have a focused and comprehensive goal, the results are not effective. Team India can play a pivoting role of getting all these stakeholders into a synergetic relationship by creating resources pool, financial or technical pools and create a clear roadmap for achieving the shared goals of equitable, inclusive and sustainable growth and development for India. Convergence is the key! The convergence of our resources and needs would create such a force that will counter and eliminate the various issues and challenges faced by our country forever!

For instance, we have hundreds of schemes, plans and policies for eradicating poverty- Governments, private organizations, NGOs, corporates, individuals, trusts, global partners all are doing their bit in fragmented ways, using various resources and various funds. Team India can get them on the same page, converge and integrate them under one umbrella goal i.e. sustainable development goal for zero hunger with a comprehensive strategy and time bound action plan. Using integrity and social accountability infrastructure ; ensuring transparent processes and zero corruption and 100% accountability-based system with robust review; monitoring and evaluation mechanism; tracking every rupee to its targeted end and outcome; Team India can act as the bridge of trust between all the sectors i.e. Government, civil, private sector, NGOs, trusts, foundations etc. and provide a common platform for them to pool their expertise, best practices and resources, find creative and innovative solutions and work towards the common goal of eradicating poverty from the country forever.

We have already established that given its resources, India can very well afford to feed, house, educate and provide health-care for all its citizens. Effective, intelligent management and utilization of all existing resources and convergence of knowledge and efforts for integrated development, that would enable over-all prosperity and security for all and build the nation anew; should be the objectives of Team India. As Mandela said- "poverty of vision and ideas is the worst form of poverty". If we could take stock of our resources and make an inventory, mapping needs VS resources or demand VS supply, it can be concluded that hunger and poverty in our country are not due to lack of resources but due to lack of creative and innovative ideas. Indeed, it is the poverty of our collective vision and will! A strong collective will with our collective efforts and the golden triangle of the private sector, government and civil society (team India along with citizens and civil society organizations) could create such abundance of resources and means that would wipe out hunger, poverty, inequality, unemployment etc. forever from our country.

Team India - Think tank should study successful poverty alleviation models and success stories around the world and select best plans and practices and come up with a comprehensive, effective strategy and action plan. There are many experts in India and around the world who have already researched and presented some of the most comprehensive, effective strategies and blueprints for all-round prosperity. This potent power of collective intelligence and collective effort can bring fresh innovative, creative solutions and create new revolutionary approaches for handling old problems. Creating a knowledge pool or technology and R& D pool with the vast scientific and technological manpower and resources existing in our country, would create such a resources pool that could take India to unimaginable heights. Getting private sector to pool their resources, focusing on people, planet and profit (the triple bottom line as it is known), aligning their businesses, social responsibility (CSR) and best practices with sustainable development goals and nation building priorities would create enough resources to tackle and eliminate every challenge existing in the country.

A sample model for poverty eradication (Task force- sustainable development and prosperity for all):

" Team India - Think tank" should create a special task force consisting of top economists, social organizations, bright and honest professionals from various institutions and corporations, retired and eminent officials, judges, defense personnel , NGOs, students, people with bright ideas for brainstorming and formulating the comprehensive strategy to combat poverty. There are so many institutions, organizations, government bodies, NGOs, corporate houses, trusts, global agencies and individuals who are doing their best to help and eradicate poverty locally and nationally. There are various schemes under various departments that are working on poverty alleviation. There are various funding agencies national, international, public, private, i.e. philanthropy, trusts, foundations, individuals, companies with corporate social responsibility funds (CSR) etc. spending time and resources to support the cause. Our team India should study, analyze and converge them with relating sustainable goals into a comprehensive strategy framework and time bound action plan. Convergence of all these existing and proposed schemes and plans, various governments and private funds (NGOs, Trusts, foundations, CSR, Global aids etc.) would create a **comprehensive and integrated national sustainable development and prosperity program** that will bring all the resources in the country under one umbrella.

To avoid scattered and fragmented approach, working in siloes practices and duplication or wastage of resources; this new comprehensive program could be structured to integrate various sustainable goals and cross-sectoral schemes run by governments - public, private and social sectors. These could be – poverty eradication and social welfare schemes which provide basic social services including quality primary and special education, strengthening the economic power of farmers and poor, providing primary health-care etc and employment schemes which provide unemployed youth opportunities in skills acquisition, employment and wealth generation. Other schemes could be rural development, concerning rural employment, transport, communication, energy, water and Infrastructure Development; natural resources development and conservation Schemes with a vision to bring about the participatory and sustainable development of agricultural, minerals and water. Similarly, various micro-finance, credit, SHG regulation and monitoring schemes should also be clubbed with the program to manage indebtedness and increase livelihood opportunities.

The participating partners along with the government- private-civil sectors should be the ministries of agriculture and rural development, bio-resources development, water resources, health, education, employment, housing, environment, finance, women empowerment, youth development, industry, science and technology, power, steel and human resources etc.

Team India can create national indicators with time bound goals and form..

An **Implementation team** for coordinating at the national and local level between all the agencies, ministries, policy makers, other relevant sectors and stake-holders.

Review and Monitoring Team to review and monitor processes, procedures, provide periodic feedback and recommendation to our task forces, assist them in the effective implementation of strategies, and plug loopholes if any.

Public Awareness team To create public awareness through media, celebrities, generate public support, forming volunteer groups, conducting workshops, educating people about various task forces, getting feedback, creating public grievances centers etc. Using the information infrastructure- interface and data tools, Team India can create easy to understand and follow citizen charters, workflow and other graphs and charts for the public to participate and monitor the outcomes.

By using social accountability infrastructure and tools, Team India along with other stakeholders can participate in policy cycle and keep a tight watch on the processes like budget allocations, service delivery, targets etc. It can use other social empowerment tools like periodic social audits, human rights checks etc. to check any misplaced priorities, misused power or policy gaps and use enforcement tools if needed to ensure inclusive and equitable development policies and processes.

Another effective tool to eradicate poverty is encouraging and enabling private-sector-led, sustainable economic growth .Many developed countries have used this model and have benefited from the opportunities that were generated by a robust private sector as they had sufficient tools, freedom and policies in place to encourage private-sector to lead their economic growth and development. India can follow their examples but at the same time, we need to be alert and reject those 'trickle down" policies and approaches that paint a rosy picture of a high GDP growth and claim to be the panacea for all economical and social ills as we have seen those generally fail to do so. We need to develop an integrated, inclusive economic growth and development model that could strike a perfect balance between the two goals of economic growth and social development (human welfare) and that lifts up the poorest sections rather than serving those at the top. In other words, the new growth and development model should focus more on the bottom of the economic pyramid (BOP) approaches, strategically balanced with the top of the pyramid (TOP) enhancing practices.

Team India must ensure that all sectors join forces and play their respective roles and responsibilities, fairly and honestly, to achieve the desired goals. For instance, private sector, by deploying the most appropriate resources, approaches and expertise in support of poverty alleviation, mapping resources and needs, demands and supply; should focus on creating productive jobs for low-income individuals, engaging local small and medium-sized enterprises (SMEs) to generate employment. Governments (states/central) should focus on improving public services, infrastructure, policies and regulation for facilitating employment generation and poverty alleviating activities and creating an enabling environment for private sector and Team India along with media and other players should focus on playing the role of a catalyst and monitoring body to ensure that both the private sector and governments fulfill their promises and expectations of society especially, of the most vulnerable and weakest sections.

Team India along with citizens and other stakeholders must decide on what must be the priorities of the nation. Poverty, inequality and unemployment are the most pressing issues in the country today and must be tackled in an urgent, comprehensive and integrated way. India's greatest challenge is to provide increasing opportunities for our ever-growing young workforce and labor force, enriching their knowledge and skills with quality education and training, raising their living standards through productive employment, and securing a good life with hope and dignity.

It is extremely important as access to food, shelter and employment is an essential component of freedom of economic choice. The absence of such opportunities means depriving our people especially, young ones of economic freedom and hope to live a dignified life. Therefore, providing employment, ensuring equality and alleviating poverty should not only be the top priorities of our governments but also, constitutionally guaranteed fundamental human rights. Team India must ensure that the policies are in line with national priorities and use the collective will and efforts of all the stakeholders to achieve these goals at the earliest. And to do so, it should leave no stone unturned and utilize every possible idea, resource, means and tools as we know no single sector i.e. governments or private can handle this task alone. It would take all the forces in the country joined together with out of the box ideas and collective knowledge and resources to handle these issues.

For instance, by utilizing new data revolution tools like satellite imaginary, remote sensing technology, mobile technology and advanced data practices, our expert team (think tank) can map needs versus resources for the various sector like industry, agriculture or manufacturing and create manpower pools i.e. labor pool, skill pool and job pool. There is a need to map demand versus supply for skill development across sectors and a focused, coordinated and comprehensive approach for skill development, industry sponsored VET (vocational training) system in schools and colleges along with employment generation can help overcome the challenge of skill development and unemployment.

There are millions of hectares of unused cultivable land in India. Almost 12 lac hectares of irrigated and cultivated land is lying unused due to state policies. That too, when we have surplus rural workforce crying for better livelihood opportunities. It is gross mis-utilization of our natural and human resources! Even less resourceful countries have managed to deploy better land and resources distribution policies for optimizing their production and employment outputs.

Today, we have the best GPS and other remote sensing technologies and infrastructure, which can map villages, towns, states & the entire nation for suitable land, climatic conditions for different crops, forest, and agro- bio- products. This resources pool i e land pool and crops-products pool along with our knowledge pool of brilliant agro – scientists, R& D technologists and manpower pool; can create hundreds of sustainable agro-bio based industries and a robust agriculture-based employment generation model. A cooperative structure for farming and dairy and development of forests and food processing can create additional jobs and help to increase per capita income of our rural people. We can use the comprehensive and integrated rural development model suggested by Dr APJ Kalam and other similar development models.

Similarly, all the issues and challenges facing the country can be analyzed and integrated into sustainable goals framework and brought under single umbrella initiatives with specific task forces with time bound action plan and review and monitoring teams. For example, Task force- clean and green India for environmental issues, Task force- peace and harmony for communalism and terrorism issues, Task force- health and hygiene for health and cleanliness issues etc.

Creating a new Paradigm

A nation is not defined by its borders or the boundaries of its land mass Rather, a nation is defined by adverse people who have been unified by a cause and a value system and who are committed to a vision for the type of society they wish to live in and give to the future generations to come."

- Fela Durotoye

It is high time we moved over from ever-conflicting issues of socialism and capitalism to find a middle way that works for all and create a win-win situation for everyone in the country. What about humanism or holism for a change where an ideal union of socialism and capitalism balances the socio-economic fabric of India and provides equal opportunities and economic empowerment to all; at the same time guiding and encouraging the highly motivated enterprising go-getters to touch the sky by providing them the tools and means and fostering their courage and acumen.

A new system where there is a perfect balance between capitalism and socialism, between the private and public sector, between governments and civil societies. A new socio-capitalist economy where both our private sector- capitalists and the governments work together towards the well-being of the country and society. A beautiful marriage of power, wealth and compassion where those who have the ability, ambition and intelligence are provided resources and freedom to generate more wealth and develop the economy while the governments along with public sector, NGOs and members of the society are focused and committed to improving the living and livelihood conditions of the entire population.

A new India where people from all walks of life, corporates, public & private sector are engaged and committed to creating an enlightened society where there is no social, economic or communal division or discrimination; all people have enough opportunities and privileges to thrive and achieve their highest potential. Where governments along with private sector and citizens work towards developing a human economy that works for all.

A human economy would have a number of core ingredients aimed at tackling the problems that have contributed to today's inequality crisis. A framework to lay down the foundation to build such a human economy is suggested by OXFAM: 190

1. Governments will work for the 99%. Accountable government is the greatest weapon against extreme inequality and the key to a human economy. Governments must listen to all, not a wealthy minority and their lobbyists. We need to see a reinvigoration of civic space, especially for the voices of women and marginalized groups. The more accountable our governments are, the fairer our societies will be.

2. Governments will cooperate, not just compete. Globalization cannot continue to mean a relentless race to the bottom on tax and labor rights, which benefits no one but those at the top. We must end the era of tax havens once and for all. Countries must cooperate, on an equal basis, to build a new global consensus and a virtuous cycle to ensure corporations and rich people pay fair taxes, the environment is protected, and workers are paid well.

3. Companies will work for the benefit of everyone. Governments should support business models that clearly drive the kind of capitalism that benefits all and underpins a sustainable future. The proceeds of business activity should go to those who enabled and created them – society, workers, and local communities. Lobbying by corporates and the purchase of democracy should be brought to an end. Governments must ensure corporations pay fair wages and fair taxes and take responsibility for their impact on the planet.

4. Ending the extreme concentration of wealth to end extreme poverty. Today's gilded age is undermining our future and needs to be ended. The richest should be made to contribute to society fairly and not be allowed to get away with unfair privileges. To do this we need to see the rich pay their fair share of tax: we must increase taxes on both wealth and high incomes to ensure a more level playing field, and clamp down on tax dodging by the super-rich.

5. A human economy will work equally for men and women. Gender equality will be at the heart of the human economy, ensuring that both halves of humanity have an equal chance in life and are able to live fulfilled lives. Barriers to women's progress, which include access to education and

healthcare, will end for good. Social norms will no longer determine a woman's role in society and, in particular, unpaid care work will be recognized, reduced and redistributed.

6. Technology will be harnessed for the interests of the 99%. New technology has huge potential to transform our lives for the better. This will only happen with active government intervention, especially in the control of technology. Governments research is already behind some of the greatest innovations in recent times, including the smartphone. Governments must intervene to ensure that technology contributes to reducing inequality, not increases it.

7. A human economy will be powered by sustainable renewable energy. Fossil fuels have driven economic growth since the era of industrialization, but they are incompatible with an economy that puts the needs of the many first. Air pollution from burning coal leads to millions of premature deaths worldwide, while the devastation caused by climate change hits the poorest and most vulnerable hardest. Sustainable renewable energy can deliver universal energy access and power growth that respects our planetary boundaries.

8. Valuing and measuring what really matters. Moving beyond GDP, we need to measure human progress using the many alternative measures available. These new measures should fully account for the unpaid work of women worldwide. They must reflect not just the scale of economic activity, but how income and wealth are distributed. They must be closely linked to sustainability, helping to build a better world today and for future generations. This will enable us to measure the true progress of our societies. [190]

We can and must build a human economy before it is too late.

We must learn from the success stories around the world, from other countries that have already implemented some of these great ideas and have achieved amazing results, to build a new India.

Building A New India

The most meaningful activity in which a human being can be engaged is one that is directly related to human evolution. This is true because human beings now play an active and critical role not only in the process of their own evolution but in the survival and evolution of all living beings. Awareness of this places upon human beings a responsibility for their participation in and contribution to the process of evolution. If humankind would accept and acknowledge this responsibility and become creatively engaged in the process of meta-biological evolution consciously, as well as unconsciously, a new reality would emerge, and a new age would be born.

- Jonas Salk in Anatomy of Reality

Team India can be the binding force that would bring all stakeholders to unite their powers and forces to build India anew and afresh. It should aim to create an evolved, enlightened, empowered and inclusive society where people from all sections are aware of their rights, roles and responsibilities and are involved in the process of nation building. By creating a democratic space, a social platform and a national framework for common goals, Team India can provide the tools and means for people to join various initiatives and task forces and contribute towards achieving the shared goals of peace, progress and prosperity for all. People of India can use this space for utilizing their individual potentials constructively to achieve our optimum collective potential. It will create such a positive and constructive force that will change India's destiny forever.

This calls for a revolution- not a destructive revolution but a constructive and positive revolution that would lead us to our conscious evolution to create a better future for all. Harnessing the collective intelligence, will and action along with collective resources, constructively to build a new India; where people from all walks of life are involved in nation-building process; would transform India into an advanced nation and a heaven on earth.

For instance, Team India can harness India's huge youth power by calling them to join various teams and task forces, contributing their time and expertise and bringing fresh ideas to the table. They can be assigned various roles like "champions of reform or development", "integrity guardians" or "peace ambassadors" and so on. Our top corporate honchos and intellectual, bright minds from our prestigious technical and management institutions like IIM and IITs etc. can join Team India's think tank and task forces and can change the face of India with their business acumen and brilliant out of the box ideas. Our semi and non-skilled manpower force can join the task forces' implementation team and build the country anew. We have a huge educated pool of women including housewives who can take time out to join various task forces like education and skill development or social issues and contribute their expertise and knowledge and participate in nation building process. The sky would be the limit for us indeed when we join forces! This would create such a revolutionary positive force that will tackle and overcome any challenge facing our country today.

Now, when there are talks of the global recession and lack of jobs going on, a million jobs can be created with such task forces for those who are willing to take up the challenges. Building a new India is a mammoth task and we need all the help- all our human resources – economists, writers, media, artists, celebrities, physicists, scientists, technocrats, educationist, finance professionals, technical, social & civil societies NGOs, students, housewives, farmers, workers joining or volunteering for team India and task forces according to their interests and inclinations to create a new India and a brighter, happier and fulfilling future for all. That's quite a job! It would not only take our country to unimaginable heights but also make each one of us happy, fulfilled and extremely proud of ourselves.

As we already explored that we have enough resources. Our need today is to manage, maintain, preserve and utilize these resources intelligently and effectively so the whole collective body of our nation is fed, preserved and maintained for further evolution. Somehow, the current issues like poverty, terrorism, unemployment etc. that are plaguing our country; in the light of our true nature and natural abundance seem subconsciously or maybe unconsciously created phenomena. It would just require a convergence of our resources, manpower and a strong will – our collective will. Rest will be, as they say, history! Nothing can stop India if people of India from all sectors join together and take up the cudgel to eliminate all these challenging issues from the face of our country.

Just imagine what a difference our team India can make to change things for better. Establishing a sound national integrity system and zero corruption - 100% transparent and accountable processes, would revolutionize the way things work in India. Having a single window, ITC based information infrastructure and using social accountability tools; people of India would not only reclaim their roles as the ultimate caretakers of national resources and revenues but also ensure fair and equitable distribution of the same to see that no one is left behind. By becoming the ultimate integrity guardians, not only we can make India corruption free but ensure social and economic justice to all too. Similarly, by reforming our political and public institutions, we can ensure better public services, management, complete transparency and accountability, ethical, fair and just practices in the country.

For instance, our Task Force – Integrity, accountability and transparency can make sure that anti-corruption strategies at all level are implemented properly. All the government departments, ministries, MLAs, MPs etc. should update the information about their activities i.e. what are their action plans, targets achieved, how much work has been done in their constituencies, their work flow, citizen's charter, their assets, earnings etc. with facts and figures. Every government minister, MP, MLA has to update his or her report card and citizen feedback reports monthly, quarterly and annually. Through Team India's interactive information interface, the public can access this information in real time and judge the politicians on their actual performance instead of the past or future promises or election rhetoric. The parliament and executive review and reform teams of Team India should monitor and evaluate the performances on a regular basis and push for reforms wherever required. It would create a transparent-accountable system where all the loopholes are plugged and public support and confidence in their representatives and governments will increase by ten folds.

Moreover , by making sure that our representatives are held accountable and answerable to people for their every action and decision , people of India can reform and transform the way our politics and parliament operate and build a new parliament that becomes the most revered and esteemed place; where the work of nation building is done with utmost sincerity and loyalty. The politicians and representatives would know that people are watching their every word, commitment and action and the only service to people and their performance would count, nothing else would do anymore!

Similarly, by assessing the integrity loopholes in our public sector, judiciary, police, and other national, law enforcement agencies and by reforming and transforming the systems and processes; a new revolution in our politics and public service would begin. As we discussed in previous chapters, by creating an accountable election system and transparent processes, combining civil activism with judicial activism and pushing for state-sponsored election campaign with open, transparent accounts and monitoring mechanism; people of India can eliminate the use of money and muscle power from the election system forever. By introducing methods like fast track justice system and high public scrutiny (with team India, media and citizens watching over and guarding the election process) for politician and candidates and making politics a high risk–low gain option, people of India can revolutionize Indian politics forever. Using social accountability tools like data analysis tool and information sharing tools, initiatives like "know your candidates" with their complete history and credentials can be made available on mobiles for people to select and elect the right candidates. It would create a filter for those with corrupt motives or shady backgrounds and open doors for honest, compassionate, socially active candidates with sincere intentions to serve their people and country. As explored earlier, if people of India can opt for direct democracy instead of the representative democracy that is the fountainhead of all political corruption, power games and vote bank politics; a new age of enlightened politics and democracy can evolve.

To build a new India, we need to create a proud, caring and cohesive society that is made up of evolved, empowered, fair and inclusive citizenship and is truly built on the foundation of freedom, democracy justice, rights and responsibilities, equality and inclusivity, shared values, unity and diversity.

Just imagine how we can all come together to lay the foundation of a new India, collectively, purposefully and synchronistically. An enlightened society where everyone is living in peace, harmony and coherence with each other; accepting and acknowledging our individual and collective responsibilities; becoming more aware and creatively engaged in the process of consciously co-creating and collaborating towards a collective social body of shared intelligence and capacities; reforming, transforming, introducing new social processes, structures and systems that would lead us to our highest collective potential future.

We need to create a neural network to utilize our collective and individual creative intelligence to the optimum- the same goes for all our resources. The human body is Nature's greatest tool, so precise every cells role is! Every DNA orchestrating a perfect symphony of organs and systems…. it is a marvel! The human body and human brain are the greatest gifts nature has bestowed on us; we just need to use them intelligently for the betterment of our country. Each one of us has the ability and capacity to live happily and abundantly and at the same time offering others the same. We have been blessed with the technology and intelligence to ride the wave of civilization into a new age of revolutionary and evolutionary transformation.

Today when man-made destructive divisions and discriminations, economic and ecological imbalance, environmental degradation, terrorism, communalism, injustice, poverty etc. are threatening the very foundation of our nation and putting us on the brink of destruction; acceptance and convergence of our collective potential and individual creativity can create the force that would take our evolution to unimaginable heights. In order for India to evolve to the next level, it is necessary to create a more peaceful and unified society, each individual must tap into his or her core of potential and bring their gifts to support and achieve our collective potential and shape the future of India.

The convergence of our collective intelligence and wisdom of eons, combined with our collective efforts will take our country to such height, which we have not ever dreamt of. As Mahatma Gandhi said – be the change that you wish to see in the world. We have to create a revolution to change the things in our country, join hands – for one common purpose, and create the nation as we all wish to see it. Similarly, the convergence of science, technology, art, business, finances, religions, our natural resources and manpower resources will go on creating a solid foundation for the time to come; on which we can build a new India – a heaven on earth.

One nation- India…..

One family- Indian…..

One religion- Humanity…

One purpose- Peace, Progress and Prosperity for all…

Such a network and force can start a revolution which cannot be stopped ….a positive force that will transmute any negative force in its wake…that will re-build India. An ideal India for each one…. by each one! Nothing can be big or impossible for such a force…. hunger, poverty, communalism or any issue, which represents negative energy in our system, will be wiped out from our country forever!

Just imagine how this new India would look like…. all coming together to create a cohesive body- a new India, restructured and rejuvenated. Our governments and political parties, instead of pulling each other down, overcoming their differences and unifying to form a political and national consensus; committed to the highest good for all, can be the backbone of this body. Our media instead of sensationalizing or getting distracted; becoming more aware, alert and responsible, can act as the nerve center of this body. Our private and public sectors converging and creating great wealth and opportunities for all; can be the bloodline of this body. Our team India with its technical pool and wisdom pool can be the brains of this collective body, serving the nation and people with utmost devotion. And above all, the people of India rising above all petty divisions and discriminations, forming 1.3 billion cells of this great collective body, working towards achieving peace, harmony and prosperity for all. All of us can join Team India and task forces according to our interests and inclinations, doing our bit and becoming the heart and hands of our mother India.

How powerful and progressive our new India would be where all existing conflicts are resolved in a best win-win manner possible; everyone involved in business shifting towards an enlightened and compassionate capitalism, a capitalism which is based on new business ethics, on human economy that is not driven to gain maximum profits but to fulfilling the evolving needs of all beings and making their goods at lowest possible prices, producing a grassroots deflation that would provide basic necessities of life and liberate our lower strata. Such initiatives and practices would create a revolution and systematic evolution with a strong, stable foundation and a healthy, balanced growth for the country.

A new India where the trinity of wisdom, prosperity and compassion formed by private sector, governments and citizens (team India), fulfilling the dreams of every citizen by working collectively towards shared goals of peace, progress and prosperity for all.

A new India where each Indian, regardless what class, caste or creed he belongs to, has access to food, shelter, job to survive with dignity at the same time, has been provided enough opportunities and resources to thrive.

A new India where we all, not only strive to better our lives by realizing our individual potential but contribute our gifts towards the betterment of all and help achieving our collective potential too. How beautiful and harmonious our new India would be, where all Indians are united and while honoring the teachings of our individual culture and doctrines at the personal level, finally realizing that all religions complement and complete each other and integrate them into a unified, universal religion- humanity.

A new India with an enlightened, empowered and evolved society where people of India have risen above all divisions, discriminations and join together to filter and eliminate the negative elements and forces from the society. It is time to embrace our higher, ultimate truth and let go of all those thoughts, choices and beliefs that are rooted in ignorance and misinterpretations and create conflicts, separatism and communalism in the society. It is time to consciously choose our highest truth and reject the old, outdated, dysfunctional and manipulative ways like pseudo-secularism and pseudo-intellectualism, selective compassion or activism that have been used for decades by our politicians and self-proclaimed custodians of religions to divide the society and play the politics of vote bank. It is time to wake up, take charge, and play our role and responsibility as the guardians and ultimate caretakers of democracy in the country.

It is said that we cannot solve the problems from the same grounds that gave births to them, therefore, we need to change the entire paradigm and move from these lower truths and perspectives to realize and embrace our highest truth. We know social stress, unemployment, poverty; vote bank politics, power games, illiteracy, ignorance etc. are the major causes behind communalism and social conflicts. We cannot eliminate these negative elements and issues by being negative but need to create such a positive force that would wipe out any such negative elements and forces from our country forever.

Team India, along with the citizens of India can create such a positive force by inviting all to join task force – peace and harmony and with the help of general public, volunteers group, media, social media, Information technology etc. should create such an environment where there is no room for communalism or social conflicts. The challenges of communalism and social discriminations are rooted in ignorance thus; it would be a war of wisdom VS ignorance as no other weapon would work! We need to create an enlightened society where alighted minds can come together and form such a force where any such darkness of social and communal conflicts cannot exist.

Our task force – peace and harmony should have people from all walks - eminent personalities, media, celebrities, educated and aware students, women, youth, academia, Intellegencia, enlightened people from all religions; coming together for educating ignorant minds and creating awareness about our higher truth and oneness. Let the cops, military force etc. do their work, our task force should focus on eliminating hatred and violence from within with the light of knowledge, wisdom and compassion. We have to remember that we are human first and foremost – communities and religions came much later in our civilization for us to be governed or manipulated by them.

As humans, we need to treat every human with at least that much dignity and make everyone see the light of truth- light of love. Nature put its faith in humans and we need to put our faith in Nature – Nature created variations/ diversity to evolve not to divide….the sun shines on all….the earth provides home to all….Nature does not discriminate between humans. All the nature's bounties….the flowers, birds, rivers, grass, fruits, grains, snowflake are for all to enjoy freely. The same creative energy has created all of us- Ram, Christ, Allah, Tao or unified field, no matter what we call it; would not change the eternal truth — it is one that we call many! Discriminating or hating another human being just because he calls it by some other name, would create a world of ignorants fighting with each other to prove their superiority. Instead, we must come together to form a wisdom pool, people from all religions must come together to filter out and counter negative elements and practices that exist in any form; in any religion, with wisdom and positive energy.

As we explored earlier, the very thought of such petty narrowness seems too ridiculous when we know that religions were introduced by great prophets to know that one behind many…..the same truth perceived and communicated through different teachers….all children perceived their father distinctively through their eyes. Religions were to create order and discipline in communities and societies; to acknowledge our oneness and the one great force that pervades everything and every being….to unite all….not to divide. Those who know the truth have to make others see too; no efforts should be left to spread the light of love and truth as through this light only we can dispel the darkness.

It is time that all of us – Team India and task force peace and harmony with writers, poets, celebrities, media, various organizations and enlightened citizens came forward, accepted our higher truth and made our people see and live this truth. Our media, social media, movies, art showing and spreading this truth as never before. After all, how long we all are going to sit in our petty wells and let things go out of hand around us, till there is some irreversible action by Nature or by certain misled heads which would put the whole country at the risk of violence or destruction? We need to root out communalism from our country. We need to root out those misguided beliefs and lies, which give birth to communalism. We need to unite our positive forces to counter every negative belief or distorted ideas that make humans turn against other fellow humans, no matter which sect, dogma or religion they belong to. Such a positive force will create a beautiful synthesis of true messages of all religions and create a new universal religion – "Humanism" based on the principles of ultimate truth, love, compassion and unity in diversity.

We need to create a wisdom revolution that would lead us to our conscious evolution and join our forces to bring the change we wish to see in the country. Instead of giving in to ignorance and false religious interpretations and manipulations, Team India and task force peace and harmony should take initiatives to build the "temples of humanity" where enlightened people from all religions can come together to develop wisdom tools and means to spread the light of truth through workshops, seminars and other media based peace and harmony initiatives to educate our children and masses. Our wisdom, love, acceptance and unity in diversity should be the greatest strength of our society not the weakness that has been misused by ages by power mongers and troublemakers. As Vivekananda said- "educate and raise the masses and thus alone a nation is possible. India will be raised, not by the power of the flesh but with the power of the spirit; not with the flag of destruction, but with the flag of peace and love".

He emphasized again and again that "The religions of the world are not contradictory or antagonistic. They are various phases of one eternal religion. The one eternal religion is applied to different planes of existence, is applied to the opinions of various minds and various races. There was never was my religion or yours, my national religion or your national religion; there never existed many religions, there is only one. One infinite religion existed all through eternity and will never exist, and this religion is expressing itself in various countries in various ways. Therefore, we must respect all religions and we must try to accept them all as far as we can".

He further explained- "The lord is the essence of unutterable love. He is ever manifest as love in all being. What other God – the creation of your mind are you then going to worship! Let the Vedas, the Koran, The puranas, and all scriptural lumber rest now for some time- let there be worship of the visible God of love and compassion in the country. All ideas of separation are bondage, that of non-differentiation is freedom (Mukti)."

How would it be that enlightened people from all religions come forward to create a **"scripture of love"** **"the book of our greatest Truth"** or **"the book of religions- One God-Many paths"** where we pick up the pearls of wisdom from all great religions, Avatars and prophets that have presented the same truth in such beautiful hues and shades and create a rainbow of love, wisdom and compassion that would light up the whole world and create a model to be followed. This book of love and wisdom should have the universal messages and teachings of all great religions i.e. the true Dharma and Karma principles and eternal song of soul of Krishna , unconditional love and compassion of Christ, unity and brotherhood of Mohammad, eternal peace and kind wisdom of Buddha- where the pages have been written not only by all the great prophets , poets, scientists, social reformers, leaders who presented and lived the same truth with different views and perspectives on different planes but keep the space for all those too who will perceive the same truth with different perspectives and views.

We should educate our children so the coming generation will accept and celebrate the truth as it is – not with any biases or prejudices tinted perspectives and let them carry the legacy forward. We cannot change the past but by changing our present, we can make our future the way we want it! We should leave no stones unturned to spread the truth and make our people become aware of the power of love and compassion and unity behind diversity, which would be the greatest strength of our society and create peace, joy and abundance for all.

It is time for conscious evolution and to embrace our higher truth. We need to combine our individual and collective wisdom to filter out any negative interpretation or ignorant beliefs that have divided our civilization into pieces and unite as one collective body of wisdom where the truth is all its forms and colors is accepted and celebrated. It is time to recreate India as the crown of the world and country of greatest wisdom again that can light the entire world with its enlightening teachings of ultimate truth and love.

It is time for people of India to come together to create a new India where no division or discrimination can exist….that works for all. Where every Indian, no matter what class, creed he belongs to, has access to a life of dignity with enough food, shelter and opportunities to not only survive but thrive.

Let us all take a pledge to create this new India ……….

Take a Pledge India

Be the change you wish to see in the world.
- Mahatma Gandhi

From revolution to conscious evolution……

Team India….an idea whose time has come!

Let us all take a pledge to create a new India …..ME and YOU ……whomsoever you are or whatever you are working as…… an economist, a writer, a media person, an artist, a celebrity, a sport man, a teacher, a scientist, a technocrat, a corporate, an educationist, a working professional, an NGO worker, a student, a housewife, a labor, a worker, a farmer ……a Hindu, a Muslim, a Sikh, a Christian….. a Dalit, a Pundit ….everyone! Remember, above all you are an Indian! No matter what color you are, what cast or creed, sect or section you belong to... India belongs to you. It is our motherland and Karamabhoomi. India does not belong to a handful of politicians or any religious sect, groups …… India's real power and strength lie in its people, in all 1.3 billion of us. We all are the makers of India's destiny. To make or break….to elect or reject …the ultimate power lies with us! We all have to come together to make it happen – to make a brighter, happier and fulfilled future for all.

Knowledge is not enough; we must apply…willing is not enough; we must do……... For long our civilization has been learning. Now is the time for action! To implement whatever we have learned from our past… to convert theory into practical……knowledge into wisdom…..thoughts into actions. Our thoughts and collective will converted into actions will create our destiny; for destiny is but the actions springing from powerful thoughts. For long, so many heroes have played their part in our country's history to bring us up to here. So many gave up their lives so we could live in freedom. So many devoted, sacrificed their lives so that we can live in better times. It is time to acknowledge their sacrifices and live the dream they passed on to us and take their legacy further. It is time to make a better world for ourselves….for our children… for our country and above all for our creator. That is the least we can do to return the precious gift of life we have been given to live and let others live with dignity, joy, peace and abundance which is the birth-right of every human. Let us rewrite the future of India where every one of us can exclaim proudly that yes, this is my country; I have built it with my own hands! We are the building blocks of this great nation. Let us all come forward and do our bit to create our dream India that our children and our forefathers would be proud of. We owe this to them and to our motherland!

Let us all come forward to create the momentum, to create a revolution and become pillars of our future India. Let us all be the heroes of the saga which is to be unfolded…. let us all be the change we would like to see in our country. Nothing is impossible for us… the world is for us to create…. we are the co-creators of our future. Let us all claim our role and responsibility in our country's evolution. We cannot wait for heroes to come and be our saviors. Let us all become the heroes and save our country. As they say, when there is a will, there is a way…. nothing can stop us from creating and actualizing our dreams. Let us pause for a while, look back at the journey till yet- take the stock of all that is now… pause and ponder over the unlimited choices and possibilities offered to us by the entire evolution process and carefully choose our future…a conscious choice made by us for a better future for our country. We have the best of means and tools to choose and create the best. Today the current state of affairs in our country are nudging us towards making the changes for the betterment of all- every single triumph over odds is a proof of Nature creating forces to pave the path for those who dare to take the road less-traveled to make the path easier for himself and for others. It's a message - to accept our highest potential and claim our greatest happiness and glory. The choice is presented to us – to accept and be what we are as one and embrace the future… the ideal future of happiness and fulfillment for all. Nature is there to support us with all its forces and resources….the whole universe will conspire to make the path for us….we the Indians…. the path breakers….the torch bearers…..each one of us is a hero…..the saviours of humanity and India.

History has witnessed whenever courageous minds stood up and took up cudgels for all that is right and just; all the universal forces have come to pave the path for them, be it Mahatma Gandhi, Nelson Mandela, Martin Luther king, Ambedkar or anyone with a genuine cause to make the whole world a better place! Frankly, there is nothing that we, the people of India cannot do.

The idea of a new India…..a free India ….free of corruption, poverty, violence, communalism, terrorism, unemployment, illiteracy, inequalities is the dream of every Indian and we have to make sure that it comes true by any means. Through resolution and diligence ………through perseverance or persistence ……. through revolution or conscious evolution. Let this vision be our collective national vision. Let us all come together to make this vision a reality…. the governments, public and private sectors, judiciary, media, intellectuals, academia, businesses, industry, teachers, doctors, workers, farmers, women and the youth of the nation – all working towards the same goal of creating a heaven on earth and make India a shining inspiration and a force to reckon with for the entire world. The land of wise and the bird of gold…. let us all put India on her throne again.

Let us all become the harbingers and light bringers for our future generations- history will always remember us for the courage…..for making the right choice at the right time!

To quote Vivekananda again:

"Let us all work hard, my brethren; this is no time for sleep.
On our work depends the coming of the India of the future.
She is there ready waiting. She is only sleeping.
Arise and awake and see her seated here on her eternal throne,
rejuvenated, more glorious than she ever was — this motherland of ours."

Arise…..Awake…..Stop not till the goal is reached."

A new heaven on earth is arising and a new India is being born…..

Epilogue

Yes, we can India….Let's do it NOW!

"We have within us extraordinary creative potentials that have yet to be massively unleashed, leading to wide-scale cooperation, innovation, sustainability and peace. All that the world truly needs to make this collective shift is a critical mass of empowered, evolutionary change agents who can envision what's possible and are willing to roll up their sleeves and take the necessary actions to make it happen."

- The Shift Network (agents of conscious evolution)

It is time for us to accept and acknowledge our collective responsibility in our country's evolution by actively participating and contributing to the process of creating a new India. It is time for us to wake up and become the "agents of change" as Barbara calls upon those who are experiencing a deep motivation to be more and find their life purpose and contribute their gifts to the conscious evolution of their country and the planet.

Today, the unconscious, distorted truths and twisted, misinterpreted religious (Dharma) ideologies have broken our great motherland into pieces and polarized our society. Misplace priorities and displaced concerns have made people of India fighting over trivial issues while the burning issues of hunger, education, unemployment, health and hygiene are being side-tracked. The state of our country today is a betrayal of our previous generation who gave up their lives for the dream of a free, peaceful and prosperous India. The time is to acknowledge and accept the gravity of situation our country is in and take collective actions towards creating a new India that lives up to the dream of our forefathers.

I am sure between those pseudo Mera-Bharat-Mahan and Oh-this-sucks-man extremes, lies a section who believes that as a part of the system, we are the system! Who believes that things can be changed, as Mahatma Gandhi said – be the change you wish to see in the world. Somewhere we need to re-evaluate things and think what have we done for our society, for our country? It's very easy to criticize if things are not right but very difficult to change them. Its time when we stopped cribbing and criticizing or living in misplaced pride and accepted the need of the hour. It is time we stopped playing victims or passive watchers and took our roles as agents of change- citizens with rights, champions of reform and integrity guardians to reform and transform our country. It is time for action. We have to take a step towards creating an evolved, enlightened and empowered society by coming together as Team India. Let's wake up and take up the cudgel to make a better tomorrow.

In Dr Abdul Kalam's words: I am echoing J. F. Kennedy's words to his fellow Americans to relate to Indians…..

'ASK WHAT WE CAN DO FOR INDIA AND DO WHAT HAS TO BE DONE TO MAKE INDIA WHAT AMERICA AND OTHER WESTERN COUNTRIES ARE TODAY'

Let's do what India needs from us. Let us make a start… Join Team India

This is time to set the ball rolling. Let us all come together as Team India and create our country anew and afresh!

If you wish to join the team, please click on the link below for the blog and face book page:

The ebook and print book is available on Amazon website :

https://www.amazon.in/see-new-India-arising-Heaven-ebook/dp/B06Y3CRC15

Author page: https://www.amazon.com/Preeti-Mahurkar/e/B06Y6B89FQ

https://yeswecanindia.wordpress.com/

https://www.facebook.com/teamindiaagain/

Twitter account : teamindiaagain

Or mail at teamindiaagain@gmail.com

Your feedback and suggestions would be appreciated. ☺

References

[1] http://www.consciouslifestylemag.com/conscious-evolution-save-humanity-planet/ ,

[2] https://www.nelsonmandela.org

[3] http://gandhiashramsevagram.org/my-dream-india/chapter-17-nonviolent-economy.php
[4] http://hdr.undp.org/en/content/poverty-and-human-development-india
[5] https://en.wikipedia.org/wiki/Tryst_with_Destiny
[6] An Uncertain Glory: India and its Contradictions, by Amratya Sen and Jean D...

[7] An Uncertain Glory: India and its Contradictions, by Amratya Sen and Jean D...

[8] https://en.wikipedia.org/wiki/Robert_F._Kennedy%27s_remarks_at_the_University_of_Kansas

[9] https://www.harpercollins.com/9789351369943/implosion-indias-tryst-with-reality
[10] http://www.livemint.com/Leisure/rexilPQLBNAGe6WcBwdwIK/Book-Review--Implosion.ht...
[11] http://economictimes.indiatimes.com/opinion/interviews/budget-2015-is-visionary-in-starting-a-social-security-network-arvind-subramanian/articleshow/46424507.cms
[12] http://thediplomat.com/2016/04/can-india-reproduce-the-east-asian-miracle/
[13] http://documents.worldbank.org/curated/en/975081468244550798/pdf/multi-page.pdf, documents.worldbank.org/curated/en/975081468244550798/pdf/multi-page.pdf
[14] http://data.worldbank.org/country
[15] http://www.worldbank.org/en/country/china/overview
[16] http://citeseerx.ist.psu.edu/viewdoc/download?doi=10.1.1.449.7305&rep=rep1&type=pdf

[17] http://www.thehindu.com/news/national/inequality-pulls-back-india-undps-human-development-report/article7988558.ece
[18] http://timesofindia.indiatimes.com/business/india-business/implement-ubi-to-wipe-out-every-tear-from-every-eye-survey/articleshow/56892354.cms
[19] https://www.affairscloud.com/wefs-the-inclusive-growth-and-development-report-20...
[20] https://www.weforum.org/agenda/2015/09/can-india-join-china-as-an-economic-superpower/
[21] https://scroll.in/article/765677/indias-middle-class-is-24-million-not-264-million-report
[22] http://reports.weforum.org/global-risks-2016/executive-summary/

[23] http://www.msn.com/en-in/news/other/25-yrs-of-economic-reforms-gap-between-big-bucks-and-impoverished-still-wide/ar-BBuWahq
[24] http://www.worldbank.org/en/publication/poverty-and-shared-prosperity

[25] https://www.oxfamindia.org/newsclipping/1044

[26] http://www.thehindu.com/news/national/indias-illiterate-population-largest-in-the-world-says-unesco-report/article5631797.ece

[27] https://www.weforum.org/reports/the-human-capital-report-2016

[28] http://www.socialprogressimperative.org/global-index/

[29] http://unsdsn.org/news/2016/07/20/ ls/

[30] Dreze Jean, & Amartya Sen. (1995). Economic development and social opportunity. Oxford University Press, New Delhi.

[31] http://elibrary.worldbank.org/doi/abs/10.1596/978-1-4648-0958-3_ch2

[32] http://www.ophi.org.uk/wp-content/uploads/MPI2016-SOUTH-ASIA-HIGHLIGHTS_June.pdf,

[33] http://www.globalresearch.ca/the-global-multidimensional-poverty-index-rising-poverty-and-social-inequality-in-india/5398001

[34] https://en.wikipedia.org/wiki/Poverty_threshold
[35] https://www.oxfam.org.au/wp-content/uploads/2017/01/An-economy-for-99-percent.pdf

[36] www.livemint.com › Money › Mark to Market, Credit Suisse report
[37] https://scroll.in/article/807490/six-indicators-of-indias-looming-demographic-disaster

[38] *Excerpted from An Uncertain Glory: India and Its Contradictions by Jean Dreze and Amartya Sen,*

[39] http://www.thehindubusinessline.com/specials/india-file/jobs-unemployment-narendra-modi/article9627739.ece

[40] *www.dailypioneer.com/avenues/only-2-of-indian-workforce-is-skilled.html*
[41] https://www.forbes.com/sites/meghabahree/2016/05/31/india-has-the-highest-number-of-slaves-globally-report/#7c2156302c3c

[42] **World Bank Country Partnership Strategy for India for the Period 2013-2017**

[43] http://timesofindia.indiatimes.com/india/Literacy-rate-up-but-so-is-illiteracy/articleshow/50749744.cms

[44] http://hlrn.org.in/documents/Housing_Land_Rights_UPRIII_HLRN.pdf

[45] http://www.cbgaindia.org/wp-content/uploads/2016/11/Ag.ISDG_.CBGA_.WORKING_PAPER_FINAL_10-NOV-2016.pdf

[46] http://www.globalresearch.ca/the-global-multidimensional-poverty-index-rising-poverty-and-social-inequality-in-india/5398001

[47] http://isdg.in/blog/report-social-watch-anton-babu-john-samuel-2030-agenda-mean-one-sixth-worlds-population/
[48] https://scroll.in/latest/818810/india-has-a-serious-hunger-problem-ranks-97-out-of-118-countries-on-the-global-hunger-index
[49] http://unicef.in/Whatwedo/10/Stunting
[50] http://www.brinknews.com/asia/indias-infrastructure-gap-a-drag-on-growth/

[51] https://www.oxfam.org/even-it-up
[52] https://www.oxfamindia.org/blog/577/oxfam%27s-%27even-it-%27-report-must-read-le...
[53] http://indiabudget.nic.in/e_survey.asp
[54] www.insightsonindia.com/.../2-shortage-medical-personnel-rural-areas-one-biggest-pr...
[55] *https://thewire.in/24924/health-budget-figures-tell-a-sick-story/*
[56] http://www.financialexpress.com/economy/economic-survey-2016-increase-spending-on-maternal-and-child-healthcare/216690/
[57] http://thediplomat.com/2016/11/india-lags-behind-china-in-social-wellbeing/
[58] http://www.oecd-ilibrary.org/social-issues-migration-health/society-at-a-glance-2016/social-spending_soc_glance-2016-19-en
[59] http://www.rteforumindia.org/sites/default/files/The%20Kothari%20Commission%20and%20Financing%20of%20Education.pdf
[60] http://edgeinmag.com/2016/08/28/innovation-excellence-and-the-long-road-for-india/
[61] http://indiabudget.nic.in/e_survey.asp
[62] http://www.livemint.com/Opinion/8S69i1ce45br6719Ca2JsJ/For-the-rich-India-is-as-...
[63] http://www.imf.org/external/pubs/ft/fandd/2016/06/ostry.htm
[64] https://thewire.in/23392/what-the-budget-tells-us-about-indias-growth-story/
[65] https://thewire.in/44003/saving-crony-capitalists-from-raghuram-rajan/
[66] http://www.igidr.ac.in/pdf/publication/WP-2016-009.pdf
[67] http://www.indiatvnews.com/business/india-nobel-laureate-amartya-sen-slams-demonetisation-says-it-declares-all-indians-as-possible-crooks-358351
[68] https://www.forbes.com/sites/timworstall/2016/11/22/indias-demonetisation-larry-summers-thinks-its-a-bad-idea/#220a06be34cb
[69] https://www.nytimes.com/2016/11/27/opinion/in-india-black-money-makes-for-bad-policy.html?_r=0
[70] http://indianexpress.com/article/india/india-news-india/both-sides-of-the-coin-what-top-economists-think-about-demonetisation/
[71] http://www.ndtv.com/india-news/nothing-to-be-proud-of-supreme-courts-indictment-of-nrega-1406219
[72] https://thewire.in/97577/farming-rural-economy-demonetisation/
[73] http://www.livemint.com/Politics/sAAliM843JTZDuTCzZWpZO/Thomas-Piketty--India-has-a-very-strong-legacy-of-extreme-i.html
[74] https://www.oxfam.org/sites/www.oxfam.org/files/file_attachments/bp-economy-for-99-percent-160117-en.pdf
[75] https://www.oxfamamerica.org/static/media/files/bp210-economy-one-percent-tax-ha...
[76] https://www.oecd.org/eco/surveys/INDIA-2017-OECD-economic-survey-overview.pdf
[77] https://scroll.in/article/815751/yes-india-has-massive-income-inequality-but-it-isnt-the-second-most-unequal-country-in-the-world
[78] https://www.weforum.org/agenda/2016/10/inequality-in-india-oxfam-explainer/
[79] http://blogs4598.rssing.com/chan-25313654/latest.php
[80] http://blogs.worldbank.org/voices/voices/ppps/jim-yong-kim-growth-must-be-much-m...
[81] https://www.weforum.org/agenda/2016/07/it-s-time-to-demolish-the-myth-of-trickle-down-economics/
[82] *https://www.oxfam.org/sites/...oxfam.../bp-economy-for-99-percent-160117-en.pdf*
[83] https://www.weforum.org/agenda/2016/10/inequality-in-india-oxfam-explainer/
[84] https://www.weforum.org/agenda/2016/10/inequality-in-india-oxfam-explainer/
[85] http://timesofindia.indiatimes.com/india/181-billion-indian-black-money-in-tax-h...
[86] http://www.thehindu.com/todays-paper/tp-business/Rich-must-open-their-wallets-more-to-remove-inequalities-Piketty/article14013634.ece

[87] http://inequality.org/business-case-annual-wealth-tax/
[88] http://news.stanford.edu/2015/01/27/inequality-bankman-policies-012715/
[89] https://www.cato.org/publications/policy-analysis/twenty-five-years-indian-economic-reform
[90] https://en.wikipedia.org/wiki/Why_Nations_Fail
[91] https://www.cato.org/publications/policy-analysis/twenty-five-years-indian-economic-reform

[92] http://www.thehindu.com/news/national/16th-lok-sabha-will-be-richest-have-most-mps-with-criminal-charges/article6022513.ece
[93] http://indianexpress.com/article/education/17000-mbas-b-techs-apply-for-114-sweeper-jobs-in-up/
[94] http://thediplomat.com/2016/04/can-india-reproduce-the-east-asian-miracle/
[95] *www.imf.org/external/pubs/ft/fandd/2001/12/wade.htm*
[96] Sharad Joshi, http://www.financialexpress.com/opinion/column-india-shining-bharat-whining/163148/
[97] *blogs.worldbank.org/developmenttalk/who-are-bottom-40*
[98] http://prakashan.vivekanandakendra.org/node/408
[99] http://www.ijhssi.org/papers/v2(11)/Version-2/G021102040053.pdf
[100] https://www.transparency.org/news/feature/asia_pacific_fighting_corruption_is_side_lined
[101] http://currentaffairs.gktoday.in/india-ranks-130th-2017-ease-business-index-10201636686.html
[102] http://blog.transparency.org/2011/12/07/what-makes-new-zealand-denmark-finland-sweden-and-others-%E2%80%9Ccleaner%E2%80%9D-than-most-countries/
[103] *prepared by Petter Langseth, Ph. D, Programme Manager, Global Programme against Corruption, Centre for International Crime Prevention, Office of Drug Control and Crime Prevention, United Nations Office at Vienna. https://www.unodc.org/pdf/crime/gpacpublications/cicp2.pdf
TI source book-2000

[105] http://www.psru.gov.sl/sites/default/files/STRATEGY.pdf, Report of Transparency International
[106] *resources.transparency.bg/download.html?id=504- TI source book 2000,*
https://www.unodc.org/pdf/crime/gpacpublications/cicp2.pdf
[107] http://www.unodc.org/pdf/crime/gpacpublications/cicp2.pdf
[108] (Guidelines from TI Source Book , UN tools, excerpts from Jeremy pope and country strategy- Sierra Leone)
https://www.unodc.org/pdf/crime/gpacpublications/cicp2.pdf

[109] http://blog.transparency.org/2011/12/07/what-makes-new-zealand-denmark-finland-sweden-and-others-%E2%80%9Ccleaner%E2%80%9D-than-most-countries/
[110] http://www.democracyweb.org/accountability-principles
[111] http://www.goodgovernance.org.au/about-good-governance/what-is-good-governance/
[112] http://documents.worldbank.org/curated/en/327691468779445304/Social-accountability-an-introduction-to-the-concept-and-emerging-practice
[113] https://openknowledge.worldbank.org/bitstream/handle/10986/6902/WPS4767.txt?sequ...
[114] https://assets.publishing.service.gov.uk/media/57a08aabed915d622c00084b/60827_DP...
[115] https://www.ids.ac.uk/files/dmfile/IETASynthesisReportMcGeeGaventaFinal28Oct2010.pdf
[116] https://www.brookings.edu/opinions/open-government-partnership-first-steps-and-t...
[117] https://www.unodc.org/pdf/crime/gpacpublications/cicp2.pdf and Guidelines from TI Source Book , UN tools, excerpts from Jeremy pope and country strategy- Sierra Leone)

[118] http://nis.transparency.bg/nis_concept_and_approach.html

[119] https://www.unodc.org/pdf/crime/gpacpublications/cicp2.pdf and Guidelines from TI Source Book , UN tools, excerpts from Jeremy pope and country strategy- Sierra Leone)
[120] https://www.transparency.org/nis
[121] https://acton.org/research/lord-acton-quote-archive
[122] https://archive.org/stream/IA.TheABCOfEconomics.410240/IA.The%20ABC%20of%20Economics.410240_djvu.txt
[123] http://www.ushistory.org/declaration/document/
[124] www.pressreader.com/india/the-times-of-india-new-delhi.../281904473950122

[125] www.constitution.org/cons/india/p4a51a.html
[126] http://www.constitution.org/cons/india/preamble.html

[127] https://en.wikipedia.org/wiki/Individual_liberty
[128] https://en.wikipedia.org/wiki/Directive_Principles

[129] Sumant Batra - http://www.eoi.gov.in/kabul/?4645?000
[130] http://mea.gov.in/Images/attach/Article_on_Constitution_of_India.pdf
[131] www.un.org/esa/socdev/publications/FullSurveyEmpowerment.pdf
www.supremecourtofindia.nic.in/speeches/speeches.../bhopal%20speech%202.9.06.p... [132]
[133] https://www.gdrc.org/u-gov/escap-governance.htm

[134] http://ras.sagepub.com/content/75/1/99.refs.html

[135] http://documents.tips/documents/abb-and-mtfreform-initiatives-on-corruption-v1.html
[136] http://indianexpress.com/article/india/india-news-india/supreme-court-pulls-up-centre-over-delay-in-payment-under-mgnrega-2799655/
[137] http://www.indiaspend.com/cover-story/chinas-vocational-training-16-times-indias-can-budget-push-help-23403

[138] http://www.india.com/news/india/a-p-j-abdul-kalams-word-of-caution-on-make-in-in...
[139] https://www.opengovpartnership.org/sites/default/files/OGP%20Indonesia%20Chairmanship%202014_final.pdf

[140] http://publicpolicy.pepperdine.edu/davenport-institute/content/foundational/enga
[141] http://www.doingbusiness.org/data/exploreeconomies/india
[142] Petter Langseth- https://www.unodc.org/pdf/crime/gpacpublications/cicp2.pdf

[143] TI source book- Jeremy Pope

[144] http://www.constitution.org/cons/india/p4a51a.html
[145] https://www.unodc.org/pdf/crime/gpacpublications/cicp2.pdf
[146] **The world Bank- Power, Rights and Poverty: Concepts and Connections** - edited by Ruth Alsop

[147] http://blog.transparency.org/2011/12/07/what-makes-new-zealand-denmark-finland-sweden-and-others-%E2%80%9Ccleaner%E2%80%9D-than-most-countries/
[148] https://www.gov.uk/dfid-research-outputs/good-practice-in-strengthening-transparency-participation-accountability-and-integrity

[149] http://www.undp.org/content/dam/undp/documents/partners/civil_society/publications/2013_UNDP_Reflections-on-Social-Accountability_EN.pdf
[150] http://reports.weforum.org/global-information-technology-report-2016/country-and-regional-trends-from-the-nri/

[151] https://www.transparency.org/whatwedo/publication/people_and_corruption_asia_pacific_global_corruption_barometer
[152] https://www.un.org/development/desa/publications/2016-e-government-survey.html
[153] https://www.brookings.edu/opinions/open-government-partnership-first-steps-and-t...
[154] The TI source book -2000
[155] https://www.law.kuleuven.be/integriteit/egpa/egpa2010/six_theoryintegritysystems.pdf
[156] Milan http://www.psru.gov.sl/sites/default/files/STRATEGY.pdf
http://nis.transparency.bg/nis_concept_and_approach.html

[157] https://www.ncjrs.gov/App/publications/Abstract.aspx?id=184687,
TI source book 2000, http://www.psru.gov.sl/sites/default/files/STRATEGY.pdf,
[158] https://openknowledge.worldbank.org/bitstream/handle/10986/9844/548080BRI0Box31560Apr0200001PUBLIC1.pdf;sequence=1

[159] https://www.shareweb.ch/site/DDLGN/Documents/Social_accountability_changing_regi...
[160] http://ras.sagepub.com/content/75/1/99

[161] http://www.opengovguide.com/commitments/establish-a-legal-framework-for-impartiality-effectiveness-and-transparency-in-elections/
[162] http://documents.worldbank.org/curated/en/327691468779445304/Social-accountability-an-introduction-to-the-concept-and-emerging-practice
[163] http://www.undp.org/content/dam/undp/documents/partners/civil_society/publications/2013_UNDP_Reflections-on-Social-Accountability_EN.pdf

[164] http://www.undp.org/content/dam/undp/documents/partners/civil_society/publications/2013_UNDP_Reflections-on-Social-Accountability_EN.pdf

[165] http://unsdsn.org/wp-content/uploads/2015/04/Data-for-Development-Full-Report.pdf
[166] https://www.researchgate.net/figure/275074488_fig1_Figure-1-The-Long-and-Short-Routes-of-Accountability
[167] http://www.transparency-initiative.org/archive/news/ogp-launch-july2011, http://www.transparency-initiative.org/archive/wp-content/uploads/2011/09/4-Campaign-finance1.pdf

[168] https://sustainabledevelopment.un.org/post2015/transformingourworld

[169] http://sdgfunders.org/reports/converging-interests-philanthropy-government-collaboration-to-achieve-the-sustainable-development-goals/
[170] https://sustainabledevelopment.un.org/post2015/transformingourworld

[171] https://sustainabledevelopment.un.org/futurewewant.html

[172] https://sustainabledevelopment.un.org/content/documents/9486ANilo%20Civil%20Soci...
[173] https://sustainabledevelopment.un.org/content/documents/9486ANilo%20Civil%20Soci...
[174] *www.undp.org/.../2013_UNDP_Reflections-on-Social-Accountability_EN.pdf*
[175] http://www.undp.org/content/dam/undp/documents/partners/civil_society/publications/2013_UNDP_Reflections-on-Social-Accountability_EN.pdf

[176] http://rio20.net/wp-content/uploads/2012/05/peoples-sustainability-treaties-on-sd-goals-zero-draft-for-comments.pdf

[177] http://www.acordinternational.org/silo/files/the-roles-of-civil-society-in-local...
[178] .https://www.opengovpartnership.org

[179] http://www.opengovernment.org.uk/wp-content/uploads/2017/02/SDG-Summary-of-OECD-...
[180] https://sdg.guide/chapter-3-tools-for-designing-sdg-strategies-and-roadmaps-a8172680d5ef

[181] http://www.acordinternational.org/silo/files/the-roles-of-civil-society-in-localizing-the-sdgs.pdf

[182] https://sdg.guide/chapter-3-tools-for-designing-sdg-strategies-and-roadmaps-a8172680d5ef

[183] https://issuu.com/uclgcglu/docs/roadmap_for_localizing_the_sdgs

[184] *https://sustainabledevelopment.un.org/.../818_11195_commitment_ROADMAP%20L...*
[185] *www.acordinternational.org/silo/.../the-roles-of-civil-society-in-localizing-the-sdgs.pd...*
[186] *https://sdg.guide/chapter-3-tools-for-designing-sdg-strategies-and-roadmaps-a817268...*
[187] *https://sdg.guide/chapter-3-tools-for-designing-sdg-strategies-and-roadmaps-a817268...*
[188] *www.psru.gov.sl/sites/default/files/STRATEGY.pdf*
[189] https://sdg.guide/chapter-3-tools-for-designing-sdg-strategies-and-roadmaps-a817...
[190] *https://www.oxfam.org.nz/.../EXECUTIVE%20SUMMARY%20-%20An%20econom...*

www.ingramcontent.com/pod-product-compliance
Lightning Source LLC
LaVergne TN
LVHW081537070526
838199LV00056B/3695